Philosophy, Science and Social Inquiry

Contemporary Methodological Controversies in Social
Science and Related Applied Fields of Research

Other Titles of Interest

DREW & HARDMAN
Designing and Conducting Behavioral Research

STOVE
Popper and After

A Major Reference Work

DUNKIN
The International Encyclopedia of Teaching and Teaching Education

Journals of Related Interest

International Journal of Educational Development
International Journal of Educational Research
Studies in Educational Evaluation
Teaching and Teacher Education

Philosophy, Science and Social Inquiry

Contemporary Methodological Controversies in Social Science and Related Applied Fields of Research

D. C. PHILLIPS
Stanford University

PERGAMON PRESS

Oxford · New York · Beijing · Frankfurt
São Paulo · Sydney · Tokyo · Toronto

300.72
P5411p

U.K.	Pergamon Press, Headington Hill Hall, Oxford OX3 0BW, England
U.S.A.	Pergamon Press, Maxwell House, Fairview Park, Elmsford, New York 10523, U.S.A.
PEOPLE'S REPUBLIC OF CHINA	Pergamon Press, Room 4037, Qianmen Hotel, Beijing, People's Republic of China
FEDERAL REPUBLIC OF GERMANY	Pergamon Press, Hammerweg 6, D-6242 Kronberg, Federal Republic of Germany
BRAZIL	Pergamon Editora, Rua Eça de Queiros, 346, CEP 04011, Paraiso, São Paulo, Brazil
AUSTRALIA	Pergamon Press Australia, P.O. Box 544, Potts Point, N.S.W. 2011, Australia
JAPAN	Pergamon Press, 8th Floor, Matsuoka Central Building, 1-7-1 Nishishinjuku, Shinjuku-ku, Tokyo 160, Japan
CANADA	Pergamon Press Canada, Suite No 271, 253 College Street, Toronto, Ontario, Canada M5T 1R5

Copyright © 1987 D. Phillips

All Rights Reserved. No part of this publication may be reproduced, stored in a retrieval system or transmitted in any form or by any means: electronic, electrostatic, magnetic tape, mechanical, photocopying, recording or otherwise, without permission in writing from the publishers.

First edition 1987
Reprinted 1988

Library of Congress Cataloging-in-Publication Data

Philips, D. C. (Denis Charles), 1938–
Philosophy, science, and social inquiry.
1. Social sciences—Research. 2. Social sciences—Methodology, I. Title.
H62.P4626   1987   300'.72   86-16939

British Library Cataloguing in Publication Data

Philips, D. C. (Denis Charles)
Philosophy, science, and social inquiry:
contemporary methodological controversies
in social science and related applied fields
of research.
1. Social sciences—Methodology
I. Title   300'.72   H61

ISBN 0-08-033410-5 Hardcover
ISBN 0-08-033411-3 Flexicover

Printed in Great Britain by A. Wheaton & Co. Ltd., Exeter

So my answer to the questions "How do you know? What is the source or the basis of your assertion? What observations have led you to it?" would be: "I do *not* know: my assertion was merely a guess. Never mind the source . . . if you are interested in the problem which I tried to solve by my tentative assertion, you may help me by criticizing it as severely as you can. . . ."

—Karl Popper,
Conjectures and Refutations

Whoso loveth correction loveth knowledge, but he that hateth reproof is brutish.

—*Proverbs*, 12:1

Preface

Woody Allen has written that unfortunately our politicians are either incompetent or corrupt, sometimes both on the same day. A parallel thought is often harbored about philosophers by their colleagues in academe—they are regarded as abstruse and irrelevant, and nearly always on the same occasions! There can be little doubt that some philosophers *are* abstruse, and no doubt the work of *some* is irrelevant. Philosophers themselves are their own severest critics on these matters; witness Sir Karl Popper's condemnation of the work of some of his Continental colleagues who, he said, fostered a "cult of un-understandability" and who stated "the utmost trivialities in high-sounding language".[1]

Nevertheless, a little charity is called for. Those outside are sometimes rather more unforgiving when reading philosophy than they are when faced with other material. No one blames quantum theorists for being difficult to follow, for it is correctly judged that the material that is being discussed *is* difficult. Sometimes a similar attitude is warranted with respect to philosophy. The material is usually abstract, at what philosophers like to regard as a "meta-level"; it cannot be mastered by skimming. But, as with many other complex fields, the arguments are easier to follow if pains have been taken to comprehend the *problems* or *issues* that are at stake.

Lest all this frighten-off the potential readers of the present book, it must be stated boldly that the issues to be discussed here *are* comprehensible to the non-philosopher—indeed, they are largely issues that have been raised by, and that are of great professional concern to, non-philosophers themselves. Furthermore, they are issues that can be discussed in a clear and lively way; there is no need to take refuge in what Popper called "impressive opaqueness".

What, then, are the issues that will be tackled here in so admirably clear a fashion, issues that are relevant and timely and upon which a philosopher claims he can shed some helpful light? In brief, they are issues that concern research and theory in the social and human sciences, and related applied fields such as educational and nursing research.

Much that is exciting is being done, and being thought, here. At the meta-level, expressions such as "crisis in the social sciences", "uneasy social science", "paradigm clash", "hotbeds of pluralistic activity", "garrulous and vacuous contributions"—and worse—are common, and indicate that important issues are being hotly debated. At a less abstract level, there are disagreements about specific theories, and research traditions that have been long-lived are under question. On the one hand, the developmental theories of Piaget and Kohlberg are facing increasing criticism from both theorists and empirically-oriented researchers; while on the other hand, cognitive scientists are hard at work, with ingenious research designs and wonderful computer programs that model human problem solving. The phenomenon of aptitude-treatment-interaction has led some previously optimistic psychological researchers to become more guarded in their aspirations. The relation between the research endeavor and policy formation has been much debated. New approaches to the design of evaluations of educational and social programs are being formulated that make the "true experiment" seem like a lumbering dinosaur, yet some folk persist in thinking that dinosaurs are wonderful creatures. Advocates for a gamut of qualitative research methodologies have become increasingly vocal, and there are many in the research community who have been forced to consult their encyclopedias and dictionaries on "Dilthey", "Weber", "Gadamer", "Wittgenstein", "emic", "hermeneutics", and "connoisseurship". Many who regarded themselves as competent data-gatherers and number-crunchers are beginning to wonder whether they are not, in fact, lackeys of an oppressive economic system, and they are trying to make out what it is that their radical colleagues see in Habermas, Althusser, and even Gramsci. Terms that were once used as proud self-descriptions have now become mild expressions of derision—"positivist", "empiricist", "Hempelian", "objectivist", "hard-nosed", "analytical". The left brain, which once seemed to occupy all of cranial space, has been relegated to a mere 50 percent in order to make a place for the right hemisphere, for whose activities there is growing respect. Even worse, in some quarters researchers have abandoned the very notion of truth as a regulative ideal, and mouthing exciting names ("Hanson", "Kuhn", "Feyerabend") they have hoisted the banners of either relativism or subjectivism.

It is apparent that all of these issues are saturated with philosophical considerations, and it is with many of the latter that the following chapters are concerned. In general, in the second and third portions of the book the reader will have little trouble in detecting a somewhat "ornery" or skeptical tone in the discussions, that sometimes borders on the cynical. A partial explanation for this lies in the fact that the author has the tendency to be fully convinced by whatever it is that he is reading at the present moment, so he has disciplined himself to back away and look for defects. And, of course, no matter how good a piece of work happens to be, there always *are* defects to be found. Sometimes these are serious, and more than offset the good features, and sometimes not. When pressed to justify this intellectual hatchetry, a Popperian framework is appealed to, whereby it can be shown that *any* position can be supported by positive reasons (Popper once said that any fool can apparently "prove" any doctrine by finding some evidence in its favor), but what really counts is how well the position can stand up to vigorous assault. For those to whom Popper does not quite have authoritative status, the passage from *Proverbs* on page v of this book may be decisive.

The book is organised into three main Parts. The titles of these are a play upon Popper's wonderful book title, *Conjectures and Refutations*; the present volume could well bear the title *Expositions and Refutations*. Part A contains an exposition of the relevant developments in philosophy against which the practice of research in the social sciences and applied fields has to be seen—the work of Kuhn, Winch, Popper, Lakatos, Feyerabend and others, and the demise of positivism. In the course of this discussion some common misconceptions and misinferences about research are touched upon, but detailed discussion of these is held over until the second part of the book. It is in Part B that the various lines of vigorous attack on the integrity of social science and educational and nursing research are described and assessed. In general, it is argued that although the critics have put their fingers on important points, they often go too far, and draw unwarranted conclusions. In Part C, theory and research in one wide but lively area is critiqued in the spirit of the Popperian critical rationalism discussed in the earlier parts of the book. (Those for whom the research that is examined is not of central interest—it focusses upon the notions of cognitive structure and development—may still find the final chapters to be of relevance for their exemplification of both the critical spirit and some of the ideas of the new philosophy of science.) At the end, a Glossary is included to aid the reader who might not be familiar with the technical or philosophical terms that were unavoidable; however, these have been kept to a minimum in the text, and an effort has been made to ensure that the context in which they are used will help to clarify their meaning.

The author of any work that is wide-ranging must owe numerous intellectual debts; the present writer is no exception, and the Acknowledgements and Notes give some indication of these. Most of the chapters are based on papers that were written for workshops and conferences over the past decade, and much of the material has appeared in print in somewhat different and preliminary form; but there have been major revisions, reorganization, and updating. An especial debt is owed to colleagues who, either in print or in discussion at these conferences, gave valuable feedback or responded constructively to the criticisms that were offered of their work; and a debt is owed, too, to students at Stanford University who discussed the material in classes and colloquia. The formulation of several of the lines of argument presented here owes a great deal to the talent of coauthors—Jennie Nicolayev and Rob Orton—who worked on two of the earlier papers that have been used as a basis for material in two chapters of this book. Finally, over several years Harvey Siegel has commented upon most of the material from his superb perspective in philosophy of science, Valerie Phillips has done her best to root out gross inelegancies and ambiguities in the prose, and Barbara Barrett of Pergamon Press has offered much encouragement.

Note

1. Karl Popper, "Reason or Revolution?", in Theodor Adorno *et al.*, *The Positivist Dispute in German Sociology* (New York, Harper and Row, 1976), p 294.

Acknowledgements

Chapters 2 and 3 are based in large measure, and with permission of the Society, upon two chapters that appeared in the 80th and 84th *Yearbooks of the National Society for the Study of Education*. These volumes were titled *Philosophy and Education* and *Learning and Teaching the Ways of Knowing*.

Chapter 4, and portion of Chapter 8, are based with permission of the editor, upon a paper that was published in the *Educational Researcher*, **12**, no. 5, May 1983.

Chapter 6 is based, with permission, upon two papers: one that appeared in *Philosophy of Education 1979* (Proceedings of the Annual Conference of the Philosophy of Education Society), and another that appeared in *Inquiry*, **19**, 1976.

Chapter 7 is based, in part, upon D. C. Phillips and Rob Orton, "The New Causal Theory of Cognitive Learning Theory", *Psychological Review*, **90**, no. 2, 1983. (Copyright 1983, by the American Psychological Association. Adapted by permission of the publisher.)

Portions of Chapter 8 are based, with permission, upon a paper published in *Philosophy of Education 1984* (Proceedings of the Annual Conference of the Philosophy of Education Society).

Chapter 9 is an expanded version of a paper first presented at a conference on "Philosophical Aspects of Educational Research" held at Simon Fraser University, B.C., Canada, and which will be published in the *Canadian Journal of Education*.

Parts of Chapter 11 are based, with permission, upon a chapter published in P. W. Musgrave, ed., *Modern Studies in the Curriculum* (Angus and Robertson; copyright McGraw-Hill Australia).

Chapter 12 is based, with permission, upon a paper "On Describing a

Student's Cognitive Structure", published in the *Educational Psychologist*, **18,** no. 2, 1983. (Copyright 1983 by Division 15 of the American Psychological Association).

Chapter 13 is based, with permission of the publisher, upon a chapter in S. and C. Modgil, eds., *Jean Piaget: Consensus and Controversy* (Holt).

Chapter 14 is based, with permission, upon a paper coauthored with Jennie Nicolayev and published in *Educational Theory*, **28,** 1978, and Cochrane, Hamm and Kazepides, eds., *The Domain of Moral Education* (Paulist Press & OISE Press).

Contents

CONTENTS

Part A
EXPOSITIONS
Recent Philosophical Developments

1

Introduction

In the opening speech of Shakespeare's *King Henry the Fifth,* the issue is raised of whether the stirring and heroic events of that monarch's reign could be conveyed adequately with the meager resources of the Globe Theater: "Can this cockpit hold the vasty fields of France? Or may we cram within this wooden O the very casques that did afright the air at Agincourt?" The bard's answer, of course, was a qualified "yes". A parallel question—hopefully with the same retort—may be raised about the present enterprise: Can a single volume, limited with respect to the number of pages available, present an adequate account of the contemporary debates about the scientific standing of the research enterprise in the social sciences and related applied fields? For there can be little doubt that momentous events have taken place here as well; there have been intellectual Agincourts aplenty, that have laid waste many long-standing beliefs about the characteristics of science and the nature of research. The literature is voluminous, and there is great subtlety and depth to many of the contributions. So, at the outset of any attempt to give an exposition and a critique of what has been happening, it is wise to follow the Bard's example and to seek pardon for daring to "bring forth so great an object".

The centrality of science

During the last few centuries of Western intellectual history, educated people typically have held an exalted view of science.[1] Together with mathematics, it has stood as the model of what a body of knowledge ought to be. In epistemological discussions in philosophy, it has been taken as an important case of "justified true belief". John Dewey wrote of science as being "authorized conviction", and he said that "Without initiation into the scientific spirit one is not in possession of the best tools which humanity has so far devised for effectively directed reflection."[2] Researchers in a variety of fields, ranging from history to psychology and sociology, have felt apologetic if their disciplines have fallen short of the ideals derived from physical science; they have engaged in the quest for laws and theories with vigor but without resounding success. In the field of education, curriculum theorists have often

2

considered science to be one of the "basics", and since the time of Herbert Spencer it has been regarded as an important component of a liberal (or liberating) education. Plato, of course, thought of science as inferior to mathematics and philosophy because it dealt with the changing and hence unreal world of sense-experience, but Plato was not speaking for epistemologists of the nineteenth and twentieth centuries. The etymology of the word "science" reveals all; Jacob Bronowski writes that "We are a scientific civilization: that means, a civilization in which knowledge and its integrity are crucial. Science is only a Latin word for knowledge."[3]

During the last three decades this epistemological status of science has come into question. Not that there was a scarcity of serious questions earlier—in some ways John Dewey pointed the direction that later inquiry was to follow. For those who paid attention, he clearly raised the issue of how our various knowledge-claims were warranted, and he suggested that there was no difference in principle between the warranting of scientific and other types of claims (including aesthetic and moral ones). But, for a variety of reasons, his work did not inspire more than a handful of those at the cutting edge of the philosophy of science during the 1950s and 1960s. For some, the landmark was the translation into English of Popper's *Logic of Scientific Discovery* in 1957; here the message was clear—scientific knowledge-claims can never be proven or fully justified, they can only be refuted. For others, the turning point was less sharply demarcated, but it was bound up with the gradual erosion of the credibility of logical positivism—the position that for several decades had appeared to be the foundation of the traditional epistemology of science. Others were finally shaken by Kuhn's *The Structure of Scientific Revolutions* in 1962, or by the work of Lakatos or Feyerabend a little later. By the mid 1970s, the "rationality of science" had become a major issue, and the literature now has grown to mammoth proportions. Newton-Smith has summarized the situation well:

> The scientific community sees itself as the very paradigm of institutionalized rationality. It is taken to be in possession of something, the scientific method, which generates a "logic of justification"... For Feyerabend, Kuhn and others, not only does scientific practice not live up to the image the community projects, it could not do so. For that image, it is said, embodies untenable assumptions concerning the objectivity of truth, the role of evidence and the invariance of meanings.[4]

Where do we stand today? How are scientific claims warranted? What rational grounds—if any—are there for a person to assent to the doctrines of modern science? Should workers in other disciplines strive to make them more like science; or should people working in the sciences finally capitulate and acknowledge that, epistemologically speaking, their knowledge claims are no more secure than those put forward elsewhere? More generally, what are the implications for the conduct of research in the "pure" and "applied" social sciences of the revolutionary works in philosophy of science of the past three or four decades? The chapters in this Part will make a start toward grappling with these issues; and at first the discussion must be expository and interpretive.

Notes and References

1. This is not to deny that there has been a degree of social schizophrenia about science—after all, the deranged scientist has been a common cultural symbol. But few if any epistemologies have been based on this model.
2. John Dewey, *Democracy and Education*. New York: The Free Press, 1966, p 189.
3. Jacob Bronowski, *The Ascent of Man*. Boston: Little, Brown and Co., 1973, p 437.
4. W. H. Newton-Smith, *The Rationality of Science*. Boston and London: Routledge and Kegan Paul, 1981, pp 1–2.

2

The New Logic of the Sciences

The twentieth century has witnessed remarkable development in the understanding of the nature of science. In the opening years the work of Einstein caused a revolution not only in the realm of physics—Bridgman was stimulated to formulate the methodology of "operationalism" (a close relative of behaviorism), and Popper was so struck by Eddington's test of Einstein's theoretical ideas that he formulated his own views on the methodology of science. At about the same time, and somewhat intertwined, the logical positivists were at work, followed closely (in time and in doctrine) by the behaviorists. Bertrand Russell contemplated science and mathematics throughout the early decades of the century, and the theory of relativity had a special place in his thought. After the Second World War, insights seemed to snowball: Carnap and Reichenbach were joined by Hempel and Nagel, and then Kuhn and Lakatos and Feyerabend and a host of other important figures came tumbling after.

By the 1980s a new understanding of the "logic" of science had been forged (although absolute finality had not been reached on many, if any, of the issues). The structure of theories, the relation between theory and evidence, the role of observation, and the processes by which science changes or develops—these were issues in the vanguard, where dramatic insights became available. The discussion of these insights can be grouped conveniently under the following headings:

Is observation in any sense foundational in science?
Are theories generated from, or determined by, evidence?
Is rational justification of knowledge claims possible?
Is justification necessarily relative to a framework?

But since much of what follows in this book is written from what can be regarded as a Popperian orientation, it would be as well to begin at the beginning (or at least, what the beginning is from this point-of-view) with a brief exposition of some of Sir Karl's insights. Then these other themes can be taken up fruitfully.

Karl Popper and critical rationality

Popper was a student in Austria during the exciting period of intellectual and political turmoil following the end of the First World War. He was familiar with Marxism, and he worked as a research assistant on a project involving Alfred Adler's psychology; as an Austrian he was no stranger to the work of Freud, and as a student of physics he was acquainted with Einstein's theories. These intellectual threads came together in 1919 when, as he tells it, he shared in the general excitement that followed Eddington's observations during an eclipse of the sun—observations that tended to confirm Einstein's views. (About the time of this eclipse a distant star was to pass behind the sun, and so be obscured, but Einstein's theory predicted that it would still be visible because its light would be bent by the gravitational field of the sun. All this could be checked at the time of the eclipse, when the normally blinding light of the sun would be absent. Many in the scientific community believed that Einstein's prediction would be shown to be wrong.) Popper ruminated on Marx, Freud and Adler, and he noted that his friends who greatly admired the ideas of one or other of these men were particularly impressed by the fact that they seemed to fit so many situations; indeed, "Once your eyes were thus opened you saw confirming instances everywhere; the world was full of *verifications* of the theory. Whatever happened always confirmed it."[1] Contrasting this situation with what had happened to Einstein, Popper realized that, in fact, this was not a strength. For Einstein's theory would *not* have fitted with anything that happened; Einstein's work was incompatible with certain possible states of affairs:

> Now the impressive thing about this case is the *risk* involved in a prediction of this kind. If observation shows that the predicted effect is definitely absent, then the theory is simply refuted. The theory is *incompatible with certain possible results of observation*. . . .[2]

For more than a decade Popper worked out the consequences of this key insight—consequences for the demarcation between science and nonscience, and for the relationship between scientific beliefs and the evidence that is offered as warrant for those beliefs. Just before the Second World War he published a book in German, and this was translated into English in 1957 as *The Logic of Scientific Discovery*. The remarkable feature of Popper's work was that he was able to develop this insight into a position that gave a credible solution to many problems about science that had caused vexation for long periods of time.

As indicated above, Popper reached the conclusion that the essence of science is testability, or more precisely the openness to refutation. A statement that is compatible with any possible evidence is not scientific, no matter how interesting it might appear; scientific statements are important—and testable—because they rule out certain possibilities. Any statement that is insulated against refutation is metaphysical. Scientific knowledge progresses by a process of formulating bold conjectures and then subjecting them to equally bold criticism and test (a test being merely a serious attempt at refutation)—a process nicely captured in the title of a book of his essays, *Conjectures and Refutations*.

This position stands the traditional view of knowledge upon its head. Normally, an item is accepted as worthy of belief (that is, it is accepted as warranted, and as being knowledge) because it is based upon firm foundations. Popper would have us tentatively accept such an item simply because we have attempted strenuously to refute it but have not been able to do so—as yet! Knowledge grows not by a process of proving items to be true, but by the "weeding" process of error elimination. That is why openness to criticism is the mark of rationality for a Popperian:

> . . . the dogmatic attitude is clearly related to the tendency to *verify* our laws and schemata by seeking to apply them and to confirm them, even to the point of neglecting refutations, whereas the critical attitude is one of readiness to change them—to test them; to refute them; to *falsify* them, if possible. This suggests we may identify the critical attitude with the scientific attitude. . . .[3]

Why is error elimination the only process by which knowledge can grow? There seems to be a third possibility lying between the weeding out of error and the insulating of beliefs from criticism and refutation—namely, the establishing of an idea as sound. Why cannot an item be shown to be true, rather than only established as untrue? In brief (the issues will be focussed upon in a little more depth in the subsequent discussion), Popper was influenced by several considerations, among which probably the most important was the traditional problem of induction ("Hume's problem"). Scientists can obtain only finite amounts of evidence from areas of nature to which they have access, and, according to the inductivist account, they make inferences from this to what holds true in portions of nature that are beyond access—to the distant past, or the future, or to the far boundaries of the universe. (The hoary example beloved of textbook writers concerns swans; from the evidence that a finite number of swans are all white, it is inductively inferred that *all* swans, that is, all future and past swans, are white. That this inference was a dangerous one was shown when black swans were discovered in Australia.) There is a problem here, nicely described in the eighteenth century by David Hume, and regarded as a blot on the escutcheon of science and philosophy over the next few centuries: Is, indeed, the inference beyond a finite body of evidence a sound one? Can we be sure that portions of nature that have not yet been observed will resemble the portions that have been? Popper shared Hume's skepticism on this matter; in his view, we can never hope to establish scientific generalizations beyond doubt—inductive inference is not a sound basis for generalization. Indeed, Popper went further:

> As for induction (or inductive logic, or inductive behaviour, or learning by induction or by repetition or by "instruction") I assert that there is no such thing. If I am right then this solves,

of course, the problem of induction. . . . The point is that there is no rule of inductive inference—inference leading to theories or universal laws—ever proposed which can be taken seriously for even a minute.[4]

So, then, knowledge claims cannot be established by means of induction; in Popper's view they can only be tested, and possibly refuted.

Popper's work has been influential, but interesting new problems have arisen that challenge some of it—a development that, of course, is consistent with the Popperian view that no human views are fully correct, that we can hope only to approach nearer to the truth but never attain it, and that we progress by criticism and refutation.

It is time, now, to turn to the exposition of these recent developments.

The role of observation

In the account of science given in textbooks for most of the century—an account supported to some degree by the philosophy of logical positivism —observation played a key role. It formed the solid foundation upon which knowledge was built, and it was the final court of appeal in disputes. There is little point in reviewing in detail the historical steps through which this "received view" decayed; it is sufficient to say that it is now widely regarded as untenable to hold that scientific theories are built up from a foundation of secure, unquestionable, objective and theory-neutral observation. Nor do any convincing grounds remain for believing that scientific theories, wherever they come from, can, after their production or invention, be reduced to (or fully stated in terms of) a set of neutral "observation statements".

These two viewpoints that recent scholarship has rejected are related, but they are not identical. The first one focusses upon the *production* of theories (i.e. they are built up from an observational foundation), while the second deals with the *logical status* of theories, however they are produced (i.e. logically they are "shorthand" ways of referring to observation statements, and in principle they can be reduced to these). The rejection of both these doctrines has led some writers to a conundrum: Science apparently is a body of knowledge about the sensible world, yet if observation plays no central role in either the production of this knowledge or in establishing its logical status, how *can* science be about the real world?

In recent years there are many who have taken this slippery argument seriously; they have held that science has no objective basis whatsoever, it is merely one ideology or worldview among many, but it has no special status or rationale warranting special respect. However, a good case can be made that the conundrum is overstated; it is not that observation plays no role at all, but that its role is not *foundational* in the sense (or senses) understood in earlier decades. Popper has said that questions inquiring about the foundations of knowledge "are wrongly put", for "they are entirely misconceived: they are questions that beg for an authoritarian answer."[5] It does not follow from this that science is ideological, or that it is a matter of whim—to eschew authoritarian grounds for belief is not to eschew *all* grounds for belief. What, then, are the insights that have been attained about observation, and what is the new understanding of the role that can be ascribed to it in the warranting of scientific knowledge claims?

To start with the rejection of the view that scientific theories are *produced from* an objective observational base: the work that immediately comes to mind here is that of N. R. Hanson. His discussion of the theory-laden nature of observation in his *Patterns of Discovery* (1958) has won the status of a classic.[6] He was not, however, the first to say the things he did. Several years earlier, in *Philosophical Investigations*, Wittgenstein even used one of the same diagrams to make the same point; Popper held much the same view; and earlier still John Dewey realized that perception was not "neutral" but that knowledge and intelligence operated so as to influence it—"judgement is employed in the perception; otherwise the perception is merely sensory excitation . . .".[7] But, for whatever reason, it was Hanson rather than these others who finally fixed the idea in contemporary consciousness.

Hanson's thesis may be stated in one sentence: "The theory, hypothesis, framework, or background knowledge held by an investigator can strongly influence what is observed." Or, in his own words, "there is more to seeing than meets the eyeball".[8] Thus, observation cannot be a "neutral foundation", nor a "disinterested arbiter" of disputes, for the process of observation is influenced (unconsciously) by the theories or hypotheses that the observer holds *before* the observations are made! By way of illustration, consider a famous psychological experiment: Slides were made from cards selected from a deck, and these were projected for very short periods on to a screen in front of various observers. The slides were all correctly identified, except for one which was a trick slide where the card was given the wrong color (for example, a black six of hearts). Most commonly the observers in the experiment saw this trick slide as a blur, or they misidentified the suit of the card. A Hansonian interpretation of this is that the observers' background knowledge (cards in the suit of hearts are red in color) influences their perception. There is some sort of interaction with the sensory data received from the slide, so that the final result is that the observers actually *see* a blur. There have been other psychological experiments in which people looking at slides of drawings saw different things depending on what particular theories they were armed with.

Until recently there has been little dispute about the truth of Hanson's thesis. Philosophers of science as diverse as Hempel, Popper, Scheffler, and Kuhn have accepted it. Recently, however, Jerry Fodor has begun to swim against the tide by arguing that indeed there are some observations, important for science, that are theory-neutral.[9] Putting this to one side, however, for some time there has been dispute about the *significance* of the thesis. A passage from Kuhn nicely expresses this; he is discussing several scientists who were looking at the same phenomena but from the perspective of different background theories, and the Hansonian issue arises as to whether they were seeing different things:

> Do we, however, really need to describe what separates Galileo from Aristotle, or Lavoisier from Priestley, as a transformation of vision? Did these men really *see* different things when *looking at* the same sorts of objects? . . . Those questions can no longer be postponed . . .[10]

One thing does seem clear: Hanson's thesis successfully undermines crude forms of empiricism and positivism, that is, those philosophical positions that suggest knowledge is built up from a neutral or objective observational base. For, according to Hanson, there is *no* such theory-neutral base. There has been no dearth of writers who are willing to spell all this out. Thus, the neo-Marxist philosopher of education Kevin Harris, in his *Education and Knowledge* (1979) assumes all empiricists are crude, and he writes that:

> The empiricist observes, collects and infers. He goes out into the world and collects his data or his facts diligently, he puts them together and analyses them, and then he draws out relations between them.[11]

It is, then, an easy matter for Harris to show (correctly) that "most of the problems with this approach come in the first step", for the observation and collection of "facts" is of course theory-laden.

At this point the arguments of those who have been inspired by Hanson often go astray.[12] It does *not* follow from the (correct) fact that science is not built up from the solid foundation of neutral and objective observation, that observation plays no role in the warranting of scientific knowledge claims. For what is overlooked by Harris (and by others—to be met in later chapters —who also wish to destroy the credibility of empiricism in a similar way) is that modern forms of empiricism do not talk of the *origins* of knowledge but of its *validation* or *justification*.[13] This is an entirely different matter, where the theory-ladenness of observation presents no problem. Indeed, it can be argued that here Hanson is a blessing; for in order to test or validate a theory (or corroborate it, as Popper would say—in his view we can never *validate*), one *must* use that theory's "way of seeing the world". For instance, when examining Freudian theory to see if it is warranted, one must use Freud's categories to deduce tests—it is illicit to use Skinnerian categories (except, of course, for a test of Skinner, or for a comparative test of the two theories, but in this latter case one would still have to use Freud as well). Neither does it follow from the truth of Hanson's thesis (if, indeed, it is true) that the very possibility has disappeared of running objective tests of a scientific theory. For no reason has been offered to support the view that because a theory is being worked with, and because, therefore, the observer will be influenced to see the world via the categories contained in the theory, then the world is thereby bound to *confirm* that theory. Israel Scheffler has put the point clearly:

What is the upshot? There is no evidence for a general incapacity to learn from contrary observations, no proof of a pre-established harmony between what we believe and what we see. . . . Our categorizations and expectations guide by orienting us selectively toward the future; they set us, in particular, to perceive in certain ways and not in others. Yet they do not blind us to the unforeseen. They allow us to recognize what fails to match anticipation. . . .[14]

There is a crucial difference between the thesis advanced here about the role of observation in testing, and the notorious view—referred to earlier—that was held by some of the logical positivists of past decades concerning "observation sentences" or "protocol sentences" (such as "red here now"). In holding that observation can still play an important role in the testing or warranting of scientific knowledge claims, despite its theory-laden nature, it is not being held that scientific theories are reducible to—that is, are logically equivalent to—statements expressible fully in observational terms. Indeed, a multitude of critics of logical positivism have driven home the point that the theoretical concepts of science have meanings that transcend definition in observational terms. Thus there are few today who would endorse the quest of yesteryear of Rudolf Carnap, who stated the theme of his first major book as follows: "The main problem concerns the possibility of the rational reconstruction of the concepts of all fields of knowledge on the basis of concepts that refer to the immediately given" (immediately given, that is, in experience such as observation).[15] Nor would many now endorse the program of P. W. Bridgman and the operationists, a program that had at its heart the belief that the meaning of any scientific construct or variable is given by the specification of the "activities or operations" necessary to measure it.[16]

But here another conundrum arises. On one hand it has just been argued that theory-laden observation can be efficacious in testing a scientist's knowledge claims. On the other hand, if these claims cannot be translated fully into observational terms, then it would seem to follow that any test that was conducted would not be absolutely authoritative. A theory that does not necessitate a precise set of observational consequences can never be decisively probed by any test, for there must always be some leeway or looseness that could allow the scientist to argue that the theory somehow was compatible with the test results (whatever they were). How, then, can it be argued that observation plays any worthwhile role in testing?

In effect, this query is a narrower version of a larger general question: In what ways are scientific theories related to evidence?

Theory and evidence

In the past few decades a whole host of problems concerning the relation between scientific theories and evidence have come to light. The overall effect of these has been to cement in place the view that theories are *underdetermined* by evidence. That is, whatever evidence is available, a variety of theories can exist that are compatible with it; furthermore, as new evidence accumulates, there are a variety of ways in which every one of these competing theories could be adjusted in order to take account of the new material—no *specific* change in any theory is necessitated by new evidence, all that new evidence necessitates is that some accommodation be made somewhere. In the light of all this, there is little wonder that the rationality of science has become a topic of importance—what grounds are there for believing that *any* scientific theory is warranted, when the available evidence can also be used to support a host of rival theories? While this problem is a serious one, it will be argued that there are no grounds for despair.[17]

Because the developments that have led in this direction are numerous, and because they tend to overlap and partially reinforce each other, it is difficult to organize a clear discussion. The simplest procedure is to enumerate the points:

(i) As indicated during the discussion of Popper, it has been recognized at least since the time of David Hume in the eighteenth century that there is a problem with the inductive support of scientific theories. A finite amount of evidence, for example that all swans that have so far been observed are white, does not, in logic, establish the claim that *all* swans are white. This is an inductive inference, and by definition the conclusion goes beyond the evidence provided—a finite number of observations on swans does not firmly establish anything about all swans. And although at first sight it seems reasonable to claim that the finite evidence makes the inductive inference probable, it is not clear how to calculate the precise degree of probability, nor is it clear that this does not beg the whole question. For the heart of the problem of induction lies in whether we have sound reason to believe that evidence about the past can throw any light at all on the future. (It would help if we could establish that nature was regular; but of course this principle itself would be a product of induction, so there is no succor here.) Popper, it will be recalled, attempted to solve the problem by dissolving it—there is no problem of induction because there is no such form of reasoning.

(ii) With the questioning of the tenets of logical positivism over the past few decades—a matter to be discussed in Chapter 4—it has been generally recognized, as discussed earlier, that the theoretical terms of science cannot have their meanings rigidly defined in observational or operational terms. Instead, theoretical terms gain their meaning from the network of relationships that tie them in with other terms in a theory. A scientific theory is a whole, it is an entity made up of interconnected parts, and as a whole it is testable. Data can be fed in, providing that the net as a whole has some link with the observable or measurable realm—it was a mistake to believe that every individual theoretical term had to be so definable. Indeed, the image of a theory as net has gained great currency; even the partly-reformed positivist Carl Hempel expressed it well:

A scientific theory might therefore be likened to a complex spatial network: its terms are represented by the knots, while the threads connecting the latter correspond, in part, to the definitions and, in part, to the fundamental and derivative hypotheses included in the theory. The whole system floats, as it were, above the plane of observation and is anchored to it by rules of interpretation. These might be viewed as strings which are not part of the network but link certain points of the latter with specific places in the plane of observation.[18]

Now, the network analogy leads directly to the so-called Duhem-Quine thesis:[19] Evidence does not impinge on any particular individual item or theoretical element in science, it impinges on the whole net. According to Duhem and Quine, it is the theory as a whole, as a single complex entity, that interfaces with evidence. The theoretical elements are not isolable, they always travel with the other items in the net. And so it is as an interrelated whole that they face up to the test of experience. Consequently, if a piece of recalcitrant evidence emerges, it can be accommodated by any of a variety of changes or modifications to various parts of the network; one scientist may want to change one part of the theoretical net, while another may advocate that changes be made elsewhere—it is always possible, by making sufficient changes in other parts, to preserve a favored portion of the net that might, at first, seem to have been thrown into question by the new evidence. Of course, the ease with which various parts of the network can be preserved may vary; in order to save one favored portion, quite severe changes may have to be made elsewhere—the tradeoffs involved might be quite difficult ones to make. But the point is that theoretical changes and developments in science are not *necessitated* by the evidence; scientists are free to use their judgment and their creativity. (The point being made here parallels the one made earlier during the discussion of the underdetermination of theories, and it will be met again during the discussion of Piaget in Chapter 13.) It would be a mistake to interpret this as indicating that scientific theories are a matter of mere whim or individual taste; to stress that individual judgment is required is not to throw away all standards, it is just to stress that decisions cannot be made in any mechanical way. However, contemporary philosophers of science generally recognize that not all "non mechanical" decisions are equally sound, and one of the current unresolved issues is the precise delineation of the rational constraints that operate on scientific judgment.[20]

(iii) A number of issues have arisen which together make a similar point about testing. There is no mechanical procedure by which a given portion of a theoretical network in science can be put to decisive test. (It is here that Popper's views have run into trouble; testing and refutation are not so watertight as some of his work implies.)[21] A scientist can use a theory, or part of a theory, to deduce a prediction that if X is done, then Y should result. But if this test is carried out and Y does not result, refutation does not automatically follow, for there are many ways the new evidence can be accommodated; similarly, if Y does result, then there are various ways in which this can be accounted for. Again, a challenge for professional judgment.

For one thing, in striking contrast to older views of "scientific method", it is now accepted that it is legitimate to "save" or "repair" a theory that appears to have failed a test by introducing an *ad hoc* hypothesis. The "new" philosophers of science, led by Lakatos and Feyerabend, have provided many detailed historical case studies which give a quite realistic picture of how science has actually been carried out by successful scientists; and it is clear from this work that the use of *ad hoc* hypotheses is not uncommon, and furthermore that often it has turned out to be fruitful. Feyerabend made the point strongly:

> The idea of a method that contains firm, unchanging, and absolutely binding principles for conducting the business of science gets into considerable difficulty when confronted with the results of historical research. We find, then, that there is not a single rule, however plausible, and however firmly grounded in epistemology, that is not violated at some time or other. It becomes evident that such violations are not accidental events. . . . On the contrary, we see they are necessary for progress. . . . More specifically, the following can be shown: considering any rule, however "fundamental", there are always circumstances when it is advisable not only to ignore the rule, but to adopt its opposite.[22]

Most philosophers of science regard Feyerabend's "anarchistic" position as too strong; and again an unresolved issue is the nature of the restraints on the use of *ad hoc* hypotheses.

Another insight concerns the use of "auxiliary" premises in the making of scientific predictions. The point here is that no test consequences follow from an isolated theory; in order to put a theory to a test some chain of reasoning has to be followed, and data and information from other branches of science—as well as from common sense, mathematics, and so forth—have to be used. (Typically measurements are made, using instruments that were designed on the basis of a host of other theories; and calculations are performed, using formulae drawn from many areas of science and mathematics.) Hempel has a striking example:[23] Semmelweis, the nineteenth-century physician who realized (before the development of the germ theory of disease) that "childbed fever" was a type of blood poisoning, deduced that if the physicians in his hospital washed their hands before attending to patients giving birth, then the patients would not get infected. He chose to use chlorinated lime as the cleansing fluid. And his test was successful—incidence of the usually fatal fever dropped dramatically. It is clear here that as well as the theory under test (that fever was caused by infection of the bloodstream of the patients), Semmelweis was making other (auxiliary) assumptions—that washing the hands of doctors would be efficacious, that chlorinated lime would do the job, and so forth. If the test had failed, if the patients still became infected, he might have rejected his theory as being incorrect when in fact it may have been one of the auxiliaries that was to blame (e.g. the chlorinated lime might have been too weak). So, to generalize the point, if a test is failed it is a matter of judgment whether to blame the theory or to "pass the buck" to one of the ever-present auxiliary assumptions.

Another problem arises if the test has positive results. For as a point of logic, the positive result does not give unequivocal support to the theory or hypothesis under test; the form of inference involved is "affirming the consequent", which is fallacious.[24] If from some theory T it is deduced that some consequence C will follow under certain conditions, and if the test is carried out and C is found to occur, it cannot be concluded that therefore T is true:

> If T then C
> C
> _____
> Therefore T

Which is not valid. (Consider "If it is raining then it is cloudy; it is cloudy; therefore it is raining".)[25]

It was by reflecting upon these matters (in part) that Popper concluded that although a scientific theory or hypothesis cannot be proven, it *can* be decisively refuted—one negative result can show that a theory is untenable. The logical form involved here would be "modus tollens", which is valid:

> If T then C
> Not C
> _____
> Therefore, not T

Thus, "If it is raining then it is cloudy; it is not cloudy; therefore it is not raining", which is logically unassailable. This Popperian "naive falsification- ism", however, will not do as an account of the logic of scientific testing. (Popper has denied that he is "naive" in this sense.) For once it is recognized that, in carrying out the test, the scientist has made use of auxiliary premises or assumptions, then the negative test results can always be evaded by ascribing the blame on to one of these, or even by introducing some new *ad hoc* assumption. Schematically:

> If T (and given auxiliary A etc.), then C
> Not C
> _____
> Therefore, either not T or not A (etc.)

Which again is perfectly valid. So, sadly, a scientific hypothesis or theory can neither be disproven, nor proven, by means of tests.

A final group of problems concerning testing have given substance to the suggestion that it cannot be judged, in isolation from the corpus of scientific theory as a whole, whether or not a piece of evidence offers support for a particular theory or hypothesis. It is not necessary to pursue at great length Hempel's "raven paradox" or Goodman's "grue and bleen paradox";[26] suffice it to state that because scientific theories are underdetermined by evidence, any single piece of evidence—any observation—may in principle support a range of theoretical statements, no matter how fanciful. (Goodman's example shows that the observation that emeralds are green may also be taken to support another theory that they are "grue", that is, green up to a certain date and blue after that!) In order to judge what the evidence can most reasonably be interpreted as supporting, it seems as if other theories must be drawn upon. (For instance, in Goodman's example, there are theories about the chemical constituents of emeralds, and theories about how the color is caused by these constituents, and it is these other theories that make the grue hypothesis unlikely—greenness is too well "embedded" a concept to be bypassed so frivolously.) But again, it is all a matter of judgment, and there is no routine or mechanical procedure a scientist can follow to link his or her evidence to the theories that are under investigation.

Rational justification

The points discussed above each highlights, in its own way, the same fundamental issue: In what sense is the knowledge embodied in the sciences rationally justified or warranted? For scientific knowledge is not based, in any logically compelling sense, on observation; neither do tests absolutely confirm nor absolutely refute it. (Popper was at least *partly* right.) It seems that, on the basis of any body of evidence, a host of rival theories could be advanced, and the accumulation of further evidence does not compellingly disqualify any of these.

At first this situation seems shocking, but calm reflection puts the matter in a different light. It has long been realized that scientific knowledge is fallible; scientists seek the truth, and often think they have found it, but when pushed they usually concede that one day they may be shown to be wrong—the tide of opinion, and of evidence, may turn against them. Thus, Newtonian physics prevailed for several centuries, but eventually it succumbed to Einstein;[27] in its turn, Einsteinian physics has started to develop flaws that some believe signal its imminent overthrow. Science does move by "conjectures and refutations" —with the important caveat that refutations, as well as conjectures, are only tentative. Contemporary philosophy of science merely shows some of the logical and epistemological reasons why this must always be so.

But there is a point of deeper significance, a point which shows why philosophy of science has been a central area in philosophy in recent decades. The developments in philosophy of science that have been outlined have led to the abandonment (in many quarters) of justificationist or foundationalist epistemologies, and have inspired the development of many "postpositivist", "postempiricist" or "antinaturalistic" epistemologies (as will be seen in later chapters). The justificationist epistemologies—and all traditional schools of thought fit under this heading—worked on the supposition that we accept items of knowledge because they are soundly based. Thus, empiricists argued that knowledge claims were soundly based if they were based on experience, while rationalists claimed that knowledge was soundly based when supported by the "light of reason". Knowledge, in other words, was identified with authority; either the authority of experience or that of reason.

The new epistemologies are non-justificationist or non-foundationalist in character, although the term "non-justificationist" is somewhat misleading. People who adhere to this position still seek justified belief; the point is that they no longer hold that beliefs can be *absolutely* justified in the sense of being proven or being based upon unquestionable foundations. Walter Weimer has expressed it well:

> Knowledge claims must be defended, to be sure; however the defense of such a claim is not an attempt to prove it, but rather the marshalling of "good reasons" in its behalf. . . . The only way to defend fallible knowledge claims is by marshalling other fallible knowledge claims—such as the best contingent theories that we possess. There are no "ultimate" sources of knowledge or epistemological authorities.[28]

It will be recalled that similar passages are to be found in Popper's writings; referring to the issue of the "ultimate sources" of human knowledge, he wrote:

> I propose to assume, instead, that no such ideal sources exist—no more than ideal rulers—and that *all* "sources" are liable to lead us into error at times. And I propose to replace, therefore, the question of the sources of our knowledge by the entirely different question: "*How can we hope to detect and eliminate error?*"[29]

There is a metaphor that has been used by philosophers of science and by scientists for half a century that nicely captures all this. The scientist is like an explorer crossing a wide expanse of water on a rotting ship. The worst plank is chosen and replaced by a little lumber found in the hold, but during the process the explorer has to place full weight on the other and hopefully less rotten plants; after one plank is replaced, it can bear the weight while another board is thrown away and replaced, but all the while the new planks are themselves rotting. An exciting situation; no wonder scientists have been regarded as paragons of intellectual virtue and fortitude, worthy of emulation by lesser mortals.

A further point can be illustrated using this metaphor. The rationality of the scientist's endeavors cannot be judged by examining what is happening at any instant (tearing out a plank in mid-ocean is not always a good idea); rather, what happens over time has to be considered (whether or not the ship is progressively made more seaworthy). This focus upon change in scientific beliefs will be examined in the following chapter; suffice it to say here that Stephen Toulmin has endorsed the view that a person's rationality is displayed in how his or her beliefs change in the face of new evidence or experience.[30] And, as will be seen, Imre Lakatos also developed his "methodology of scientific research programs" to deal with this sort of situation; he stressed that there is no "instant rationality". A scientist is free to make the best adjustments to a theory that he or she can—by abandoning an auxiliary assumption, by adding an *ad hoc* ingredient, or even by just ignoring temporarily the embarrassing evidence. The crucial thing is whether such changes make the theory or research program more progressive, in the sense that it is now able to predict and explain phenomena that previously it could not deal with. Lakatos wrote:

> ... the idea of instant rationality can be seen to be utopian. But this utopian idea is the hallmark of most brands of epistemology. Justificationists wanted scientific theories to be proved even before they were published; probabilists hoped a machine could flash up instantly the value (degree of confirmation) of a theory, given the evidence; naive falsificationists hoped that elimination at least was the instant result of the verdict of experiment. I hope I have shown that *all these theories of instant rationality—and instant learning—fail.* . . . rationality works much slower than most people tend to think, and, even then, fallibly.[31]

Unfortunately, rotting planks are not the only hazard facing the ship of science. The shoal of relativism will have to be traversed during the next stage of the journey.

Relativism and "good reasons"

The position that was advanced in the previous section seems reasonable: A scientist defends a knowledge-claim by making the best case that is possible—by marshalling good arguments, relevant observations, solid experimental results, and so forth. And, where necessary, the scientist makes adjustments to the "web of science" (or to the "scientific research program") in the way that seems most appropriate and fruitful. The psychologist, educationist, and philosopher Donald Campbell has written a passage that captures these themes well:

> Non-laboratory social science is precariously scientific at best. But even for the strongest sciences, the theories believed to be true are radically underjustified and have, at most, the status of "better than" rather than the status of "proven". All common-sense and scientific knowledge is presumptive. In any setting in which we seem to gain new knowledge, we do so at the expense of many presumptions. . . . Single presumptions or small subsets can in turn be probed, but the total set of presumptions is not of demonstrable validity, is radically underjustified. Such are the pessimistic conclusions of the most modern developments in the philosophy of science.[32]

But by what criteria are these things to be judged? On what grounds can it be decided that indeed the arguments are cogent, that the evidence is relevant, and that the results are solid? For we have seen that the case can be made that these things are not clearcut—they are matters of professional judgment, and there can be disagreements. And it is here that the discussion needs to turn to the work of Thomas S. Kuhn and Imre Lakatos.

Notes and References

1. K. Popper, *Conjectures and Refutations*. NY: Harper Torchbooks, 1968, p. 35.
2. Ibid., p. 36.

3. Ibid., p. 50.

4. K. Popper, *Unended Quest*. La Salle, Illinois: Open Court, 1976, pp. 145–147.

5. K. Popper, *Conjectures and Refutations*, op. cit., p. 25.

6. N. R. Hanson, *Patterns of Discovery*. Cambridge: Cambridge University Press, 1958.

7. J. Dewey, op. cit., p. 143.

8. N. R. Hanson, op. cit., p. 7.

9. Jerry Fodor, "Observation Reconsidered", *Philosophy of Science*, **51**, 1 March 1984, pp. 23–43.

10. T. S. Kuhn, *The Structure of Scientific Revolutions*. Chicago: The University of Chicago Press, 1962, p. 119.

11. Kevin Harris, *Education and Knowledge*. London: Routledge, 1979, p. 5.

12. The evils of "rampant Hansonism" will be discussed further in Chapter 8.

13. A variety of perspectives on modern empiricism are presented in H. Morick, ed., *Challenges to Empiricism*. Indianapolis: Hackett Publishing, 1980.

14. I. Scheffler, *Science and Subjectivity*. NY: Bobbs-Merrill, 1967, p. 44.

15. R. Carnap, *The Logical Structure of the World*. Berkeley: University of California Press, 1969, Preface, p.v. This book was first published in 1928; Carnap later softened his views.

16. P. W. Bridgman, *The Logic of Modern Physics*. NY: Macmillan, 1927, p. 34.

17. For discussion of some issues, and a suggested solution to the problems, see C. Glymour, *Theory and Evidence*. Princeton NJ: Princeton University Press, 1980.

18. Carl Hempel, *Fundamentals of Concept Formation in Empirical Science*. Chicago: University of Chicago Press, 1952, p. 36.

19. So named for the turn-of-the-century Continental physicist-philosopher Pierre Duhem and the contemporary Harvard philosopher W. V. O. Quine, who both developed forms of this thesis.

20. For example, see Harvey Siegel, "Brown on Epistemology and the New Philosophy of Science", *Synthese*, 1983, **56**, pp. 61–89.

21. There are places, though, where Popper has seen this, and where he stresses the tentative nature of refutation.

22. Paul Feyerabend, "Against Method", in M. Radner and S. Winokur (eds.), *Analyses of Theories and Methods of Physics and Psychology*, Minnesota Studies in Philosophy of Science IV. Minneapolis: University of Minnesota Press, 1970, pp. 21–22.

23. Carl Hempel, *Philosophy of Natural Science*. Englewood Cliffs, NJ: Prentice-Hall, 1966, chs. 2, 3.

24. But see C. Glymour, op. cit., where he offers a "bootstrapping" theory of how evidence can be used to confirm a theory.

25. Jum Nunnally has a nice psychometrically-oriented example involving a hypothetical theory relating anxiety and stress. See his *Psychometric Theory*. NY: McGraw-Hill, 2nd. edition, 1978, p. 104.

26. A readable discussion of both of these can be found in K. Lambert and G. Brittan, *An Introduction to the Philosophy of Science*. Englewood Cliffs, NJ: Prentice-Hall, 1970, ch. 4.

27. Of course, Newtonian physics lives on as a very useful approximation, and the same fate may befall Einstein's work; "overthrow" in science does not always mean complete abandonment.

28. Walter B. Weimer, *Notes on the Methodology of Scientific Research*. Hillsdale, NJ: Lawrence Erlbaum, 1979, p. 41.

29. K. Popper, *Conjectures and Refutations*, op. cit., p. 25.

30. See the opening quotation in Toulmin's *Human Understanding*. Princeton, NJ: Princeton University Press, 1972.

31. I. Lakatos, in I. Lakatos and A. Musgrave, eds., *Criticism and the Growth of Knowledge*. Cambridge: Cambridge University Press, 1972, p. 174.

32. Donald T. Campbell, "Qualitative Knowing and Action Research", in M. Brenner, P. Marsh, and M. Brenner, eds., *The Social Context of Method*. NY: St. Martin's Press, 1978, p. 185.

3

The New Dynamics of Science

About a quarter of a century ago a new respect for the historiocity of science was born. This is not to say that previously there had been insensitivity to the fact that scientific understanding has been growing and changing, but with hindsight it is clear that the way in which change occurs was not fully appreciated, nor was the full significance of the phenomenon.

If a person—or a group—changes a belief from X to Y, then the question arises as to how it is known that Y is better (more adequate, or closer to the truth). If it is believed that changes in belief should be made on rational grounds, the question surfaces as to whether belief in Y is more rational than belief in X (given that only a finite amount of evidence is available, and given that the evidence accessible to mortals is rarely if ever fully reliable or convincing). Is a person who refuses to change to Y in the face of the new evidence, but who sticks with X, acting irrationally? The specter even arises that many cases of change in belief are not ones that can be helpfully explicated in terms of rationality at all—perhaps they have to be seen more in sociological or psychological terms.

Debates over these issues have a broad significance; they transcend the field of science. As mentioned earlier, science is usually regarded as a paragon of human knowledge, so if the dominant view about the nature of scientific knowledge undergoes revolutionary change who can say whether other fields of activity will remain unaffected? The philosopher Harold Brown put it succinctly:

> Scientific change cannot be analyzed in terms of logic or empirical methodology. . . . If this view, or one even close to it, is correct, it raises serious problems about the validity of scientific knowledge and the rationality of the scientific enterprise. Indeed, if we extend the extreme historicist thesis to encompass all knowledge, as we must if we are to take it seriously, it is difficult to understand how any knowledge or any theory of knowledge is possible.[1]

Kuhn, Wittgenstein, and the emergence of relativism

Kuhn's book, *The Structure of Scientific Revolutions* (1962), has meant many different things to many different people (a sampling of these views will occupy attention in Chapter 8). Undoubtedly one of its chief messages has been the importance of the framework or paradigm in the context of which a scientist's work takes place. For Kuhn challenged the view that the history of science is a story of unremitting progress, marked by a steady "accumulation of individual discoveries and inventions."[2] Instead, his perception was that throughout history scientists have been working within a series of discontinuous or incommensurable paradigms. At any one time, Kuhn argued, a particular paradigm acted as a framework that determined the key concepts and methods, the problems that were significant, and so on. Scientists at work within any paradigm were filling out the details and perhaps slightly extending it, a process Kuhn called "puzzle solving":

> Few people who are not actually practitioners of a mature science realize how much mop-up work of this sort a paradigm leaves to be done or quite how fascinating such work can prove in the execution. . . . Mopping-up operations are what engage most scientists throughout their careers. They constitute what I am here calling normal science. Closely examined, whether historically or in the contemporary laboratory, that enterprise seems an attempt to force nature into the preformed and relatively inflexible box that the paradigm supplies.[3]

For scientists working within a particular paradigm difficulties or anomalies arise from time-to-time, but these are usually set aside as being of minor importance. Eventually a revolutionary scientist treats them as a sign of decay, and is inspired to produce a new paradigm—a new framework of concepts and methods and so forth. The development of this new paradigm, and its competition for dominance with the older one, constitutes a scientific revolution.

Kuhn's notion of a paradigm has proven to be extremely controversial. One critic has noted that he used this key term in at least twenty-one different senses.[4] But the reaction here has been comparatively mild in comparison to the invective heaped upon the relativistic aspects of Kuhn's work.

For if a paradigm delineates the key concepts of a science and the methodological rules to be followed, then it is apparent that the adherents of one paradigm must think harshly of any rival paradigm—by the rules and criteria appropriate to the first, the second is likely to appear deficient, and of course vice versa. As a consequence, the movement of a scientist from one paradigm to another is, in sense, not a rational affair. The making of the judgment that presumably accompanies a rational shift in position is dependent upon the existence of rules or criteria, and these are always embedded *within* a paradigm. So it is not clear how adherents of one paradigm could *rationally* decide to switch positions, for the criteria they have to use would necessarily be inappropriate for the new paradigm. Kuhn put the issue vividly:

> Like the choice between competing political institutions, that between competing paradigms proves to be a choice between incompatible modes of community life. Because it has that character, the choice is not and cannot be determined merely by the evaluative procedures characteristic of normal science, for these depend in part upon a particular paradigm, and that paradigm is at issue. When paradigms enter, as they must, into a debate about paradigm

choice, their role is necessarily circular. Each group uses its own paradigm to argue in that paradigm's defense.[5]

Paradigm change becomes a-rational, rather like political or religious conversion.

Even most of those who regard Kuhn's work as flawed, and who see his notion of scientific paradigms as being so vague as to be almost worthless, are forced to acknowledge that scientists *do* work within the context of sets of theories and assumptions that play an important role in shaping the direction and form that their work takes. Thus, a Freudian psychologist will work with the concepts and methods of this theoretical framework, and will tackle problems that appear to be important from its perspective. And the radical behaviorist will work within a different framework. Kuhn, of course, went further than this, for he argued that rival paradigms are incommensurable—scientists in each will not be able to engage in rational dialogue across the boundary. Scientists in different paradigms, according to Kuhn, live and work "in different worlds".

Whether or not one goes the whole distance with Kuhn, he certainly put his finger on a problem concerning the rational or at least the objective status of scientific knowledge. For if the pursuit of science involves the assessing of "best arguments" and the giving of cogent criticism (as argued in the previous chapter), and if the scientist's criteria are greatly influenced by the framework in which he or she is housed, then it cannot be posited that the arguments advanced by a scientist from one framework are better (or "truer") than those put forward by someone from a different frame, for there are no framework-independent criteria (i.e. no "absolute" or "external" criteria) by which to decide between the two cases. Once again, the problem discussed in Chapter 2 arises—the claim of science to have solid knowledge seems to be overstated. The best that can be claimed, it appears, is that *relative to a given framework or paradigm*, a particular argument or a particular knowledge claim is well warranted. This Kuhnian line of thought has, indeed, led to the ship of science running aground on relativistic shores.[6]

Fortunately the whole train of argument is dubious, although a great deal of ink has been spilled over it in the past two decades. The crucial issue is whether Kuhn's incommensurability thesis is accepted; for if so—if two paradigms or frameworks are so disparate that rational discussion between them (and particularly the giving and receiving of sharp and cogent criticism) is impossible—then the relativistic conclusion is bound to be reached. If, however, the thesis is rejected (and as will be indicated shortly, there are good reasons to believe that it should be) then although it still needs to be acknowledged that scientists work within frameworks, it no longer follows that they are unable to engage in rational discourse with each other. And if rational discourse *is* possible, then in principle there is no insurmountable obstacle to the making of defensible interparadigmatic judgments about which knowledge claims are the best-supported ones. There is no mechanical procedure available for doing this, of course, but rationality has never been appropriately conceived as being a mechanical process.

There have been many lines of attack on Kuhn's incommensurability thesis.[7] Scheffler has argued that because two scientists differ in the paradigms to which they adhere—and because they thereby differ with respect to their "first order" concepts and criteria—it does not follow that they disagree at higher or deeper levels of abstraction (the "second order" level) about the basic criteria that are to be used in judging the merits of scientific work. There is, according to this view, no breakdown in communication at the really fundamental levels.[8] Toulmin has stressed that although two paradigms may differ with respect to many important items (witness Newtonian and Einsteinian physics), there will be many items that they possess in common (both Einstein and Newton accepted much of the corpus of physics, mathematics and logic). These common ingredients ensure that the paradigms overlap, rather than being incommensurable, and the channel for communication is left open: "paradigm-switches certainly need not lead to inescapable incomprehension."[9] Still other writers have attacked the theory of meaning that lies at the heart of much thinking about incommensurability and relativism—the theory, sometimes called semantic holism, that if a term (e.g. "energy") is embedded in several different theories or paradigms, then its meaning in all of these cases will be quite different because meaning is determined by the whole "web" in which the term is located. (It is interesting to note that this theory of meaning—related to the Duhem-Quine thesis discussed earlier—is one that has come down from the positivists and their view of scientific theories as networks; many contemporary relativists who accept this theory are fond of saying that there was nothing they admired about the positivists, an issue to be touched upon in the next chapter.) Much of Newton-Smith's book *The Rationality of Science*, to mention only one recent source, is devoted to a discussion of this theory of meaning which he calls "radical meaning variance". He points, *inter alia*, to a consequence of the theory that has been widely recognized: Rival paradigms cannot be incompatible if the meanings of their terms are different. For if a particular key term appears in rival paradigms, then because in each it would be used in such different ways, and it would be embedded in such different conceptual webs, in effect it would be a different term in each setting, and so there would be no bar to accepting both the "rival" paradigms for they are not *really* rivals! In other words, if paradigms are incommensurable a person is free to accept both of them:

The meaning of a theoretical term was said to be determined by the entire set of sentences within the theory containing the term. Consequently any change in the postulates containing a given theoretical term was claimed to bring a change in the meaning of that term. Thus, if

Einstein and Newton discourse about mass, force and all that, they fail to disagree. They are simply equivocating. On this account of the matter the assertion by the Newtonian "Mass is invariant" and the assertion by the Einsteinian "Mass is not invariant" are not logically incompatible, as the meaning of "mass" is not constant across the theories.[10]

This is an effective argument because it is stated in terms that must be accepted by any follower of Kuhn who is enamored of semantic holism. There are independent grounds, however, for denying that semantic holism gives an adequate account of how concepts acquire meaning. The term "electron"—to take a simple but fair example—was introduced into science not as a meaningless term which would gain significance from the theoretical network in which it was located (a view, as has been intimated, that requires that as the web changes the term changes in meaning). Rather, the term was introduced to refer to whatever entity was present in the physical realm and was the cause of certain detectable effects—such things as sparks of static, electrostatic attraction, and so on. As theories were developed, these did not change the meaning of the term "electron" (its denotation remained the same); rather, they threw light on the properties of this purported entity. On this view, then, the Newtonian and Einsteinian certainly understand each other when they debate (about "mass", to revert to Newton-Smith's example). They merely are disagreeing about the properties that entities possess, and thus there is no incommensurability. The long and short of it is that the followers of Kuhn are between a rock and a hard place: either semantic holism is wrong, in which case there is no incommensurability, or else semantic holism is right, in which case there is no incommensurability either!

There is another important point to be made about relativism. In practice no one can consistently lead a life in strict adherence to the relativist position, for it is self-defeating. Relativists hold that their viewpoint is true, that is, true for everyone, and not just for them. And, furthermore, no relativist would accept the argument from a colleague who had presented an incorrect or faulty piece of work that "It is only faulty or incorrect for you, but from my perspective it is sound".[11] It is apparent that the making of corrections to the work of others, and the detection of error, disappear as options for the consistent relativist.[12] Certainly there are few scientists who would be prepared to be so charitable to their rivals as to forego the right to offer criticisms in the course of day-to-day professional activity. On the contrary, on all sides in science there is commitment to truth as a *regulative ideal* (as Popper and others have termed it); scientists try to determine the truth and to hold true beliefs—their disputes are about whose views *are* true, or are *to be regarded tentatively* as being true. Toulmin sums up a recent brief discussion of some of these issues pertaining to relativism with the words "it is hard to see how Kuhn can ultimately hold his critics at bay".[13]

Kuhn and Winch

Kuhn's treatment of science as a community endeavor, and his treatment of scientists who are working within the same paradigm as forming a community of like-minded investigators, highlights the similarity between his position and that of members of the Wittgensteinian tradition in philosophy. In his *Philosophical Investigations* (1951), Wittgenstein did not discuss paradigms, but rather, games—the multitude of games that are played with language, such as giving orders, reporting events, speculating, testing hypotheses, making jokes, "asking, thanking, cursing, greeting, praying."[14] Presumably each of these activities had its own set of rules or criteria (no matter how fuzzy a set); so, it would be inappropriate to judge the game of making hypotheses about nature in terms of the criteria appropriate to the game of making jokes. Furthermore, Wittgenstein claimed that a language game is part of a "form of life". In essence, then, games are a species of paradigm, or more likely vice versa.

Peter Winch has approached various issues in philosophy of social science from this general Wittgensteinian orientation, and his work brings out clearly the similarity between the Wittgensteinian and Kuhnian theses. In his influential book, *The Idea of a Social Science*, which appeared about four years before Kuhn's volume, and also in several papers written later, Winch made use of some fascinating examples—a sociologist studying religions, and a Western anthropologist studying the "primitive culture" of the Azande. The sociologist or anthropologist, on one hand, is working within a particular scientific framework (or game or form of life or paradigm, to use the Kuhnian and Wittgensteinian terminology somewhat liberally), whereas, on the other hand, the religious zealot or the Azande tribesman is working and living within another.

The point Winch wanted to make about cases such as this was a sophisticated one not fully appreciated by his opponents.[15] It is not that Western scientists cannot communicate or offer valid criticism cross-culturally; but before they can do so, these scientists must be able to identify relevant aspects of the form of life under study, and to do this they must make use of the criteria accepted within that particular form. For instance, if a Pharisee is chanting or performing some ritual action, is that an example of a religious practice? To identify it as such, the sociologists of religion have to make use of the criteria for demarcating the religious practices not that they use, but which are used in the Pharisee's culture (or to use the now common terminology, an emic rather than an etic approach is necessary). Hence, as Winch puts it:

> But if the judgments of identity—and hence the generalizations—of the sociologist of religion rest on criteria taken from religion, then his relation to the performers of religious activity cannot be just that of observer to the observed.... A historian or sociologist of religion must

himself have some religious feeling if he is to make sense of the religious movement he is studying and understand the considerations which govern the lives of its participants.[16]

A follower of Kuhn would make exactly the same point; to take a dramatic case, if psychologists in the Skinnerian behavioristic paradigm (assuming it is a paradigm)[17] wished to criticize the types of evidence considered by Freudians, they would have to use—and hence understand—the Freudian criteria for judging the admissibility of evidence. (This point was also alluded to in the previous chapter.)

In general terms, then, the essentials of Winch's position (which would be endorsed by many followers of Kuhn) are as follows: (a) Before we can criticize some activity or belief, in either our own society or a foreign culture, we first have to identify what game (or form of life or paradigm) it belongs to; (b) In order to do this we must use the appropriate rules or criteria, and these will be the ones that are *internal* to that form of life; (c) When we come to criticize the identified activity or belief, we may well see that it is inappropriate to judge it in terms of the rules apposite to Western science (or to some favored branch of science)—there are many forms of life or paradigms, and it may turn out that there is incommensurability; (d) The point of a paradigm or form of life is only apparent to those *within* that particular form.

This general Wittgensteinian-Winchian-Kuhnian orientation has been strongly attacked by critics from across the philosophical spectrum, and especially by those occupying Popperian wavelengths.

It is clear that one such, I. C. Jarvie, did not fully appreciate the intricacies of Winch's position, but nevertheless his critical points have considerable force. While he admits that much of Winch's argument is "a plausible, even a beguiling one",[18] Jarvie correctly notes that essentially it makes external criticisms of forms of life an impossibility. Thus, the practice of some primitive tribe—the making of a sacrifice before the planting of crops, for example —cannot be criticized by an outsider on moral or religious or even agricultural grounds; for it may well be that the form (or paradigm or game) being engaged in has a point that cannot be translated as being the same as the point of our Western science or agriculture or morality or religion. The ritual could be part of a form of life or game that we do not have, and which we therefore cannot identify in our own terms, and hence cannot properly criticize—in short, their form of life might be incommensurable with ours. (And even if the ritual was in a game that we also play, it would be very hard to establish this.) As Jarvie puts it, Winch's view is that "our universe of discourse cannot appraise other universes of discourse, or appraise itself as the only true universe of discourse. Reality is built into a universe of discourse."[19] And a little later he adds that Winch "maintains in his book that understanding a society is a kind of conceptual empathy which imprisons you in a universe of discourse that cannot evaluate itself."[20] On this reading of Winch, there is little that separates him from Kuhn; and of course the relativism shines through.

From the point-of-view of the Popperians, this is an entirely unsatisfactory position. It will be recalled that the essence of rationality, for them, is the delivery and acceptance of strong criticism, particularly that which is aimed at the bases or foundations of a position. But this is precisely what seems excluded by the Winchian-Wittgensteinian-Kuhnian relativistic view and the case for incommensurability that is central to it; no wonder that Popperians have been bitterly opposed to the ideas of all three men. Jarvie summarizes the counter position well; there is, he argues,

> something like a community of rationality shared by all men, but recognized or fostered by different societies in varying degrees (none being perfect). This rationality consists at the very least in learning from experience, and especially from mistakes.[21]

It is this that makes possible the escape from the prison of incommensurability (a matter discussed more fully earlier in the chapter), and it is the common thread of rationality that allows rational argument to take place across frameworks, not only between "primitives and primitives, primitives and westerners, but even between Einsteins and Bohrs."[22]

Some applications to educational and social science research

Before continuing the exposition of post-Kuhnian developments in the understanding of the dynamics of scientific change, it may be fruitful to sketch a few of the perspectives on actual research in education and the social and human sciences that are opened up by the ideas already encountered. (Some of the more relativistic applications of Kuhn and Winch will be held over until Chapter 8).

(1) The issue of whether or not different paradigms or frameworks or forms of life are incommensurable has direct relevance for researchers. The social and human sciences are replete with contrasting approaches, methodologies, and theories, and in many cases it is not clear whether these are, in fact, conflicting or complementary (or "orthogonal"). Certainly it is common for researchers to identify their "rivals" as being in a different paradigm, without much attention being paid to what this might mean. The field of history has been shaken by the work of the revisionists (who are, perforce, faced by those whose work they want to revise), and of feminist historians, and others; psychology is the home of behaviorists, neo-behaviorists, information-processing researchers, Adlerians, Freudians, and so on; in sociology the descendants of the functionalists face up to neo-Marxists, symbolic interactionists, sociobiologists. . . . In the field of evaluation of educational and social programs there has been a conscious effort to develop a variety of rival approaches, and so models taken from the aesthetic domain and the legal sphere live alongside experimental and quasi-experimental approaches, and a host of case-study methodologies. In all fields there is growing tension between the so-called "qualitative" and "quantitative" paradigms.

A somewhat hoary example brings out the issues starkly. Consider followers of Freud and Skinner (possibly these are declining bands, but by no means are they extinct, and rumors persist that contemporary cognitive science is about to rediscover Freud). At any rate, researchers who accept the radical behaviorist framework deny that it is scientific to speculate about "inner" causes, especially "ghostly" entities that are in principle unobservable (such as ego, id, and death wish); and of course they focus on behavior and its observable antecedents and consequences. Many Freudians take the diametrically opposite view; some would argue that the Skinnerians have adopted an untenable positivistic account of the nature of science, and that they fail to take seriously phenomena about human beings that all of us are directly acquainted with through personal experience. There are some Freudians, however, who acknowledge that they are not playing the "scientific game"; the point of their game is different, and can be appreciated fully only from inside its boundaries.

A follower of Winch, Wittgenstein, and Kuhn would gleefully point to the incommensurability of frameworks that is illustrated here. On the other hand, a follower of Popper and Jarvie (and perhaps of Toulmin) would argue that while there is severe disagreement between the behaviorists and the Freudians, there is no incommensurability; both sides understand each other, they just happen to think the rival view is wrong. If the positions were incommensurable, then it would be possible (as argued earlier) to accept *both*.

(2) It is evident that cross-cultural study raises thorny issues.[23] Some types of research avoid the problems, essentially being studies within some Western framework or paradigm that require straightforward cross-cultural observational data. A simple example would be the study of various national dietary habits and their correlation with the incidence of types of intestinal cancers. (Is the incidence of stomach cancer in Japan due to the high consumption of ingredients we do not imbibe so frequently, such as teriyaki sauce?)

The situation is entirely different if the behavior being studied is inseparably bound up with the rules, mores, or understandings within that culture. The study of discipline in schools, of interaction between teachers and pupils or teachers and parents, of moral behavior and moral cognition—these and a host of other research problems are plagued by the difficulties discussed earlier. For even to describe the observed behavior involves categorizing it ("X is an example of pupil disobedience to authority", "Y is an example of parental disinterest in the school curriculum"), and this in turn involves understanding the distinctions made and the rules followed within the culture or group under investigation. What a researcher in one framework may consider to be disobedience to authority, may count as healthy independence to someone looking from a different perspective—the emic and the etic yield different categorizations. Given all this, it is sobering to reflect on the difficulties that Lawrence Kohlberg and his associates faced when they attempted to show that the stages in the development of moral cognition in children are invariant across cultures; this research depended heavily upon a standard test instrument (embodying the famous "Kohlbergian dilemmas") which Kohlberg administered to children in the USA, Taiwan, Mexico, and Turkey. How can it be judged that the questions had the same significance to youngsters from such culturally diverse groups? This is a vital methodological issue, and it is not clear that Kohlberg tackled it in a sufficiently sophisticated way. (Kohlberg's work will be used as an important case study in Part C of this book.)

The cross-cultural work of Michael Cole and his co-workers makes an interesting comparison.[24] Working in Liberia, Cole quickly realized that "standard" tasks given to Western children in experiments on cognitive development had completely different significance in the African setting, and he abandoned them and instead adopted an "ethnographic" approach to his psychological research.

(3) The literature on paradigms, games, and forms of life also is directly relevant to the field of education by way of the light it throws on certain curriculum issues. In particular, the "structure of knowledge" theorists— Joseph Schwab and Philip H. Phenix in the United States,[25] and Paul Hirst, R. S. Peters, and J. P. White in Britain[26]—treat the various forms of knowledge that traditionally constitute the main body of school and university curricula in a way that closely relates them to Kuhnian paradigms and Wittgensteinian forms of life.

Schwab and Hirst have given similar analyses of the structure possessed by a form of knowledge. In general terms, they stress that each form has a set of distinctive concepts which are related in, again, distinctive ways; and they hold that each form has its own characteristic "methodological" features, such as tests against experience and manipulative techniques. The difficulties associated with this position have been thoroughly aired in the literature of philosophy of education over the last decade or so (and some of these will be taken up in the detailed case study in Part C).

For the present purposes, the relevant issue is that the various forms of knowledge (Hirst identified some seven separate forms—mathematics, the physical sciences, history, and so on), each with their own distinctive structures, give incommensurable views of reality, and to understand the viewpoint of each form it is necessary to become immersed in it (to absorb, one might say, its distinctive "form of life"). In the words of Peters and Hirst:

> What we are suggesting is that within the domain of objective experience and knowledge, there are such radical differences in kind that experience and knowledge of one form is neither equatable with, nor reducible to, that of any other form. In each case it is only by a grasp of the appropriate concepts and tests that experience and knowledge of that kind become available to the individual. Achievements in one domain must be recognized as radically different from those in any other.[27]

This position has important implications. Hirst and Peters recognize that some subjects (geography is a good case) are really "fields" to which several disciplines or forms of knowledge can make a contribution. In other terminology, subjects such as geography are "multidisciplinary" fields. But it would appear to follow from the analysis of Hirst and Peters that a genuine interdisciplinary subject (that is, an integrated blend of several forms) is a *logical* impossibility, for the forms of knowledge are incommensurable.

The dynamics of research programs

Within the field of philosophy of science, attention in the post-Kuhnian period has not focussed solely upon questions about the nature, and incommensurability, of paradigms. The whole manner in which the corpus of science undergoes change (and possibly development) has been thrown open to vigorous debate; and accompanying this debate has been a renewed effort to use case studies from the history of science to inform the discussion. Once again, a brief sampling will be presented from the available material, before the discussion turns to the application of the relevant ideas to the field of educational and social science research.

In his now classic paper "Falsification and the Methodology of Scientific Research Programs", written for a conference discussing Kuhn's views, Popper's colleague Imre Lakatos reached a number of important and controversial conclusions about the nature of scientific inquiry.[28] Thinking of himself (or, at least, publicly presenting himself) as merely extending Popper's philosophy of science, Lakatos argued that there is no magical method of "instant rationality" and that there is no watertight way to take a piece of scientific work and decide upon its merits. Work that appears to be of crucial importance at one time may shrink into insignificance; work that now is apparently sound may later be judged as faulty; and the grounds offered by a scientist for ignoring difficulties or even clear counter-evidence may seem entirely cavalier at one time, but remarkably insightful at some other date.

So Lakatos turned to *ongoing* science, to *programs* of scientific research. Here it *is* possible to make judgments; the direction in which the program has been moving over time can be assessed as either progressive or degenerative. Changes or "improvements" to a research program, the strategems adopted to accommodate difficult experimental findings, and so forth, should always be progressive; they should be content-increasing by anticipating new facts. In Lakatos's view, a scientific research program is rather like a game with evolving rules. Central to the activity are certain ingredients that the players do not want to change under any circumstances (in baseball, for example, there are certain rules and procedures that cannot be changed without the game losing its identity and changing into something entirely different). To preserve this "hard core", there must be other elements that are expendable or subject to change in the light of experience. (Baseball has its "designated hitter" rule, rules governing the replacement of pitchers, and so on.) These form the "protective belt". And finally, changes in the program are directed by the "positive heuristic". (In baseball, presumably, changes in the game are directed by the heuristic principle of making it more of a thrilling competition and spectacle.) This is how one of Lakatos's colleagues summarizes his theory, in a memorial volume of essays:

> According to this methodology the basic unit of scientific discovery is not an isolated theory but rather a research program. Such a program, developing under the guidance of its heuristic, issues in a series of theories. Each such theory though it may contain an irrefutable ("metaphysical") part, will be refutable, but the typical response of the proponent of the program to an experimental refutation will be to amend his theory—leaving certain assumptions (the "hard core" of the program) unchanged, whilst replacing other ("auxiliary") assumptions.[29]

In this same memorial volume, the controversial nature of Lakatos's position is underscored by a number of criticial essays, including several by former colleagues and students. A variety of historical examples are dissected to see if, in fact, they bear out Lakatos's account. Books offering alternative models of scientific change have appeared.[30] (In Part C of the present volume, Lakatos's methodology will be illustrated in more depth by being applied to the analysis of the Kohlbergian research program on the development of moral reasoning.)

One more or less sympathetic critic who deserves special mention is Paul K. Feyerabend, who developed many of his own views through vigorous dialogue with Lakatos. Feyerabend calls himself an anarchist, and he asserts that while it is not, perhaps, the most attractive political view, it "is certainly excellent medicine for *epistemology*, and for the philosophy of science".[31] In a footnote added at a later date, he wrote that he now preferred to think of himself as a Dadaist, to avoid certain unpleasant connotations of the term "anarchist".

Feyerabend goes further than Lakatos, and asserts that there is no way at all in which we can pass definitive judgment on the work of scientists. "Anything goes," he constantly argues, for there is no way in advance that we can determine what methods will force nature to yield her secrets. And the greater the diversity of methods and theories that are being used, the better the quest will be, because there will be constant challenge, criticism, stimulation, and interchange.[32]

> The idea of a method that contains firm, unchanging, and absolutely binding principles for conducting the business of science meets considerable difficulty when confronted with the results of historical research. We find then, that there is not a single rule, however plausible, and however firmly grounded in epistemology, that is not violated at some time or other. It becomes evident that such violations are not accidental events. . . . On the contrary, we see that they are necessary for progress.[33]

To sum up this brief discussion, then, it would seem that although there is little overall unanimity, it would not be reckless to assert that contemporary philosophy of science emphasizes the importance of research programs progressively opening up new phenomena, the exposing of assumptions (including ones that are difficult to give up as well as the ones that are expendable), and the giving and receiving of strong criticism (and especially valuable here is "external" criticism, criticism from outside one's own theoretical frame). Together with all this goes a rather more charitable attitude than existed in the past; scientists can no longer be condemned automatically if they are caught making *ad hoc* hypotheses. The main focus of attention in all this obviously is the process of scientific change.

Change and progress in research

Over recent decades there has been a constant stream of criticism of the whole social science and educational research enterprise; this will form the topic of discussion in the second part of this book. The misconceived, misdirected, trivial, and fruitless nature of much research has been touted in a variety of journals; to mention just one example, the "house journal" of the American Educational Research Association, the *Educational Researcher*, has (creditably, from a Popperian viewpoint) carried an unusually high number of articles lambasting the work of various members of the Association. There have been conferences and symposia to discuss the lack of impact of research on practice.[34] And a number of books either offer guidance about fruitful ways to critique research,[35] or suggest how to redirect research efforts,[36] or else they attack the very cornerstones of educational and social science research methods.[37] To this list must now be added work inspired by Lakatos's "methodology of scientific research programs".

The benefits that can be expected to accrue from application of this new critical methodology can be highlighted through contrast with good work done from a more conventional position. In their book *Appraising Educational Research*, Millman and Gowin set out to train students of education to think critically about cases of educational research. The book reprints eight research papers—none of them "straw men" but all in some way useful pieces of work—and then a critique is given of each in a "question and answer" format. The critiques focus upon such issues as whether the research achieves its stated aims, the type of evidence or data adduced and whether it is compelling or ambiguous, whether the overall design of the research is sound, and the use of key concepts throughout the research report.

Clearly, all these matters are important, especially for researchers in training who must learn to profit from both the positive and negative features of preceding work; but there are some vital issues that are left unaddressed.

One striking feature of the eight individual case studies presented by Millman and Gowin is that they are, indeed, *individual*. Their book does not grapple with the *dynamics* of research—the fact that research usually is inspired by a theoretical position, and is part of an ongoing program or loosely defined movement. Furthermore, a researcher usually will criticize earlier work, and will try to improve upon it (the full ruminations that are gone through probably will not appear in the final published paper); and in turn the researcher's own efforts will be subjected to scrutiny by the peer-group, and will be rejected, or revised, or emulated. If full justice is to be done to educational and social science research, then some way must be found to incorporate evaluation of the ongoing stream of work plus the basic theoretical orientation that has inspired it (and which might be modified a little as a result of it). Even a casual reader of Lakatos and Feyerabend, not to mention Kuhn and Popper, cannot help but become sensitized to these issues.

A brief example may help to clarify the newly emerging mode of criticism or appraisal. (In Part C, as already mentioned, another and more detailed application will be made of Lakatos's methodology.)

In 1969 the age-old "environment versus heredity" dispute was revitalized by the appearance in the *Harvard Educational Review* of Arthur Jensen's paper "How Much Can We Boost IQ and Scholastic Achievement?".[38] This, together with the related work of H. J. Eysenck in Britain, suggested that intelligence (as measured by IQ tests) was in large part genetically determined. The issue was taken up vigorously by supporters of the environmentalist school of thought. Rebuttal followed upon rebuttal; the *Harvard Educational Review* alone was able to fill two volumes with reprints of the articles it had published on the matters in dispute. It is apparent that the two rival viewpoints can be treated as competing research programs; the dynamic interaction between them (one position rebutting the other, and in turn trying to fortify itself against new arguments and data from the opposition) can be evaluated in terms of Lakatos's methodology. Are the rival programs progressing or degenerating? Are the changes in the respective "protective belts" such that new phenomena are uncovered? Peter Urbach, a colleague of Lakatos, made a study along these lines and concluded that the hereditarian or Jensenist position was stronger, considered as a research program with its own dynamic.[39] However, a supporter of Feyerabend and Lakatos would emphasize that this does not mean the environmentalist position is the *wrong* one; there are no sure criteria for judging the longterm outcome of rivalry between several research programs. One that is weaker now may be stronger later.

Conclusion

The last two chapters have recounted the main lines of development of the new understanding of the epistemology of science, indeed, the new epistemology of all human knowledge. It is fitting to allow Popper to sum-up:

> epistemology becomes . . . the theory of the growth of knowledge. It becomes the theory of problem-solving, or, in other words, of the construction, critical discussion, evaluation, and

critical testing, of competing conjectural theories. . . . This is how we lift ourselves by our bootstraps out of the morass of our ignorance; how we throw a rope into the air and then swarm up it—if it gets any purchase, however precarious, on any little twig.[40]

Notes and References

1. Harold Brown, "For a Modest Historicism", *The Monist*, **60**, October 1977, pp. 540–541.
2. T. S. Kuhn, *The Structure of Scientific Revolutions*. Chicago: University of Chicago Press, 1962, p. 2.
3. Ibid., p. 24.
4. Margaret Masterman, "The Nature of a Paradigm", in I. Lakatos and A. Musgrave, eds., *Criticism and the Growth of Knowledge*. Cambridge: Cambridge University Press, 1970.
5. Kuhn, op. cit., p. 93.
6. Mandelbaum distinguishes three types of relativism in "Subjective, Objective, and Conceptual Relativisms", in M. Krausz and J. Meiland, eds., *Relativism: Cognitive and Moral*. Notre Dame, Indiana: University of Notre Dame Press, 1982.
7. For a good overall view, see Harvey Siegel, "Objectivity, Rationality, Incommensurability, and More", *British Journal for Philosophy of Science*, **31**, 1980, pp. 359–375.
8. I. Scheffler, *Science and Subjectivity*. Indianapolis: Bobbs-Merrill, 1967, pp. 81–83.
9. Stephen Toulmin, *Human Understanding*. Princeton, NJ: Princeton University Press, 1971, p. 123.
10. W. H. Newton-Smith, op. cit., p. 11.
11. But see the argument that relativists can escape this, in the Conclusion to D. Thomas, *Naturalism and Social Science*. Cambridge: Cambridge University Press, 1979.
12. This is discussed further in Chapter 8.
13. Stephen Toulmin, "From Form to Function: Philosophy and History of Science in the 1950s and Now", *Daedalus*, Summer 1977, p. 156.
14. Ludwig Wittgenstein, *Philosophical Investigations*. NY: Macmillan, 1968, p. 23.
15. See the exchange between Winch and I. C. Jarvie in R. Borger and F. Cioffi, eds., *Explanation in the Behavioral Sciences*. Cambridge: Cambridge University Press, 1970, pp. 231–248.
16. P. Winch, *The Idea of a Social Science*. London: Routledge, 1967, pp. 87–88.
17. Although it has some of the requisite features, there are reasons to doubt it is a paradigm. See B. Mackenzie, *Behaviorism and the Limits of Scientific Method*. London: Routledge, 1977, especially ch. 1.
18. I. Jarvie, "Understanding and Explanation in Sociology and Social Anthropology", in Borger and Cioffi, op. cit., p. 235.
19. Ibid., p. 236.
20. Ibid., p. 246.
21. Ibid., p. 238.
22. Ibid., p. 239.
23. There are some excellent articles in B. Wilson, ed., *Rationality*. Oxford: Blackwell, 1970; and S. Benn and G. Mortimore, eds., *Rationality and the Social Sciences*. London: Routledge, 1976.
24. M. Cole *et al.*, *The Cultural Context of Learning and Thinking*. NY: Basic Books, 1971.
25. See J. J. Schwab, "Structure of the Disciplines: Meanings and Significances", in G. Ford and L. Pugno, eds., *The Structure of Knowledge and the Curriculum*. Chicago: Rand McNally, 1965, pp. 1–30.
26. P. H. Hirst, "Liberal Education and the Nature of Knowledge", in *Philosophical Analysis and Education*. ed. R. D. Archambault, London: Routledge, 1965, pp. 113–138; R. S. Peters and P. H. Hirst, *The Logic of Education*. London: Routledge, 1970.
27. Peters and Hirst, op. cit., p. 65.
28. I. Lakatos, "Falsification and the Methodology of Scientific Research Programs", in Lakatos and Musgrave, eds., *Criticism and the Growth of Knowledge*, op. cit., pp. 91–196.
29. J. Worrall, "Imre Lakatos (1922–74)", in R. Cohen, P. Feyerabend, and M. Wartofsky, eds., *Essays in Memory of Imre Lakatos*. Boston: Reidel, 1976, pp. 5–6.
30. See, for example, Larry Laudan, *Progress and Its Problems*. Berkeley: University of California Press, 1977.

31. P. Feyerabend, *Against Method*. London: Verso, 1978, p. 17.

32. This is a theme of Feyerabend's paper "How To Be a Good Empiricist", in P. Nidditch, ed., *The Philosophy of Science*. Oxford: Oxford University Press, 1974, pp. 12–39.

33. P. Feyerabend, *Against Method*, op. cit., p. 23.

34. See Fred Kerlinger, "The Influence of Research on Education Practice", *Educational Researcher*, **6**, September 1977, pp. 5–12; and Philip Jackson and Sara Kieslar, "Fundamental Research and Education", ibid., pp. 13–18.

35. E.g., Jason Millman and D. Bob Gowin, *Appraising Educational Research*. Englewood Cliffs, NJ: Prentice-Hall, 1974.

36. L. G. Thomas, ed., *Philosophical Redirection of Educational Research*, 71st Yearbook of the NSSE, Part 1. Chicago: University of Chicago Press, 1972.

37. See R. Harre and P. Secord, *The Explanation of Social Behavior*. Totowa, NJ: Littlefield, Adams, 1973; D. Morrison and R. Henkel, eds., *The Significance Test Controversy*. Chicago: Aldine, 1970.

38. A. Jensen, "How Much Can We Boost IQ and Scholastic Achievement?", *Harvard Educational Review*, **39**, Winter 1969, pp. 1–123.

39. P. Urbach, "Progress and Degeneration in the IQ Debate", Parts I and II, *British Journal for the Philosophy of Science*, **25**, June 1974, pp. 99–135, and September 1974, pp. 235–259.

40. K. Popper, "Epistemology Without a Knowing Subject", in his *Objective Knowledge*. Oxford: The Clarendon Press, 1972, pp. 142, 148.

4

The Demise of Positivism

There is a mystery that can serve as an allegory for the fate of positivism in the middle decades of the twentieth century. It concerns the death of the Czar and his family at the time of the Russian Revolution. The "received account" is that all of them died after being taken prisoner, but rumors persisted that Princess Anastasia survived and lived to a ripe age in hiding. Presumably she changed her name, but those close to her would have known her true identity. Once a Romanov, always a Romanov.

The parallel is this: Without giving away all the secrets of the plot to be unravelled in the subsequent pages, it has been claimed by many that a philosophical position, positivism, was dominant during the middle third of the century (if not back through the turn of the century), and that it had a profound but pernicious influence on conceptions of the nature of science. Major researchers in education and the social sciences, it can be argued, were in turn influenced by this erroneous view of science. Luckily, however, positivism eventually sickened and died—perhaps at the hands of, but certain making way for, the new accounts of the nature of science that have been discussed in the preceding chapters; its death also allowed more revolutionary views to blossom. Thus Rabinow and Sullivan, in their *Interpretive Social Science: A Reader*, write that "the dominant direction in twentieth-century science and philosophy has been the thorough undermining of the Comtean (i.e. positivistic) ideal of science." [1] And in the Preface to his book *Notes on the Methodology of Scientific Research*, the psychologist Walter B. Weimer also provided a succinct summary of this general view:

> Our knowledge of the nature of science and its growth has increased in recent years, and traditional conceptions of science and its methodology have been examined, found wanting, and are in large part being abandoned. [2]

This, then, is the "received view", but it should be noted that rumors abound concerning positivism's continued healthy existence in hiding. Peter Halfpenny writes:

> And even if in its simpler philosophical forms it is dead, the spirit of those earlier formulations continues to haunt sociology, in a full range of guises. . . . [3]

Researchers Lincoln and Guba also accept this prognosis:

We shall take the position that the positivist posture, while discredited by vanguard thinkers in every known discipline, continues to this day to guide the efforts of practitioners of inquiry, particularly in the social or human sciences.... since these methods are based on metaphysical principles that are dissonant with principles guiding the vanguard development of substantive (discipline) thought, it is imperative that inquiry itself be shifted from a positivist to a postpositivist stance.[4]

Kenneth Gergen states that positivistic "assumptions are highly pervasive and continue to furnish the general rationale for theory and research in the sociobehavioral sciences."[5] Henry Giroux goes even further; the "culture of positivism", he states, must be viewed as a "dominant ideology", but it has been thoroughly absorbed and "now represents an integral part of the social and political system of the United States."[6] Giroux has given the term "positivism" a rather broad meaning, but it is also clear that he views it as thriving—mushroom like—in the dark.

It is evident, then, that the received view concerning the death of positivism can be disputed. A little detective work is called for. In the discussion that follows, first the variety of positions that often are identified as "positivistic" will be outlined, then these will be examined to determine which have stopped breathing. Finally, there will be a brief discussion of some mistaken claims about the death of positivism that have been made in the educational and social science literature (a more detailed discussion will follow in Chapter 8).

What was positivism?

Writing in the *Encyclopedia of Philosophy* in 1967, the distinguished historian of philosophy John Passmore wrote that "Logical positivism, then, is dead, or as dead as a philosophical movement ever becomes."[7] And in similar vein, Popper stated in 1974:

Everybody knows nowadays that logical positivism is dead. But nobody seems to suspect that there may be a question to be asked here—the question "Who is responsible?" or rather, the question "Who has done it?"[8]

And then Sir Karl added a twist worthy of the best of mystery stories: "I fear that I must admit responsibility."[9] To add a third and final expert witness, the psychologist Brian Mackenzie made a study of the ways in which positivism had influenced the behaviorists, and in his view the key goals and tenets of positivism turned out to have been "frustrated", "proved incoherent", "of dubious generality", and without "much practical value"—all mortal wounds, indeed, for a philosophical position.[10]

It appears undeniable, then, that there was a death. Perhaps the mystery with which the chapter began is easily resolvable: some researchers continue to believe in positivism because the demise was not widely advertised. But there is another possible solution: possibly there were several things using the same name, *a la* the Romanovs, so that although one (or more) may have died, one (or more) might have survived—but found it healthier to change identity.

Thus the question arises as to what it was that died. What, in short, was positivism? Here some important complexities arise. On the whole, philosophers have been clear about the variety of things that have passed under the name of "positivism", but researchers across the social sciences and related applied fields have been a little less discerning—sometimes with unfortunate consequences. Peter Halfpenny has noted that "there are so many different understandings about how the term can or should be used", and he adds that anti-positivists "use the term loosely to describe all sorts of disfavoured forms of inquiry."[11] It will pay to "set the house in order" right at the outset.

This is not the place to recount the intricacies of late nineteenth- and twentieth-century thought, but it seems that researchers could have one or the other, or sometimes even all, of the following things in mind when they refer vaguely to the "death of positivism" or "the abandonment of traditional conceptions" and the like. These can be sketched in only the barest outline:

1. *Comtean-type positivism.* The nineteenth-century French philosopher Auguste Comte had an elevated respect for science, and he believed the scientific method could be applied to human affairs, including the study of morals. The sciences, he argued, focus upon observable, objectively determinable phenomena. He regarded all sciences as being related, and as forming a sequence that has developed historically from mathematics, through astronomy, the physical and then the biological sciences to sociology (which term, of course, he invented). The later sciences grew out of the earlier ones, but were not reducible to them. Herbert Spencer, John Stuart Mill, Ernst Mach, the logical positivists, and John Dewey, all had certain affinities with Comte (although they had their differences as well). These individuals are dead, but the ghosts of some of their ideas still walk the earth.

2. *Logical Positivism.* This movement, which is sometimes called "consistent empiricism" and "logical empiricism", developed in Austria and Germany in the 1920s, but as is well known the base of the movement was in Vienna. The members of the Vienna Circle came from different scientific backgrounds: Schlick from physics, Carnap and Waissman from mathematics and philosophy, Neurath from sociology, Godel and Hahn from mathematics, Kraft from history, Frank from physics. Later Reichenbach, Hempel, Ayer and others were associated with the movement. Logical positivism was never marked by unanimity of opinion—there were many active but friendly disagreements, and this must be borne in mind when the expression "logical positivism" is used. Wittgenstein's early work had great impact on members, and Popper discussed issues with them (they even published the first and German version of his *Logic of Scientific Discovery*) but he disagreed with them on basic issues.

As an organized movement, logical positivism was killed off by the rise of

Hitler and the murder of Moritz Schlick by a deranged student. But many of the ideas lived on and were developed in the 1940s and 1950s in the later writings of the scattered members.

(a) The logical positivists were marked by a great hostility towards metaphysics. Michael Scriven described the situation colorfully:

> The Vienna Circle or *Wiener Kreis* was a band of cutthroats that went after the fat burghers of Continental metaphysics who had become intolerably inbred and pompously verbose. The *kris* is a Malaysian knife, and the *Wiener Kreis* employed a kind of Occam's Razor called the Verifiability Principle. It performed a tracheotomy that made it possible for philosophy to breathe again.[12]

However, it was not only the detrimental influence of metaphysics on philosophy that was decried. The logical positivists wanted to expunge it from science as well—a goal that many contemporary researchers in education and the social sciences would still share.

(b) Related to this, as Scriven pointed out, the logical positivists adopted the verifiability principle of meaning. The point of this was that in their efforts to drive a wedge between science and metaphysics, it probably seemed promising to try to show that purported statements in the latter category were meaningless, while those in the former were not. Popper has commented on their endeavor as follows:

> they were trying to find a criterion which made metaphysics meaningless nonsense, sheer gibberish, and any such criterion was bound to lead to trouble since metaphysical ideas are often the forerunners of scientific ones.[13]

The principle they hit upon stated that something[14] is meaningful if and only if it is verifiable empirically (i.e., directly, or if charitable, indirectly, by observation via the senses), or is a tautology of mathematics or logic. This has been parodied as "if it can't be seen or measured, it is not meaningful to talk about." For many commentators this truly is the heart of "positivism", and it certainly manages to dispose of metaphysics (which, by definition, is "beyond physics" and is unverifiable by means of empirical data).

The use of operational definitions in the social and behavioral sciences is related to the verifiability principle, and so is the pragmatic criterion of meaning which was devised in the United States much earlier by Charles Sanders Peirce and which was adopted by William James and John Dewey. (The pragmatist Charles Morris was quick to note the similarity between logical positivism and pragmatism, and his view became widely shared.[15] All this is significant, because some folk in education and the social sciences who revel in the fact that logical positivism is dead are very fond of Dewey.)

It should be added that the verifiability principle had a stormy history, and it went through a number of changes in attempts to insulate it against the well-founded criticisms that it provoked. The principle was eventually discredited among philosophers, but it lingered on in the social science research community in one or other of its manifestations.

(c) When formulating the verifiability principle of meaning, the logical positivists were forced to grapple with the issue: "What will *count* as a satisfactory verification?" Their answers usually involved reference to a class of elementary "observation statements"; that is, in discussing how a given idea could be validated and hence shown to be meaningful, the logical positivists usually claimed that the verification had to be in terms of simple, "rock-bottom", elementary, direct and indubitable descriptions of sense experience. (This pipe-dream, it will be recalled, was touched upon in Chapter 2.) Again this doctrine has had a checkered history, and the logical positivists themselves disagreed about it. Here is Carnap's formulation:

> we have to proceed from that which is epistemically primary, that is to say, from the "given", i.e., from experiences themselves in their totality and undivided unity. . . . The elementary experiences are to be the basic elements of our constructional system. From this basis we wish to construct all other objects of prescientific and scientific knowledge.[16]

(d) Least understood by researchers is the fact that, on the whole, the logical positivists were not realists with respect to the status of theoretical entities. Consider the entities postulated in subatomic theory; these are not directly observable, and even indirect confirmation is a complex business. So, rigorous use of a verifiability principle of meaning poses a problem here—what do we mean when we speak of protons, electrons or quarks? Can they be regarded as real entities if there is a problem with respect to their verification in terms of direct and simple and indubitable sense experience? Alternatively, should they be interpreted as theoretical fictions? There is a parallel problem about the laws of nature, for universal generalizations of the form "all X are Y" cannot be verified (usually we cannot check on all members of the class X). Thus, many of the logical positivists were led to take a nonrealist stand; several became instrumentalists—theoretical entities (and also laws) could be thought of, as Ayer put it, "simply as conceptual tools which served for the arrangement of the primary facts."[17] Similarly, scientific theories could not be true or false, but as tools they could be economical, useful, or instrumentally helpful; theories were hypotheses designed to predict facts (facts being sense experiences, or rather reports of sense experience in terms of propositions), but they could not be conceived of as true descriptions of an underlying physical reality. Hans Reichenbach put it as follows, in a passage that contrasts the "erroneous" metaphysical viewpoint with the sounder positivistic one:

> Speculative (i.e. metaphysical) philosophy is characterized by a *transcendental* conception of knowledge, according to which knowledge transcends the observable things. . . . Scientific philosophy has constructed a *functional* conception of knowledge, which regards knowledge as an instrument of prediction and for which sense observation is the only admissable criterion of nonempty truth.[18]

There were many other doctrines of the logical positivists, involving the nature of (and the relationships between) mathematics, logic and philosophy.

But these are not directly pertinent to the points to be developed in what follows.

3. *Behaviorism*. Sometimes the expression "positivism" has been used when the real target is behaviorism. Certainly the two positions have much in common. The behaviorists have favored operationalism—in fact, they did much to pioneer it—and have been hostile to abstract theorizing in the sciences (for they believe it smacks of metaphysics). Watson, in his famous paper of 1913 that launched the movement, urged psychologists to abandon the notion of "consciousness" because there were no clearcut observational criteria for using it; he wrote that so far as making observations was concerned it mattered neither "jot nor tittle" whether one supposed consciousness was present or not. Only behavior is observable, and only by focussing on this can psychology become objective. The opening lines of his paper are notorious:

> Psychology as the behaviorist views it is a purely objective experimental branch of natural science. Its theoretical goal is the prediction and control of behavior.[19]

In this respect, then, the behaviorists were fairly consistent positivists (and logical positivists at that), but their rejection of "inner" causes and psychological events is somewhat misleading. Given the state of psychology in the first three or four decades of the twentieth century, it might have been credible to suppose that the realm of "inner events" could not be made testable, but a lot of things have happened since then. The work of Tolman, and especially the development of the notion of a computer program by Turing and others, has given hope that theories about "inner events" and "programs" can eventually explain, and even predict, how a person will behave under certain conditions (for example, in the sorts of experimental situations engineered by cognitive psychologists). A latter-day logical positivist, then, need not be hostile toward psychological theory but could grant it the same status, say, as quantum theory in physics. It follows from this that it cannot be argued, in reverse as it were, that because the rejection of "inner" processes and events is a mistake in psychology, therefore positivism is an indefensible position. (It may be, of course, but the point is that this argument does not establish it.)

4. *Empiricism*. Finally, "positivism" is sometimes used as a label for "empiricism". This is a particularly misleading usage. "Empiricism" refers to a broad spectrum of epistemological positions to the effect

> that either our concepts or our knowledge are, wholly or partly, based on experience through the senses and introspection. The "basing" may refer to psychological origin or, more usually, philosophical justification.[20]

Within this spectrum, different philosophers mean somewhat different things when they use the term. At any rate it is clear that logical positivism is a type of empiricism, and that not all types of empiricism are positivistic. Thus the death of logical positivism leaves many varieties of empiricism unscathed—a point that has been overlooked by some enemies of positivism, to their cost (as will be seen in Part B).

Which aspects of positivism died, and how?

Some of the four positions that have been identified as receiving the label "positivism" have died, but others are still alive in one form or another. And because each of the four are complex positions, even the ones that have died have not departed "holus bolus"—bits and pieces of them have managed to escape the Grim Reaper. The true picture (always stranger than fiction) is quite complex.

1. Consider, for a start, Comtean positivism. As a general position it is no longer espoused, but like an old soldier it faded away rather than died. On the other hand, social scientists are fond of pointing both to the special complexities their disciplines have when contrasted with the physical sciences, and to the recent extension of scientific inquiry into these domains. Comte would be pleased. Some, like Dewey, regard scientific inquiry as normal everyday inquiry writ large, so that finding a solution to a problem in quantum mechanics is in principle no different from solving a moral problem or from solving how to get to a pressing appointment on the other side of town. Comte would be delighted. Finally, while some social scientists are reductionists, there are many, particularly in sociology, who follow Comte in that they regard their discipline as being irreducible to some more "fundamental" science.

2. Turning to logical positivism, the verifiability principle suffered the same fate as the "Elephant Man"—it became a contorted monstrosity that choked to death under its own weight. As indicated earlier, it led to problems about the meaningfulness of scientific laws and theories. Furthermore, logical positivists were never clear about the status of the principle, for if it was to be regarded as a meaningful principle about what was meaningful, then by its own test it was not (for it was not testable or verifiable)! Popper never accepted the principle as pertaining to meaning, but as seen earlier he did restate it and use it as a way of demarcating science from metaphysics. For Popper, scientific statements are ones that are testable in the sense of being potentially refutable; all else is metaphysics. But unlike the logical positivists, Popper did not regard metaphysics as lacking in meaning or importance. Indeed, he wrote scathingly of the verifiability principle of meaning:

> A further and less interesting point . . . was the sheer absurdity of the use of verifiability as a meaning criterion: how could one ever say that a theory was gibberish because it could not be verified? Was it not necessary to *understand* a theory in order to judge whether or not it could be verified? And could an understandable theory be sheer gibberish?[21]

It is common for contemporary social scientists of all methodological persuasions to agree with the logical positivists—perhaps too readily—that metaphysics has no place in their work. In his *Foundations of Behavioral Research*, Fred Kerlinger was writing on behalf of many:

> The scientist, when attempting to explain the relations among observed phenomena, carefully rules out what have been called "metaphysical explanations". A metaphysical explanation is simply a proposition that cannot be tested.[22]

However, this general disdain for metaphysics may be too facile; for one thing, the recent neo-Kuhnian philosophy of science (discussed in the previous chapter) contains the reminder that scientific research programs may be based on certain "hard core" assumptions and heuristic principles that are not subject to empirical refutation (and which, therefore, are close to being metaphysical). The later Wittgenstein, too, made remarks that soften the empirical-metaphysical distinction.[23]

3. Next, behaviorism has obviously fallen from grace. It has faced a barrage of criticism from philosophers: Norman Malcolm and others have shown that although children might learn to use third person language ("she is angry") by observing the behavior of others (as Skinner's behaviorism held), this could not be how they learn first person usage of these terms ("I am angry" is not sensibly construable as a conclusion reached on the basis of self-observation along the lines "I must be angry, for I am speaking loudly and I am flushed"); and Skinner's attempt to account for human verbal behavior in terms of operant conditioning was decisively criticized in 1959 by Noam Chomsky. However, descendants of the behaviorists still flourish. Calling themselves "neo-behaviorists" or "cognitive behaviorists", they no longer avoid reference to inner psychological causes and events, but as indicated earlier they construe these so as to allow empirically detectable consequences. (In other words, in much scientific practice a weakened form of the verifiability principle lives on.) Albert Bandura's work (to be met again in Part B) provides a good illustration of these points; in *Social Learning Theory* he writes:

> Because some of the inner causes invoked by theorists over the years have been ill-founded does not justify excluding all internal determinants from scientific inquiry. . . . With growing evidence that cognition has causal influence on behavior, the arguments against the influence of internal determinants began to lose their force.[24]

4. Finally, what happened to empiricism? Is it no longer held that our concepts or knowledge claims are justified in terms of experience? There are problems here, of course, which the earlier chapters did not attempt to hide—problems about the rationality of belief, and the justification for change of belief when no empirical evidence is fully compelling—and debate rages over these difficult matters.[25] The point is, however, that it is difficult to deny *some* role to empirical data or evidence in the growth of human knowledge; the issue centers on *what* role. Critics of positivism sometimes get carried away, as will be seen later, and in their eagerness to celebrate its demise they throw the empiricist baby out with the positivist bathwater.

Mistaken claims about the death of positivism

Up to this point it has been argued that, of the various doctrines which from time-to-time have been called positivistic, some have been (properly) crushed by the weight of criticism, but others have survived and even have been accepted by the critics. However, not all researchers have been aware of this, and some wild implications have been drawn when they have commented upon the death of positivism. To put it bluntly, some of the most boisterous celebrants at positivism's wake are actually more positivistic than they realize, or have more in common with the positivists than they would care to admit. In some respects this legacy of positivism is a good thing (for, like most complex doctrines, it was not all bad); but in some respects the movement away from positivism has not gone far enough. Most of these issues will be taken up, and illustrated, in Part B.

In the meantime, let it suffice to say that often when there is a death there is an inquest. And the "last will and testament" of the deceased is scrutinized by the courts so that no spurious claims are honored. No matter how unpopular the positivists now are, we owe them the same courtesy; and calm assessment reveals that they were not entirely rogues. Perhaps the closing words of R. W. Ashby's discussion of the logical positivists (in the view of many the worst rogues of the lot) bear repeating as an epitaph:

> the logical positivists contributed a great deal toward the understanding of the nature of philosophical questions, and in their approach to philosophy they set an example from which many have still to learn. They brought to philosophy an interest in cooperation. . . . They adopted high standards of rigor. . . . And they tried to formulate methods of inquiry that would lead to commonly accepted results.[26]

Notes and References

1. P. Rabinow and W. Sullivan, eds., *Interpretive Social Science: A Reader*. Berkeley: University of California Press, 1979, pp. 8–9.
2. Walter B. Weimer, *Notes on the Methodology of Scientific Research*. NJ: Lawrence Erlbaum Associates, 1979, p. ix.
3. Peter Halfpenny, *Positivism and Sociology*. London: Allen & Unwin, 1982, p. 120.
4. Y. Lincoln and E. Guba, *Naturalistic Inquiry*. Beverley Hills, Ca: Russell Sage, 1985, pp. 15–16.
5. Kenneth Gergen, *Toward Transformation in Social Knowledge*. NY: Springer-Verlag, 1982, p. 11.
6. Henry Giroux, *Ideology, Culture, and the Process of Schooling*. Philadelphia: Temple University Press, 1981, p. 42.
7. John Passmore, "Logical Positivism", *The Encyclopedia of Philosophy*. NY: Collier-Macmillan, 1967, p. 56.
8. Karl Popper, "Autobiography", in P. A. Schilpp (ed.), *The Philosophy of Karl Popper*. La Salle: Open Court, 1974, p. 69.
9. But see R. Haller, "New Light on the Vienna Circle", *The Monist*, 1982, 65(1), pp. 25–35.
10. Brian Mackenzie, *Behaviourism and the Limits of Scientific Method*. London: Routledge and Kegan Paul, 1977, p. 119.
11. P. Halfpenny, op. cit., p. 11.
12. Michael Scriven, in P. Achinstein and F. Barker, eds., *The Legacy of Logical Positivism*. Baltimore: The Johns Hopkins Press, 1969, p. 195.

13. K. Popper, *Unended Quest*, op. cit., p. 80.
14. It cannot be said that *"statements* or propositions are meaningful if...", because many would argue that unless they are meaningful they are *not* statements.
15. See the discussion in D. Gruender, "Pragmatism, Science, and Metaphysics", *The Monist*, 1982, **65**(2), pp. 189–210.
16. R. Carnap, *The Logical Structure of the World and Pseudoproblems in Philosophy.* Berkeley: University of California Press, 1969, pp. 108–109.
17. A. J. Ayer, *The Central Questions of Philosophy.* Harmondsworth: Penguin Books, 1976, p. 110.
18. H. Reichenbach, *The Rise of Scientific Philosophy.* Berkeley: University of California Press, 1963, p. 252.
19. J. B. Watson, "Psychology as the Behaviorist Views It", reprinted in W. Dennis, ed., *Readings in the History of Psychology.* NY: Appleton-Century-Crofts, 1948, p. 457.
20. A. R. Lacey, *A Dictionary of Philosophy.* NY: Scribner's, 1976, p. 55.
21. K. Popper, *Unended Quest*, op. cit., p. 80.
22. F. Kerlinger, *Foundations of Behavioral Research.* NY: Holt, Rinehart & Winston, 2nd ed., 1973, p. 5.
23. L. Wittgenstein, *On Certainty.* NY: Harper Torchbooks, 1972, sections 94–99.
24. A. Bandura, *Social Learning Theory.* Englewood Cliffs, NJ: Prentice-Hall, 1977, p. 10.
25. For problems, see H. Morick, ed., *Challenges to Empiricism.* Indianapolis: Hackett, 1980; for a recent "solution" see J. Watkins, *Science and Scepticism.* Princeton, NJ: Princeton University Press, 1985.
26. R. W. Ashby, "Logical Positivism", in D. J. O'Connor, ed., *A Critical History of Western Philosophy.* NY: The Free Press, 1964, p. 508.

PART B
REFUTATIONS
Misunderstandings and Misinferences

5

Introduction

At a conference held half-a-century ago, Karl Popper read a paper that he later expanded into his important book *The Poverty of Historicism*. This volume addressed many issues, but the one that is relevant here is anti-naturalism;* Popper was concerned to examine—and of course criticize—the various lines of argument that were surfacing to the effect that the methods typical of investigations in the natural or physical sciences were not applicable to the social sciences:

> ... students who work in one or another of the social sciences are greatly concerned with problems of method; and much of their discussion of these problems is conducted with an eye upon the more flourishing sciences, especially physics. ... But in the theoretical social sciences, outside economics, little else but disappointment has come from these attempts. When these failures were discussed, the question was soon raised whether the methods of physics were really applicable to the social sciences.[1]

Popper went on to point out that in the minds of many the question arose "Was it not perhaps the obstinate belief in their applicability that was responsible for the much-deplored state of these (social) studies?"[2]

Believing that scientific method is simply rationality "writ large", that all knowledge progresses (logically) the same way that natural science progresses, Popper had little sympathy for the anti-naturalistic position. His strategy was simple, and at the time probably effective: He showed that each of the difficulties and special conditions in the social sciences that anti-naturalists pointed to as debarring transfer of the methods of the physical sciences, were in fact also to be found in those physical sciences where they had *not* led to the abandonment of "scientific methods" of inquiry—thus the arguments for non-transfer were spurious. Popper also realized that it was crucial, when the viability of naturalism was under consideration, for a sound view of the nature of science to be held. (Obviously, if the nature of science has been misconceived, and if a "straw man" has been set up, then it might be an easy matter to show that the social sciences are not naturalistic; but this would be a Pyrrhic victory.)

A half-century later, anti-naturalism not only remains popular, but is

*In many social science contexts the term "naturalistic" signifies use of qualitative, and avoidance of experimental and quantitative, methods of data collection. This is *not* the sense in the following discussions, unless the term is used this way in a quotation.

enjoying something of a resurgence. One student of sociological method observed in 1973 that

> it must be acknowledged that many social scientists would disclaim the physical sciences model. For example, sociologists at present are undergoing an intensive and enduring rethinking of their objectives by way of reaction to the empiricist influence that has shaped their discipline in the last thirty years. The most common disclaimer to be heard is that "understanding" is a sufficient objective for certain social scientists. . . .[3]

The questioning atmosphere seems to have been given a boost by three general factors. In the first place, many social scientists have become aware of the developments in philosophy of science that were expounded in Part A, and they have drawn a relativistic moral: There are no absolutely reliable methods of inquiry, indeed, *all* methods are on an equally uncertain footing—so there is no philosophical bar to using non-naturalistic methods. Second, the English-speaking world has been taking a stronger interest in modes of thought that have been nurtured on the Continent, of which possibly the most relevant for the present concerns have been hermeneutics and phenomenology (both of which have been seen—rightly or wrongly—as being non-naturalistic). Witness to this is the spate of books on the use of interpretive methods in social science research. Finally, within the social sciences themselves, new practical difficulties have arisen in the conduct of research that researchers believe do not have to be faced in the physical sciences, and with which the methods of the physical sciences seem unable to deal.

The following chapters take up these matters from a critical (if not skeptical) Popperian viewpoint. Do, in fact, the three general factors force social scientists to adopt an anti-naturalistic stance? The critics of naturalistic social science have not always recognized the "Catch 22" that faces them; for if the "new philosophy of science" is on the right track—and, as indicated, many of them believe that by and large the new points are sound—then, in this new and liberal sense of "science", there would seem to be little bar to the social sciences being regarded as scientific. On the *old* and now discredited view of science it no doubt *was* quixotic to suppose that the social sciences could be naturalistic; but of course not even the physical sciences were naturalistic in this sense (for this account of naturalism was inadequate)! In the book referred-to earlier, Popper put in a way that could hardly be bettered:

> Whether a student of method upholds anti-naturalistic or pro-naturalistic doctrines. . . . will also depend on his views about the methods of physics. I believe this point to be the most important of all. And I think that the crucial mistakes in most methodological discussions arise from some very common misunderstandings of the methods of physics.[4]

Notes and References

1. K. Popper, *The Poverty of Historicism*. London: Routledge, 1961, pp. 1–2.
2. Ibid. p. 2.
3. Charles Lachenmeyer, *The Essence of Social Research: A Copernican Revolution*. NY: Free Press, 1973, p. 196.
4. Popper, *Poverty of Historicism*, op. cit., p. 2.

6

Pragmatic Difficulties in Research

From time-to-time in any of the sciences, researchers are likely to face problems that seem insuperable given the methods that are available in their current armamentarium. This situation naturally leads to a certain loss of heart, and to flirtation with methods and ideas that in more certain times would not be touched with a barge-pole. A clear example is provided by the history of the biological sciences over the past two hundred years; at times the complexity of living organisms seemed unmanageable, so that researchers abandoned the "mechanistic" orientation and swung over to rampant romanticism and vitalism. But when a breakthrough occurred in "hardnosed" methodology, the pendulum swung back.

A somewhat similar situation is occurring in the social and human sciences, although many would deny that their move away from the "hardnosed" pole represents a flight to romanticism. Be that as it may, there can be little doubt that critics of naturalistic research methodologies in the social sciences and the related applied fields are becoming more vocal, and some of their critical fuel is drawn from the difficulties that have arisen in the course of day-to-day conduct of research. L. J. Cronbach expressed this dramatically in an essay "Prudent Aspirations for Social Inquiry" (1982):

> Fortunately, today's (social science research) profession is coming to see the rationalist, scientistic ideal as no more than an infantile dream of omnipotence. The present mood, one hopes, bespeaks an institution on the brink of adulthood, ready to claim a role within its capabilities and aware that waiting for its Newton is pointless as waiting for Godot.[1]

The issue, of course, is whether this prudence is worse than the original disease. Possibly, close inspection will reveal that naturalistic methods are not so decrepit as they are made out to be.

These pragmatic difficulties, then, are worth examining in detail. There are several of them: the complex and interactive nature of human attributes, the difficulty of measuring the ineffable, the policy or decision-making orientation of the social sciences, and the limitations of the experimental method in studying human and social affairs. They will be discussed in two stages.

50

The interactive universe

It is almost platitudinous to state that humans are complex, and that as a consequence studying their behavior is a headache in comparison to studying the actions of non-sentient matter. (Popper is one of the few to have denied this; he argued that people generally are rational, while particles of matter are not, so that investigators have a headstart when studying human action.) A new dimension to this issue of human complexity was opened up during the Presidential Address to the American Psychological Association in 1957, when L. J. Cronbach spoke on the topic "The Two Disciplines of Scientific Psychology".[2] In what has since become a classic source, Cronbach argued that it was simplistic for researchers to look for straightforward effects, such as which of several possible treatments will maximize a particular response of a certain type of organism. Members of a species have individual differences, and so some individuals may have their responses maximized by treatment A, but others by treatment B or C. Thus, some children in a classroom might respond well to one particular teaching method, but other members of the class, with different individual characteristics, might respond to other methods. In other words, aptitudes or abilities or characteristics of individuals interact with the treatments, and Cronbach called for more research aimed at identifying these aptitude-treatment interactions (ATI).

In 1974, when receiving the Distinguished Scientific Contribution Award of the same Association, Cronbach reviewed the great volume of work that had been done over the intervening years.[3] This paper, too, has become a widely-quoted classic. Interaction effects, which often are of considerable magnitude, have been identified in a variety of contexts; furthermore, these effects are themselves interactive, in other words a particular ATI may be affected by other variables or individual differences such as sex or socio-economic status. Finally, to make matters even more complex, interactive effects often have time as a significant variable—a generalization that was true in 1940 may not hold in 1960, and by 1980 may have changed yet again. Thus, the immunity of a population to disease may change over time, or the aspirations of children of a given socio-economic class may shift over several decades, and parenting behavior may alter; and all these things are involved in complex networks of interactions that will, perforce, undergo change.

A colorful analogy may be helpful; the interactive psychological world envisioned by Cronbach can be modeled by a concentration or prison camp on a remote island. Suppose that the inmates are being systematically deprived of sufficient quantities of drinking water. This treatment will not effect everyone in the same manner; there will be interactive effects. Thus, there may well be a sex difference, and women might respond to the dehydration in a different manner from men (they might be more, or less, resistant to thirst). However, not all the men and all the women respond in the same way. There is likely to be a further interaction with age; young women might have a different resistance from older ones, who in turn will differ from younger and older men. Then there will be other interactions—body weight (obese people will interact with the treatment differently from slimmer folk); state of health; and perhaps even IQ (smarter folk may figure out ways of cutting down their need for water, for example by not jogging around the camp). Thus intelligent, slim, healthy, young women will react differently from . . . .

Imagine, as the final complexity in this horrendous psychological parable, that the island community with its scarce water resources is isolated for a long period of time. Characteristics of the prisoners may change over the years—weaker individuals will succumb, and the older inhabitants twenty years down the line may have quite different characteristics compared to the older inhabitants of the present day, and so interactive effects true of the present senior citizens will not be true of those in the future. The networks of interactions will have changed. Truly, Descartes' malicious demon could not have engineered a nastier situation for the behavioral scientist or education researcher to deal with.

(i) The limits imposed by interactions

In an interactive world such as this, to pin down a stock of generalizations applicable to the social scene is no easy matter. Even with only a few relevant variables to consider in some relatively simple problem area, a large number of interactive effects of considerable magnitude are possible; and it would take an impossibly large experiment—far exceeding the limits of any resources a behavioral scientist conceivably could command—to gather the relevant data. (The present political climate in the US makes it unlikely that many tens of thousands of children will be removed from their homes and given to researchers to assign to various controlled conditions for relatively long periods of time; on the other hand, the army might be willing to provide the several regiments necessary to deal with the logistics of such an experiment.)

In one particularly significant passage, Cronbach outlined his conclusions:

> Our troubles do not arise because human events are in principle unlawful; man and his creations *are* part of the natural world. The trouble as I see it, is that we cannot store up generalizations and constructs for ultimate assembly into a network. It is as if we needed a gross of dry cells to power an engine, and could only make one a month. The energy would leak out of the first cells before we had half the battery completed. So with the potency of our generalizations. If the effect of a treatment changes over a few decades, that inconsistency is in effect a Treatment × Decade interaction that must itself be regulated by whatever laws there be. Such interactions frustrate any would-be phenomenal picture he tries to explain.[4]

It appears, then, that Cronbach was asserting that although there may be laws underlying social phenomena, we cannot realistically hope to discover them.

> A general statement can be highly accurate only if it specifies interactive effects that it takes a large amount of data to pin down. Some effects in the network will change in form, in a span

of one or two generations, even before enough qualifying clauses have been added to describe the effect accurately.[5]

The best that can be hoped for is to "pin down the contemporary facts", and even this will be exceedingly difficult. In terms of our parable, the behavioral scientist can attempt to describe the present complex patterns of interactive effects which influence the dehydration of the individual prisoners, but the patterns will be changing even as the scientist studies them, so he or she will be condemned to the labors of Sisyphus and will constantly be repeating the work without making significant headway.

N. L. Gage, writing in his well-known *The Scientific Basis of the Art of Teaching*, identified this as a "melancholy" view, and he spelled out what it means when applied to research on classrooms: the perpetrators of this view (i.e., Cronbach and his co-workers)

> hold that the complexities of teaching have been shown to be intractable. Any hope of mastering these complexities is forlorn—doomed to founder in a morass of higher-and-higher-order interactions, historical relativisms that make today's truth tomorrow's falsehood, laws of learning that fail to hold, and profound misconceptions of the character of what the behavioral sciences can properly aspire to. Thus, we are told, the best we can hope for is not prediction and control but mere temporary understanding.[6]

And Richard Snow, Cronbach's co-worker in the ATI field, reported in the *Educational Researcher* that after he had led a colloquium on ATI findings, "a well-known learning theorist remarked . . . 'If you're right, I quit, because this makes it all too complicated—theory becomes impossible!'"[7]

(ii) Revamping the role of the social scientist, and the nature of theory

The closing section of Cronbach's 1974 paper was titled "Realizable Aspirations for Social Inquiry", and in it he expressed the view that has been alluded to in the preceding discussion, namely, that social scientists can realistically hope only to "pin down the contemporary facts" in "each generation", and to provide a modicum of insight and wisdom on a par with that provided by "the humanistic scholar and the artist".[8] The narrow identification of social science with natural science is inappropriate—a point that emerges even more strongly in Cronbach's writings since 1974 on the role of the evaluator of educational and social programs.

It has been common to treat evaluators as a specialist group of scientific researchers; indeed, the new Society to which Cronbach made some revealing remarks in 1976 had called itself the "Evaluation Research Society". Cronbach did not mince words:

> Science is only part of the story and, I would say, a subordinate part. If evaluation is not primarily a scientific activity, what is it? It is first and foremost a political activity, a function performed within a social system.[9]

And the function of evaluators is to make "the system function better". Social reforms or social programs are put into operation in particular sites which may differ radically from each other, and where the conditions may be undergoing rapid change. (Once again the island prison camp comes to mind.) Under these circumstances, it is a waste of effort, not to mention other resources, to worry unduly about internal validity or even perhaps the refinement of research designs. Faced with such shifting conditions, we should try to learn as much as we can that will be of use in planning further social interventions. Doing social research or evaluation work, according to this view, is not like doing laboratory work in the natural sciences.

In his most recent writing on this general topic, Cronbach has gone even further—he shows signs of heading in the same direction as hermeneutically-inspired writers. He calls the desire to discover laws that operate in the social domain a "Saturnian ideal", suitable for extra-earthly creatures but quite out of the question for *us*. He suggests that laws do not lie at the bottom of regularities in human affairs:

> Much of the similarity in persons' actions comes from shared experiences, and customary behavior . . . is modified by a process of contagious reinterpretation of roles and goals. Traditional natural science encounters no irregularities of this character. Although particles are attracted to other particles, they don't fall in love . . . a culture uses language to define appropriate objects for sexual love. To explain conduct, a phenomenology—especially an appreciation of the nouns and verbs our subjects call upon to organize experience—is indispensable. . . .[10]

This line of argument will not be pursued here, but will be taken up again in Chapter 9. The focus in the present discussion will remain upon his influential 1974 argument based on the phenomenon of ATI.

Richard Snow, who coauthored with Cronbach the mammoth volume *Aptitudes and Instructional Methods*[11] does not fully endorse the latter's conclusions about the implications of ATI research for our conception of the possibilities of social science, but his remarks tend in the same direction. As Snow put it in his paper in the *Educational Researcher*, "ATI does not make theory impossible; it makes general theory impossible",[12] and he would emphasize the word "general". The researcher interested in the field of instruction should concentrate on detailed description of "specific instructional situations" and "specific groups of people". Out of this work there might emerge theories that are quite specific with respect to time and place. In the very long term, a theorist might be able to "cluster" specific theories of this type and derive "more abstract notions". But Snow stressed that "there would never be a general, top-down instructional theory, created in academia and applicable, or inapplicable, in particular schools".[13]

(iii) Why melancholy is uncalled for

It must be asserted at the outset that the arguments of Cronbach and Snow are not convincing. Several lines of thought can be put forward to counter their "melancholy" and anti-naturalistic position.

(a) In the first place, although the label "aptitude-treatment-interactions" is new, the actual picture of reality presented by Cronbach and Snow does not differ in essentials from the picture that has emerged over the centuries in the field of physical science. Here, too, there are interactions—pressure and volume interact to affect the behavior of a gas—but temperature in turn is another interacting factor, and so is the initial mass of the gas and its purity. Furthermore, depending upon the precise chemical nature of the gas (another interacting factor), some surprising events may occur at specific temperatures and pressures—some gases will condense into liquids while others sublimate directly into solids.

The difference between the social and physical domains is merely that the *types* of factors that interact are different, although, of course, the "merely" is not entirely without significance. With respect to gases, the interacting factors are physical; with respect to people, interactions are not confined to the physical realm—there is more at work than such things as temperature or climatic factors, age, and body weight. Creativity, intelligence, motivation, previous socialization, state of mental health, cognitive repertoire, and so on, are also possible sources of interactive effects. Furthermore, humans are role-playing and rule-following creatures, while presumably gases neither consciously set out to follow Boyle's Law nor debate which role is appropriate for them in a given experimental setting.

Now, many philosophers have held that such differences as these between the social and physical realms are so great as to render it impossible to produce social science that is in any sense parallel or analogous to physical science. Peter Winch is probably the best known recent figure in this tradition, as will be recalled from Part A. (Other anti-naturalistic arguments will be met in the following chapters.) However, the argument offered by Cronbach and Snow is entirely different. It is not so much the *nature of the factors* operating in the social realm that makes impossible the attainment of scientific theory, it is—in the main—the fact that these entities are *interacting*. And, as argued above, it would seem that interactive effects have not prevented the development of theory in other branches of science; neither Boyle nor Newton knew all the interactions in their respective fields before they successfully theorized.

There is one caveat that should be entered here. It is obvious that Cronbach places a great deal of emphasis upon the fact that one important interacting factor in the social sciences is *time*; as he puts it, generalizations decay. But time is also a variable that effects certain processes in the physical world, and biological phenomena (both in individuals and in populations or species) change over time—matters with which natural scientists have been able to cope satisfactorily.

There is an interesting variant of this line of argument concerning interactions in physical science that was developed by Karl Popper in his *Poverty of Historicism*, and it recently has been revived by N. L. Gage in his controversy with Cronbach and Snow.[14] Processes in the natural world in essence are arenas where a host of forces interact, and scientists cannot make accurate predictions because of the ensuing complexities. But this does not mean that theories are either unattainable, or useless when they are found. Popper uses the example of a storm shaking a tree and causing an apple to fall and bruise on the ground; Gage uses an autumn leaf wafting to the ground. In both cases, there are gravitational effects, air resistance, wind currents, biochemical actions in the plants that determined when the apple and leaf would fall, and so on. The situation in social science research undoubtedly is of similar complexity.

(b) The main source of trouble for Cronbach and Snow is that they take an unduly inductivist or Baconian position concerning the nature of scientific inquiry. Cronbach paints a picture of the social or behavioral scientist collecting the relevant facts and then settling down to produce a theory. The scientist, he stated in a quotation given earlier, attempts to "store up" facts about the contemporary scene "for ultimate assembly into a network". His analogy of filling a room with dry cells for ultimate use in working an engine is a powerful way of driving this account home for his readers. Given this inductivist account of science, it is indeed a serious problem if the facts that are being stockpiled for use in later theorizing start to degenerate or decay because of time being a further interacting factor.

The inductivist view, however, runs counter to the "prevailing view" in philosophy of science. As Karl Popper put it in his autobiography, "we never argue from facts to theories, unless by way of refutation or falsification." Popper goes on to label this mistaken view as "Lamarckian", for it essentially stresses *"instruction* by the environment". His own view is, he claims, Darwinian in that it stresses *"selection* by the environment":

> From the point of view of this methodology, we start our investigation with *problems*. We always find ourselves in a certain problem situation; and we choose a problem which we hope we may be able to solve. The solution, always tentative, consists in a theory, a hypothesis, a conjecture.[15]

This conjecture is tested; relevant data are collected, resulting in either refutation, modification, or (if the test is passed) slightly less tentative acceptance of the original conjecture.

Would, then, acceptance of a Popperian (and Darwinian) approach to theory construction and abandonment of the Baconian one, open an escape route from the melancholy position described by Cronbach and Snow? There is a need to return once more to the "island paradise" described earlier.

If a scientist were to be sent to study the concentration camp, she would be faced by Cronbach's and Snow's problem—her descriptive generalizations would decay while she was going about collecting others. However, it would not be long before she obtained enough of a sense of conditions on the island to form some hypothesis such as, that the hot and dry conditions favor survival of prisoners of a certain body type. This could be tested, and exceptions noted and investigated further. More refined hypotheses might emerge, even hypotheses about the direction of change in the prison population over time, and these could then be tested.

It can be argued that Cronbach's original dilemma concerning the impossibly large experiments that would need to be carried out to pin down ATI in the social domain only arises if the scientist has no hypotheses. If all theoretical possibilities have equal probability, then all have to be investigated. Thus, all relevant data have to be assembled, and, of course, the effort required undoubtedly would be mammoth. But when the experimenter has guidance from hypotheses, matters are greatly simplified. The scientist might speculate along these lines: "The island is hot and dry. These conditions will favor survival of younger people rather than older and frailer prisoners; and fat prisoners will fare worse than those with relatively low body weight. And, of course, clever prisoners may hit on good survival strategies, but a clever, fat, old prisoner would have to be *really* smart to thrive under these conditions." Following Popper, the scientist could set out not to "prove" or "verify" these predictions but to *refute* them. Complex experiments would not need to be carried out, but rather the hypotheses under investigation would give guidance as to what data it would be appropriate to gather. Thus, old prisoners, and fat prisoners, could be sought out; or death statistics could be investigated to see whether proportionally more prisoners in these categories had succumbed. The Cronbach-Snow problem is avoided; Popperian or Darwinian emphasis on refutation of hypotheses has avoided the pitfalls of Baconian or Lamarckian inductivism.[16]

The point is central, and it is worth making somewhat more rigorously. Suppose there are, in a simplified social setting, only five interacting factors which will be labeled A through E. Furthermore, at a given time t.1, each of these factors can have any one of three values, signified by 1, 2, or 3. Thus, there is $A1, A2, A3, B1, B2, \ldots$ Even with only five factors, the number of possible interactions is large: 3^5 or 243 if all five factors are involved in any interaction ($A1, B1, C1, D1, E1$; or $A2, B1, C1, D1, E1$; or $A2, B2, C1, D1, E1$; and so on).

Now, if an experimenter has a neutral attitude toward all of these possibilities (that is, if all are regarded as equally likely to occur), and if the experimenter refrains from hypothesizing, then a large experiment would have to be run to determine the specific interactions which do occur out of these 243 possibilities. (In measurement terms, a factorial design would be appropriate.) However, such a procedure would take time and enormous resources; and in an interactive universe, by time t.2 it is likely that the nature of the interactions will have changed—more or fewer factors now may be involved, or the factors may be spread over a greater range of values, and so forth. The atheoretical researcher would then have to run another large experiment at time t.2 and so on *ad infinitum*.

However, suppose the researcher hypothesized early in the research, and came to the tentative conclusion that the only interaction likely to occur out of the 243 possibilities was, say, A5, B4, C3, D2, E1. Furthermore, suppose the researcher also hypothesized about the likely changes in this interaction over time. A relatively simple study would suffice to check all this (if a factorial design were used, many cells could be left empty, and matters would be simplified further if an absolute criterion were suggested by the hypothesis under test). If it was found that A5, B4, C3, D2, E1 did not occur, but instead the interaction was A5, B4, C3, D2, E2, then the original hypothesis would be refuted and the researcher would have learned an important lesson. One or two further hypothesizing and testing cycles might be sufficient to allow the development of a theory or hypothesis that survives serious testing.[17] All of this bears out the worth of the two aphorisms enunciated by Karl Popper to the effect that we learn from our mistakes, and the important thing is to make our mistakes as rapidly as possible.

But there is one other aspect of the foregoing discussion which needs to be underscored: the researcher needs to produce reasonable hypotheses or theories. And it is here that one of the oft-heard criticisms of research in social science (and domains like educational research and nursing research) floats to the surface—such research is carried out, if not in a theoretical vacuum, at least in an environment where the theories are extremely weak. The way to overcome this is to place renewed emphasis on the importance of good theorizing, whereas Cronbach's ATI paper would seem to encourage the researcher to further neglect this already weakened aspect of research.[18]

(c) To return to Cronbach's main argument: If theories are to be found, they will apply only to very specific contexts—general theory will be beyond our grasp because of the multitude of interactions, and because, in particular, time is an interacting factor. To cite an example, a theory about the behavior of children of a certain social background and ability, on a particular task, in a particular school, at a particular time, cannot be expected to hold true for other children with other abilities in other schools and on other occasions.

At one level this is true. Specific regularities may not hold in new sites where the particulars are different. But this is no reason for concluding either that theory at some more general level is not possible (Snow acknowledges that the *possibility* exists), or that such a general theory will only emerge *after* the specific or particular theories have been developed.

Evolutionary biology is an instructive example here. Charles Darwin was faced with a situation a great deal more complex than that dealt with by the researcher on the fictitious island prison camp; he was studying, in effect, the class of all living organisms and their interactions with the environment. Each particular species has a host of characteristics, and, of course, individual members differ with respect to each other; and within a species, and across species, there are an enormous number of interactive affects with the environment. Furthermore, as indicated by the fossil record, both the characteristics of living things, and the nature of their interactions with their environments, have changed dramatically over time. Nevertheless, without waiting for the full set of generalizations applicable to specific members of specific species in specific environments at specific times, Darwin actively hypothesized on the basis of incomplete knowledge, and came up with a successful general theory. And it should be noted that his theory accounts for the alteration of species over time!

The process that worked so well for Darwin should at least be tried in education and the social sciences. Researchers should take heart from William James's remarks about the general who never fought a battle for fear of injuring his troops:

> Not so are victories either over enemies or over nature gained. Our errors are surely not such awfully solemn things. In a world where we are so certain to incur them in spite of our caution, a certain lightness of heart seems healthier than this excessive nervousness on their behalf.[19]

And, as Popper has shown, it is only by making errors in their hypotheses that researchers can hope to advance.

Setting criteria and measuring the immeasurable

A completely different set of problems that has led some in the social sciences to move in the direction of anti-naturalism, centers around issues of measurement. By way of introduction, consider the remarks of W. Edwards Deming, written after a lifetime of experience in the social sciences and evaluation:

> there has never in man's history been an era of greater effort toward safe drugs, safe automobiles, safe apparatus, safety on the job, decrease in pollution, war on poverty, aids to underprivileged children, and all sorts of well-meant social programs. The problems of evaluation of these efforts are compounded by failure to define terms operationally, as well as by failure to lay down criteria by which to weigh gains and advantages against losses and disadvantages. A drug that helps thousands may be harmful to a few people. Is it safe?
> Any adjective that is to be used in evaluation requires an operational definition, which can be stated only in statistical terms. Unemployed, improved, good, acceptable, safe, round, reliable, accurate, dangerous, polluted, inflammable, on-time performance (as of an airline or train) have no meaning except in terms of a stated statistical degree of uniformity and reproducibility of a test method or criterion.[20]

In *The Poverty of Historicism*, Popper gave a number of examples of social experiments which are not too dissimilar to ones that Deming used throughout his paper—a man opening a grocery shop, a monopolist raising the price of his product, the improving of working conditions in an attempt to increase output, and the like.[21] But Popper did not address the issues of definition that Deming raised—such as what degree of increased profit (or other benefit) will count as success for the monopolist (and for how long must it be maintained); or what living standard, for how long, will the grocer require before he decides he was right to have gone into business? Of course, the very reasonable line could be taken that Popper did not discuss this because he regarded the point as obvious. In order for claims to be testable or refutable in principle, or for criteria to be useful, the terms in which they are couched must have unambiguous and unchanging meaning.

It would be a mistake to regard this definitional issue as a valid one but presenting only minor difficulty, although in some cases no doubt it does. There are several contexts in which it is particularly vexing. The first is where there are both benefits and disadvantages which in some way need to be weighed against each other, as in Deming's example of a new drug which is beneficial to many but very harmful to a few. Many piecemeal social reforms contemplated in recent years have this character—reform of the taxation structure so that everyone contributes at the same rate, introduction of more visual aids in schools (which benefits certain types of pupil but slows down others), use of a new method of teaching children to read (which gets them to read much sooner but seriously harms their ability to spell). The calculation of whether such reforms are successes, or overall benefits, raises issues similar to those that the members of the utilitarian school in ethics have been struggling with over a considerable period. Cost-benefit analysis, and games and decision theory have all been tried, with indifferent success.

The argument can be made that this problem of opposing debits and credits is more pressing now than it was in previous ages, because in advanced Western-type societies we can no longer expect to achieve many massive, clearcut reforms. In the words of Peter H. Rossi:

> We are today groping for new and presumably better treatments for a variety of social ills and have enough wealth to correct some of the obvious faults of our society. But, ironically, no matter how heavy our consciences now, we can no longer expect reforms to produce massive results. We have passed the stage of easy solutions. . . . Provide schools and teachers to all children and illiteracy goes down dramatically; but to achieve a level of education high enough to assure everyone a good job is a lot more difficult. Diminishing returns set in . . .[22]

To which can be added—what Rossi did not say—that society being the complex thing it is, giving a small benefit to one group will often entail extracting some type of payment from another. And so we need to be clear about how much benefit, and how much payment, we expect in order to judge the change as being beneficial overall. (It can be noted in passing that the same problem arises when comparing several alternative programs of social reform. Each may have different advantages and disadvantages, and so the choice between them may come to depend on having some criteria for preferring one set of costs and benefits as against the others).[23]

The unambiguous specification of key terms in criteria of success or failure also runs into serious problems in those contexts where operationalization of the kind envisioned by Deming and others would either have a trivializing effect, or would entirely fail to encapsulate the things of value that were happening.[24] Thus, consider a program that is pilot-testing a program for teaching spelling to young elementary school students; the method might or might not meet with success in getting children to spell, but it also might have other educational effects which may be difficult—or even impossible—to measure adequately at the present time. The children might be happier, more spontaneous, more creative, more actively enquiring for themselves, and more attentive to the opinions of others, and operational definitions of these concepts may leave a great deal to be desired.

This general problem of definition and clarification of criteria is recognized as one of the most serious in the whole field of evaluation.[25] Educationalists interested in literature and the arts are particularly likely to point to it, by objecting to the trivial nature of operational definitions that have been put forward in their own fields (the qualities developed in students in these fields are, it is often claimed, "ineffable"). There has also been strong criticism from those who are interested in the legislative process, who have argued that the aims of pieces of social legislation are usually very complex and cannot be measured by simple means. As David K. Cohen put it, when discussing Title 1 of the Elementary and Secondary Education Act (ESEA) (US Congress, 1965):

> It is, therefore, difficult to conclude that improving school's production of poor children's achievement was the legislation's major purpose. The legislative intent embraced many other elements: improving educational services in school districts with many poor children, providing fiscal relief for the central cities and parochial schools, reducing discontent and conflict about race and poverty, establishing the principle of federal responsibility for local school problems. The fact that these were embodied in a single piece of legislation contributed heavily to its passage, but it also meant that the resulting program was not single-purpose or homogeneous.[26]

Hence, "achievement scores are not an adequate summary of the legislation's diverse aims".[27] It may be very difficult, or perhaps impossible, both to determine what the aims were and to usefully operationalize them.

Partly as a result of these problems, a growing number of social scientists are turning to qualitative rather than quantitative research for guidance in determining whether pilot programs have been successful and are worth continuing. One of the pillars of quantitative social research, Donald Campbell, put it this way in the opening lines of his *Kurt Lewin Award Address* at the annual meeting of the American Psychological Association in 1974:

> in program evaluation methodology today, there is a vigorous search for alternatives to the quantitative-experimental approach. In academic social science there is renewed emphasis on the methods of the humanities and increased doubts as to the appropriateness of applying the natural science model to social science problems. . . . these terms are shorthand for a common denominator among a wide range of partially overlapping concepts: For *quantitative* read also scientific, scientistic, and *naturwissenschaftlich*: for *qualitative* read also humanistic, humanitistic, *geisteswissenschaftlich*, experiential, phenomenological, clinical,

case study, field-work, participant observation, process evaluation, and common sense knowing.[28]

Campbell's significant remarks will be discussed further in Chapter 9; suffice it to say here that there has been a spate of books discussing the use of qualitative methods, especially in the evaluation field.[29]

One important form that support for qualitative techniques has taken has been the advocacy for more reliance upon the role of experts. For the expert—so it is claimed—has mastered the laws, theories, quasi-laws, and subtle nuances that are important in a field but which are difficult to express publicly in a precise way. In fact, Olaf Helmer and Nicholas Rescher go so far as to give the concept of expertise a central place in the epistemology of the "inexact sciences".[30] A related form of the same anti-naturalistic idea has surfaced over the past decade or so as an interest in adopting techniques from the legal sphere,[31] and from literary and artistic criticism, for use in the social sciences. Thus, in a keynote address at the 1975 meeting of the American Educational Research Association, an organization noted for fostering quantitative research, Elliot Eisner made a case for the development of educational connoisseurs, who in the course of evaluating educational innovations would practice "educational criticism" instead of quantitative assessment; a few years later he put it this way:

> Effective criticism, within the arts or in education, is not an act independent of the powers of perception. The ability to see, to perceive what is subtle, complex, and important, is its first necessary condition. The act of knowledgeable perception is, in the arts, referred to as connoisseurship.[32]

Here the stress on the qualitative is close to merging with another typical anti-naturalistic thesis, namely, that social life must be understood intuitively.

Sometimes a Winchian or Wittgensteinian type of argument is presented in support of these anti-naturalistic theses: A form of life, such as a classroom or the life of an urban minority group, cannot be judged effectively by an outsider; only an investigator who takes an emic approach can be successful, and can come to grasp the subtle and perhaps ineffable qualities of a "foreign" form of life. Anthropological work is also cited as a backing; for instance, Clifford Geertz writes of his own field, ethnography:

> It is merely to say that the anthropologist characteristically approaches such broader interpretations and more abstract analyses from the direction of exceedingly extended acquaintances with extremely small matters. He confronts the same grand realities that others—historians, economists, political scientists, sociologists—confront in more fateful settings: Power, Change, Faith, Oppression, Work, Passion, Authority, Beauty, Violence, Love, Prestige; but he confronts them in contexts obscure enough . . . to take the capital letters off them.[33]

Geertz's concept of "thick description" (that is, description which is impregnated with theory and hypothesis), which in turn he took from the philosopher Gilbert Ryle (somehow Popper gets left out of the genealogy, although he had a very similar notion), is often cited; and to top it all, Polanyi's notion of "tacit knowledge" usually makes an appearance. (Polanyi's work will be met in more detail later.)

There is, of course, a great deal that is sound in the anti-naturalistic stress upon the importance of qualitative techniques (and one does not have to be an anti-naturalist to appreciate their value). The anthropologist, the historian, and even the drama critic, can look at what a teacher and pupils are doing, or at how members of an ethnic minority cope with government housing and health officials, and so on. The central problems concern not the interest or even the suggestive value of the results they turn up, but rather (i) the validity of their results, for it is well known that social science experts, critics, and connoisseurs can violently disagree, and, (ii) whether in fact these qualitative methods can succeed in situations where quantitative methods are difficult or impossible to apply.

Clifford Geertz himself has been sensitive to the methodological problems here. Writing about the view that the settings in which qualitative workers gather data are "natural laboratories", he stated:

> The "natural laboratory" notion has been . . . pernicious, not only because the analogy is false—what kind of a laboratory is it where *none* of the parameters are manipulable?—but because it leads to a notion that the data derived from ethnographic studies are purer, or more fundamental, or more solid, or less conditioned . . . than those derived from other sorts of social inquiry. The great natural variation of cultural forms is . . . not, even metaphorically, experimental variation, because the context in which it occurs varies along with it, and it is not possible (though there are some who try) to isolate the y's from the x's to write a proper function.[34]

It is here that a Popperian orientation is fruitful, and somewhat rescues the naturalistic approach. Some qualitative investigators present the evidence that *supports* their interpretations, unmindful of Popper's warning that anybody can always find *some* evidence to support their view. What counts, however, is whether a serious search for *disconfirming* evidence turns up anything. To cite Geertz yet again (from a passage that seems often overlooked by those who could most profit from it),

> Cultural analysis is (or should be) guessing at meanings, assessing the guesses, and drawing explanatory conclusions from the better guesses, not discovering the Continent of Meaning . . .[35]

The results of this guessing process are hypothetical, not warranted truths, and they should be subject to further testing. David Krathwohl, a former president of the American Educational Research Association, put all this succinctly in his discussion of "organized skepticism" (a captivating expression that seems to have originated with Robert Merton):

> Organized skepticism is a basic norm that makes science a unique source of knowledge. It is the responsibility of the community of scientists to be skeptical of each new knowledge claim, to test it, and to try to think of reasons that the claim might be false—to think of alternative

explanations that might be plausible as the one advanced. This challenge to new knowledge is *sought* in science rather than avoided as it is in other methods. . . . [36]

It seems not unreasonable to believe that qualitative studies can be carried out in this healthy skeptical spirit, and so be scientific or naturalistic!

One point remains to be taken up. Geertz remarked that natural settings are quite unlike laboratory settings, for they are marked by lack of control over the relevant variables. Many other methodologists, from across the social sciences, have made the related point that the experimental method is singularly inappropriate for the study of human affairs. In particular, in action settings such as are commonly encountered in the evaluation of educational and social programs, experimental designs have been tried, and generally have been found wanting. In real life, it is hard to impose random assignment of subjects (even volunteers) to experimental and control groups; it is difficult to cut down attrition; it is impossible to ensure that the only difference between the various groups in the study is that the relevant ones get the experimental treatment (there is the famous example of the "performance contracting" experiment where some schools in the study had teachers' strikes, and one school was devastated by a hurricane—all of which took place without consultation with the experimenter); there are ethical problems connected with forging ahead with the experimental treatment in order to get statistically manipulable results when early results indicate that the treatment is harmful; and finally, even at its best the true experiment yields information only about what *was* the situation in a *particular* group or sample, but often this is not the most useful information:

> Social knowledge is used in circumstances other than those originally studied. New sites and new clienteles have to be served, and the original site changes with time. Extrapolation is speculative even when the effect is established beyond question in the original context. [37]

In addition, even well-done experiments yield limited information; for example, if a treatment fails to produce a significant effect, unless supplementary information was gathered the experimental results will not indicate the reasons for the failure.

To some, "practical" difficulties such as these (if, indeed, this is the best way to think of them) have led to a loss of faith in naturalistic methods. For the experiment was often regarded as *the* dependable source of information, and when it fell, faith in science sometimes went with it. Once again, Popper's words are relevant:

> The question about the sources of our knowledge can be replaced. . . . It has always been asked in the spirit of: "What are the best sources of our knowledge—the most reliable ones, those which will not lead us into error, and those to which we can and must turn, in case of doubt, as the last court of appeal?" I propose to assume, instead, that no such ideal sources exist—no more than ideal rulers—and that *all* "sources" are liable to lead us into error at times. And I propose to replace, therefore, the question of the sources of our knowledge by the entirely different question: "How can we hope to detect and eliminate error?" [38]

If Popper is right, and if this is the basis of all scientific inquiry, then the pragmatic difficulties that have been discussed here are no bar in principle to the social sciences and educational research being naturalistic endeavors. The conception of naturalism that is held has to change, not the conception of what the social sciences can prudently hope to achieve.

Notes and References

1. L. J. Cronbach, "Prudent Aspirations for Social Inquiry", in William Kruskal, ed., *The Social Sciences: Their Nature and Uses*. Chicago: Chicago University Press, 1982.
2. L. J. Cronbach, "The Two Disciplines of Scientific Psychology", *The American Psychologist*, **12**, (11), November 1957.
3. L. J. Cronbach, "Beyond the Two Disciplines of Scientific Psychology", *The American Psychologist*, **30**, (2), February 1975.
4. Ibid., p. 123.
5. Ibid., p. 126.
6. N. L. Gage, op. cit., p. 91.
7. R. L. Snow, "Individual Differences and Instructional Theory", *Educational Researcher*, **6**, (10) November 1977, p. 12.
8. L. J. Cronbach, "Beyond the Two Disciplines . . ." op. cit., p. 126.
9. L. J. Cronbach, "Remarks to the New Society", *Evaluation Research Society Newsletter*, **1**, April 1977, p. 1.
10. L. J. Cronbach, "Social Inquiry by and for Earthlings", in D. Fiske and R. Shweder, eds., *Metatheory in Social Science*. Chicago: University of Chicago Press, 1986, p. 85.
11. L. J. Cronbach and R. E. Snow, *Aptitudes and Instructional Methods*, NY: Irvington, 1977.
12. R. L. Snow, op. cit., p. 12.
13. Ibid.
14. K. Popper, *The Poverty of Historicism*, op. cit., p. 117; N. L. Gage, "Paradigms Found: New Prospects for Educational Research," paper presented at APA Conference, Toronto, 1978.
15. K. Popper, *Unended Quest*, Illinois: Open Court, 1976, p. 86.
16. This discussion, and the material that follows, grossly oversimplifies the statistical processes involved in hypothesis-testing in the social sciences.
17. The affluent reader can purchase the board game "Clue", the successful playing of which seems to depend upon adopting the hypothesizing and testing cycle.
18. Here Snow differs somewhat from Cronbach; he anticipates that theory *might* eventually be forthcoming, but when and if it comes it will be "from bottom up".
19. W. James, "The Will to Believe", reprinted in *Essays on Faith and Morals*, Cleveland and NY: Meridian Books, 1962, p. 50.
20. W. Edwards Deming, "The Logic of Evaluation", in E. L. Struening and M. Guttentag (eds.) *Handbook of Evaluation Research*. Beverly Hills: Sage, (1), p. 55.
21. K. Popper, *Poverty of Historicism*, op. cit., pp. 59, 86.
22. P. H. Rossi, "Evaluating Social Action Programs", in F. G. Caro (ed.), *Readings in Evaluation Research*. NY: Russell Sage Foundation, 1971, pp. 276–7.
23. See J. S. Coleman, "Evaluating Social Action Programs", in F. G. Caro (ed.), op. cit., esp. p. 282. Also A. M. Rivlin, *Systematic Thinking for Social Action*. Washington, DC: The Brookings Institution, 1971, esp. Ch. 3.
24. For further discussion of the charge of trivialization see D. C. Phillips, "Operational Definitions in Educational Research", *Australian Journal of Education*, (12), 1968.
25. For examples, see the papers by Suchman, Weiss, and others in Carol Weiss, ed., *Evaluating Action Programs*. Boston: Allyn and Bacon, 1972.
26. D. K. Cohen, "Politics and Research: Evaluation of Social Action Programs in Education", in ibid., p. 145.
27. Ibid., p. 142.
28. D. T. Campbell, "Qualitative Knowing in Action Research", in M. Brenner *et al.*, eds., *The Social Context of Method*. NY: St. Martin's Press, 1978, p. 184.
29. See, for instance, T. Cook and C. Reichardt, eds., *Qualitative and Quantitative Methods in*

Evaluation Research. Beverley Hills, Sage, 1979; also E. Guba and Y. Lincoln, *Effective Evaluation.* SF: Jossey-Bass, 1982.

30. O. Helmer and N. Rescher, "On the Epistemology of the Inexact Sciences", *Management Science,* **6,** 1959.
31. See R. Wolf and G. Arnstein, "Trial by Jury: A New Evaluation Method", *Phi Delta Kappa,* **57,** (3), November 1975.
32. E. Eisner, *The Educational Imagination.* NY: Macmillan, 1979, p. 193.
33. Clifford Geertz, *The Interpretation of Cultures.* NY: Basic Books, 1973, p. 21.
34. Ibid., pp. 22–23.
35. Ibid., p. 20.
36. D. Krathwohl, *Social and Behavioral Science Research.* SF: Jossey-Bass, 1985, p. 21.
37. L. J. Cronbach, "Prudent Aspirations for Social Inquiry", op. cit., p. 66.
38. K. Popper, *Conjectures and Refutations,* op. cit., p. 25.

7

Neo-Hegelian Critiques*

It has often been remarked that the social domain differs from the physical with respect to its degree of complexity. While some, like Popper, have regarded this assertion as dubious, there have been others—as was seen in the previous chapter—who have come to believe that social and human affairs are so complex that the prospect for the development of a social science (with an array of laws and theories) is far from bright.

There even are some who would argue that Cronbach and Snow do not go far enough in their work on interaction effects. It was suggested earlier that ATI occur between discrete factors like sex, SES, IQ, and age; and although there are potentially many such interacting factors, the situation does not seem to differ markedly from what happens in the physical domain. But a different conception of interactions is possible—indeed, it is one that has had major impact upon Western philosophy and social science for well over a century. It emanates from the early nineteenth-century German philosopher G. W. F. Hegel, and especially from his "principle of internal relations".

Hegelian organicism

A distinction can be drawn between internal and external relationships. The relationships or interactions between the factors in ATI are external, for the factors themselves are not affected by the interactions. In a classroom, according to the ATI picture, the effectiveness of an educational treatment may be influenced by interactions between the sex, age and IQ of the students, but the sex and age and IQ do not thereby change. In contrast, however, in internal relationships the interacting factors are themselves partly *constituted* by the interactions, so that these factors are different when interacting from what they are when independent or isolated. A simple physical example is provided by gravitational phenomena; an object's weight (as opposed to mass) is determined by the other things that are nearby and which gravitationally effect it, so that a stone will weigh X when on the surface of the earth, but when it is in closer (internal) interaction with the moon (on the lunar surface, for instance) it will weigh Y. The significant point for what follows is that many

*Portions of this chapter are based on earlier material co-authored by Rob Orton.

would regard the examples that have just been given as "topsy-turvy"; they see the physical realm as being more usually the home of external relations, and the social domain as being riddled with internal relations.

Groups of objects that are externally related to each other have sometimes been called "mixtures" or "collections" or "aggregates"; the image is of a heap of sand, where the individual granules hardly effect each other, and where each will retain most of its individual properties (size, shape, density, color, chemical composition, etc.) irrespective of the properties of its neighbors in the pile.

On the other hand, groups of objects that are internally related have been called "wholes", "organic entities", "dynamically interrelated", "holistic systems" and the like. The properties of such internally related systems are interesting, for an object that is embedded in such a system is no longer a separate object—it is a *part*. If it is removed from the system, in other words if the internal relations are severed, then it is no longer a part; it becomes a separate object, with different properties, for it no longer has the internally determined properties it had as part of the whole. And, of course, the whole would change as well, for a part has been excised, and so some internal properties have been lost. Hegel's early twentieth-century follower, the idealist philosopher McTaggart, put it this way:

> Let us take X, Y, and Z as representing all the infinite number of qualities possessed by some substance A, including those which are derivative from the relations in which A stands. . . . If we now enquire what A is, a complete answer must be given by giving the nature of A, and this consists of its qualities. X, Y, and Z are taken as a complete list of these, and thus the nature of A is X, Y, and Z. Let us suppose any of the qualities altered, either by addition or subtraction or substitution, so that the complete list would be represented by W, X, Y, Z, or by X, Y, or by W, X, Y. Thus the nature of the substance which had such qualities would be different from the nature of A. Therefore the substance in question could not be A.[1]

It follows from the logic here that "a whole is more than the sum of its parts".[2] For the whole not only contains properties that the parts would have if they were isolated from each other, but it also contains the emergent relational properties that appear when these parts come together in internal relationship. (Imagine entities A and B having two non-relational properties each; when they come into relationship in a whole there will be *five* properties at least—the four non-relational properties plus at least one relational property.) The philosopher of science Rom Harre was reflecting this viewpoint when he wrote recently that "a social collective is not a statistical aggregate of individuals. It is a supra-individual, having a distinctive range of properties."[3]

William James was less impressed with Hegelian organicism or holism; for a while after its rise to popularity in the English-speaking world in the late nineteenth century he was almost alone in withstanding its charms. He saw that the logic of internal relations was such that the properties of all things are created by the "through-and-through" relations into which they enter, and his sense of the ridiculous led him to write this parody of Hegel:

It costs nothing, not even a mental effort, to admit that the totality of things may be organized exactly after the pattern of one of these "through-and-through" abstractions. In fact, it is the pleasantest and freest of mental movements. Husband makes, and is made by, wife, through marriage; one makes other by being itself other; everything is self-created through its opposite—you go around like a squirrel in a cage. . . *What, in fact, is the logic of these abstract systems? It is, as we said above: if any Member, then the Whole System; if not the Whole System, then Nothing.* [4]

More will be said later about the logic of internal relationships.

Twentieth-century social science has not always shared James's sense of humor; Hegelian ideas have been taken deadly seriously. Thus Yvonna Lincoln and Egon Guba claim that researchers in the "vanguard"—the postpositivists—elect "to carry out research in the natural setting or context of the entity for which study is proposed", for their

ontology suggests that realities are wholes that cannot be understood in isolation from their contexts, nor can they be fragmented for separate study of the parts (the whole is more than the sum of the parts). . . . [5]

There is *some* justification for all this—social phenomena *are* complex, and the complexities are compounded and interacting. The record over the past century and a half indicates that whenever there has been dissatisfaction with the methods that are available to deal with great complexity, there is a reversion back to Hegel (or else, a similar position to Hegel's is reinvented anew). While acknowledging the genuine difficulty of the issues here, the following discussion will argue that the continued romance with Hegel is bound to bring little satisfaction.

Systems Theory

Modern systems theory appears to have developed directly as a result of dissatisfaction with the traditional analytic or naturalistic or mechanistic method of studying complex systems. As T. Harrell Allen put it in 1978,

GST (General Systems Theory) is grounded in holistic methodology. We see today a shift in the social and behavioral sciences towards holism. . . . This means one is forced to conceptualize in terms of wholes, forming connections to other wholes, heretofore thought to be isolated phenomena. It results in a rejection of the atomistic and mechanistic perspective. [6]

The traditional approach has been to divide the system into discrete parts (or "corpuscles" or "atoms"), each of which is then studied in isolation from the others; the whole system is regarded as being the sum of these parts (or, alternatively, the sum of the parts is regarded as determining the nature of the whole system). As an illustration a supporter of the mechanistic method might well choose the example of a watch. The features of the parts of the watch determine, so the argument runs, the features of the watch as a whole; for example, the accuracy and weight of the whole watch are determined by the accuracy and weight of the parts.

Ludwig von Bertalanffy looms large in the development of what is now known as General System Theory (GST). It is not surprising that he started his career as a biologist (or that he was educated in Germany where Hegel's thought was widely studied); for it is in biology, particularly, that an apparently good case can be made *against* the mechanistic method and *for* the opposing organismic or holistic or systems view. Consider the kangaroo as an example of a complex biological system. It could be argued by an organicist or systems theorist that the features of the parts of this organism are determined by the characteristics of the whole organism, for the parts are internally interrelated so as to form a "through-and-through" whole—each part helps to determine the others. But the organicist would not stop here. An attack would be mounted upon the mechanist's example of the watch; for even here, the interrelations between the parts are important, although they are not internal relationships. Barely adequate for the study of a watch, mechanism is hopeless when it comes to dealing with internally related entities. In von Bertalanffy's words,

> Mechanism . . . provides us with no grasp of the specific characteristics of organisms, of the organization of organic processes among one another, of organic "wholeness", of the problem of the origin of organic "teleology", or of the historical character of organisms . . . We must therefore try to establish a new standpoint which—as opposed to mechanism—takes account of organic wholeness, but . . . treats it in a manner which admits of scientific investigation.[7]

The new "standpoint" which von Bertalanffy called for in order to do justice to "organic wholeness" was, of course, GST. In a later work he called for the full and rigorous development of the organismic view, and he believed that organismic principles were applicable not only to the study of biological systems, but to *all* systems, including systems studied in the social and behavioral sciences. He wrote:

> a stupendous perspective emerges, a vista towards a hitherto unsuspected unity of the conception of the world. Similar principles have evolved everywhere, whether we are dealing with inanimate things, organisms, mental or social processes. What is the origin of these correspondences?
>
> We answer this question by the claim for a new realm of science, which we call General System Theory. . . . A "system" can be defined as a complex of elements standing in interaction. There are general principles holding for systems, irrespective of the nature of the component elements and of the relations or forces between them.[8]

His call for the development of GST evidently fell upon receptive ears, for a considerable body of literature rapidly accumulated. Systems theorists developed a number of techniques and principles for dealing with holistic complexity, although none of these were new or led to great breakthroughs in scientific practice. The flow diagram was taken to new levels of detail, and useful terminology was developed—"input", "output", "throughput", "positive" and "negative feedback", "closed" and "open systems", and the like. The notion of entropy was borrowed from thermodynamics (the most likely state of a system is one of greatest entropy). The principle of "equifinality" was formulated, according to which a system usually can reach a given state via a variety of pathways (hardly a new insight). And the notion of hierarchical order was developed; Arthur Koestler, an admirer of von Bertalanffy's, was particularly struck by this and in his book *The Ghost in the Machine* he coined the term "holon" for a complex system. According to Koestler, a holon is a system which, when seen by looking down from a "higher" hierarchical level, appears to be a part of a more embracing system, but from a "lower" level it appears to be a whole. Thus, a holon is a "Janus-faced" entity.[9]

In strongly attacking the mechanistic method, the systems theorists and others generally erected a "straw man" and gave an impoverished account of what this entailed. Consider the words of Andras Angyal, writing in his book on personality theory (an early piece in this tradition):

> Since the basic idea of the holistic attitude is quite generally known, it will be sufficient here to indicate its meaning with but a single example. Let us draw on a surface a horizontal line A, and an oblique line B in such a manner that the two lines intersect. One can study and describe the properties of line A and those of line B. However, a knowledge of the whole resulting from these two lines, namely of the angle which the two lines form, does not emerge from such a study. The angle is something entirely new, and its properties cannot be derived from the properties of the lines which constitute it. . . . Just as complete information concerning the two lines which form the angle does not give us any knowledge about the angle itself, so knowledge of physiology, psychology, and sociology cannot result in a science of the total person.[10]

The striking thing here is that Angyal did not consider the direction of the two lines, or their spatial juxtaposition, to be included in the "complete information" about them. But mechanists or atomists have always considered such relationships between the parts to be vitally important, a point that holists choose to overlook. Edward Madden made this same point about shortsightedness in relation to Gestalt psychologists (who also adhere to a form of holism); and he has shown that in classical Newtonian dynamics (a prime example of mechanism and naturalism if ever there was one), relational factors such as the position and momenta of the various elementary particles were considered as vital pieces of information.[11]

"Reciprocal Determinism" in Cognitive Learning Theory

Another context in which Hegelian ideas have appeared (or rather, have been reinvented, for there is no evidence that Hegel was consciously applied) is in the recent writings of the cognitive learning theorist Albert Bandura. In the *American Psychologist* of April 1978, Bandura made a far-reaching suggestion: In the interest of understanding human behavior, older notions of causation had to be abandoned, and a new "genetic analytic principle" accepted, namely, the principle of "reciprocal determinism".[12]

Bandura's case ran as follows: According to one popular model, human behavior can be explained as a unidirectional function of internal and environmental factors. "In the unidirectional notion of interaction", Bandura noted, "persons and situations are treated as independent entities that combine to produce behavior".[13] A second model conceives of behavior as a slightly more complex function of personal and environmental factors. Three components are examined instead of two—personal factors (such as internal cognitive states), situations, and person–situation interactions. In both these models, however, causation is conceived as being unidirectional. In a third model, which Bandura devoted most of his paper to explaining, "behavior, internal personal factors, and environmental influences all operate as interlocking determinants of each other." This social-learning view of interaction Bandura called "reciprocal determinism."[14] He pictured the situation along the following lines:

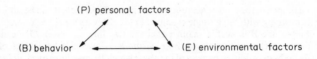

From the perspective of reciprocal determinism, environmental factors (E), behavior (B), and personal or cognitive factors (P), are seen as interdependent. As an example, Bandura considered TV-viewing behavior. Viewing behavior—that is, what TV station a person selects—is partly a function of personal preference, but it can also be argued that personal preferences are shaped by one's viewing behavior. Furthermore, the stations that are selected for viewing influence what programs all of the networks will televise (TV stations are very "market" oriented). Thus it can be said that behavior influences the environmental factors. These environmental factors in turn influence what stations and programs are available for a viewer to select between, and thereby they help to shape viewing tastes (personal factors). In this way it can be shown that the interaction between personal factors, behavior, and environmental factors is not unidirectional but reciprocal.

The most striking difference between unidirectional and reciprocal analyses of behavior, Bandura suggested, shows up in processes that regulate themselves. A mechanical example of self-regulation is a wall thermostat controlling room temperature. A human example might (at first sight) be a writer who set a goal to produce a certain number of pages before rewarding herself in some way. In a unidirectional analysis of these cases, behavior is conceived as being governed by its antecedent and consequent conditions. The behavior of the thermostat, for example, can be explained by knowing the temperature of the room before and after its activity (together, perhaps, with some laws relating to the physics of the device). Similarly, the case of the writer would be tackled by determining how many pages had been set as a goal at the start of the day, and how many were actually written. From the point-of-view of reciprocal determinism, however, this approach to the cases is simplistic. The wall thermostat probably can be understood by knowing the antecedent and consequent conditions, but in the case of the writer the unidirectional account is quite inadequate (according to Bandura).

Bandura devoted much of his effort in the paper to combating the reduction of human behavior to a type of machine behavior (*a la* the thermostat). In human behavior, he argued, one must distinguish between the mechanics and the agency of behavior regulation, for "people do not simply react mechanically to situational influences—they actively process and transform them."[15] Self-regulation cannot be bypassed without sacrificing considerable explanatory and predictive power:

> The more complex the activities that are self-regulated, and the less particularized the regulatory decision rules, the more judgmental factors enter the process, and the more the process departs from the mechanical servo-cybernetic metaphor.[16]

Bandura's point here seems to be that the relation of the self-system to the environment is too complex to be captured in a mechanical or radical behavioristic model. Rather than pursue the cybernetic approach, Bandura sketched out the reciprocal influences between external factors and self-regulatory processes. The self-regulated individual effects the environment; but in turn the environment serves to help develop the self-regulatory functions, to provide support for the self-regulatory systems, and to selectively activate and disengage self-reactive influences. Bandura wrote:

> Because personal and environmental determinants affect each other in a reciprocal fashion, attempts to assign causal priority to these two sources of influence reduce to the "chicken-or-egg" debate. The quest for the ultimate environmental determinants of activities regulated by self-influence becomes a regressive exercise that can yield no victors in explanatory contests, because for every ultimate environmental cause that is invoked, one can find prior actions that helped to produce it.[17]

Bandura's discussion in the *American Psychologist* was unsatisfactory, partly because he never clearly established that the traditional pattern of causal explanation cannot be made to work. Consider the example of TV-viewing behavior. As discussed before, personal factors such as an individual's likes and dislikes certainly influence which channels are selected for viewing; the causal arrow here is going from P to B. However, it can also be argued that viewing behavior influences the environment (the TV programs), so that B causes E. Furthermore, as the environment influences personal tastes, the arrow also goes from E to P. But an alternative exists to this reciprocally determined system—an alternative where the traditional notion of causation does not break down. For though it is true that personal viewing tastes influence behavior and that behavior (through the environment) also influences viewing tastes, it is *not* true that these two causal sequences occur at the same instant. It is highly unlikely that the influence of, say, a taste for madcap British humor that causes one to turn on "Monty Python" at 9:00 one evening is also, at the very same time, causing the network to televise this program. After all, the TV schedule was made out months in advance, and the initial decision to air it may have been made on the basis of a programmer's hunch that people would come to like it. The environment at 9:00 on that evening was more or less given, and it was independent of that precise piece of viewing behavior, although it still could be true that over the long haul viewing behavior does influence the TV environment. More generally, it appears that almost any example of so-called reciprocal determinism can be taken and, by carefully pinning down the times at which the various factors interact, it can be shown to be a series of unidirectional causal influences. Bandura's triangular diagram, then, is more accurately rendered as a linear sequence:

T.1 . . . . . . P causes B
T.2 . . . . . . B causes E
T.3 . . . . . . E causes B and P

It is apparent that the need to modify the traditional concept of causation has not been established by Bandura's argument.

Yet there might be something more. Bandura's position with respect to reciprocal determinism might have been inspired by a concern similar to one that has been found in the physical sciences, where complex problems are formulated in terms of functional laws. Consider what happens when a stone is thrown into the air. It could be said that the gravitational attraction between the stone and the earth is causing the two bodies to come together, but it would be more in accord with scientific practice to use the formula:

$$F = G.M_1.M_2/D^2$$

and to show that this enables one to explain why the stone falls. The mathematical formulation captures the functional relationships in the relevant system. Bertrand Russell made this point in his essay "On the Notion of Cause", written around the turn of the century. Russell argued that the traditional notion of cause is outdated and it is only because philosophers do not understand enough mathematics that they continue to think in terms of causes rather than functional laws:

> The law of gravitation will illustrate what occurs in any advanced science. In the motion of mutually gravitating bodies, there is nothing that can be called cause, and nothing that can be called effect; there is merely a formula. Certain differential equations can be found, which . . . render the configuration at any earlier or later instant theoretically calculable.[18]

However, it is not clear that this line of argument carries the day either. It seems that when such functional laws are used to explain specific cases, they are used in ways that reduce the cases to instances of unidirectional causation. To clearly display the logic here, consider a case that is much simpler than the ones that Bandura and Russell use as examples—namely, Boyle's law. It is true that the pressure and volume of a gas are related by a simple formula (pressure is inversely proportional to volume), and it is impossible to say in general that one of these factors is causally more important than the other—that a change in either parameter is the cause of an accompanying change in the other (for of course the reverse could be true). However, if one was explaining a specific case such as the workings of an automobile engine and was asked why the pressure increased in the cylinders just before the sparkplug touched off the gases, one's reply would be "because the volume decreased when the piston moved up in the cylinder." The law

$$P = c/V$$

still holds, but the question asked is not why both P and V changed, but rather, why the pressure increased. To answer this question, it is necessary to use the law to establish a unidirectional causal statement. In a different situation, of course, one might use the same law to explain why a volume of gas decreased by citing increase in pressure as the causal factor. In *The Cement of the Universe* Mackie makes this point when arguing against Russell's abandonment of the notion of cause. He notes that functional laws usually entail the holding of various unidirectional causal laws (such as increase in pressure causing a decrease in volume). In addition, Mackie argues that functional laws are limiting cases of unidirectional causal influences, and he points out that functional laws may be viewed as generalizations of unidirectional causation.

Bandura offers no convincing arguments against this approach. He fails to show that the cases he visualizes cannot be conceptualized in the manner outlined. Several caveats are necessary here, however. First, human behavior *is* complex, and when the interrelationships between several people are involved (for example, two parents and a child interacting over the dinner table), there are so many variables and so many interactions that in practice it may be impossible to formulate precisely the causal links or to do the necessary calculations. This is a practical difficulty (on a par with the difficulties that worried Cronbach and which were discussed in the previous chapter), and it does not show that the endeavor is misguided in principle. (Indeed, in replying to this general line of criticism of his work, Bandura placed great emphasis on the issue of complexity, and he reproduced an enormously complex diagram showing the multitude of interactions in the human circulatory system—which, one is to suppose, he takes to be on a par with, or even simpler than, many psychological systems.)[19] Second, in arguing that Bandura has not made his case about the limitations of the traditional notion of causation, the point has not been to wholeheartedly endorse the application of this traditional notion to human affairs. It has been argued by many philosophers (as will be seen in Chapter 9) that causal models are entirely inappropriate for explaining human action; the point here simply has been to show that Bandura's line of argument is not a telling one.

Finally, it should be noted that Bandura also discussed reciprocal determinism in his book *Social Learning Theory*. One out of the six chapters was devoted to this topic, but, although the author believed he was arguing for his "new" view of causality, his words actually support the rival case that has been offered here. For the thrust of his argument was not that B, P, and E reciprocally determine each other at the same time, but rather it was that there is usually an ongoing history of interaction and that B, P, and E have come to be what they are by virtue of a long series of interactions over time. (This is, to be sure, an important point, but it is not the point that Bandura believed it to be!) Perhaps because the term "history" is not in common use among research psychologists, the argument was presented without benefit of this straight-forward word. Instead:

> Rather, to elucidate the process of reciprocal interaction between personal and environmental influences, one must analyze how each is conditional on that of the other. The methodology best suited for this purpose specifies the conditional probabilities that the interacting factors will affect the likelihood of the occurrence of each other *in an ongoing sequence.* [20]

And again,

> Analysis of *sequential* interchanges in social relationships provides one example of reciprocal influence processes. Studies of dyadic exchanges document how the behavior of one member *activates* particular responses from the repertoire of the other members which, in turn, *prompt* reciprocal counteractions that mutually shape the social milieu. [21]

Perhaps even more telling is Bandura's remark that "in the regress of prior causes, for every chicken discovered by a unidirectional environmentalist, a social learning theorist can identify a prior egg." [22]

The Past Reborn

It is not their critics, but rather it is Bandura and von Bertalanffy and the systems theorists themselves, who have unwittingly uncovered "a prior egg." Apparently without realizing it, they have rediscovered Hegel's principle of internal relations; and, even more strikingly, they have developed arguments and examples that are almost identical to ones used almost a century ago by scientists who also were impressed by complexity and who *consciously* looked to Hegel for help. For in the late nineteenth and early twentieth centuries a host of neo-Hegelian holists or organicists (who were anti-naturalistic) were moved to criticize what they had variously called "simple-minded Galilean-ism" and the "additive method of science". [23] In 1884, the young J. S. Haldane (on the threshold of a distinguished scientific career) published an essay "Life and Mechanism" in the influential journal *Mind*. Using a variety of biological examples, he tried to show that "the ordinary conceptions of physical science are insufficient when applied to the phenomena of life", and that other conceptions must be substituted. [24] In attempting this, he was clearly anti-naturalistic. What was needed, Haldane argued, was the conception that Bandura later called "reciprocal determinism". Haldane chose the shorter term "reciprocity", although on occasion he used pretty much the same language as Bandura:

Not only, however, do surroundings and organisms successively act and react on one another, but the organism, as we have seen, reacts on the surroundings in a certain manner—in such a manner, namely, as to bring it about that the surroundings act again on the organism. . . . the surroundings in acting on the organism are therefore at the same time acted on by it. The organism is thus no more determined by the surroundings than it at the same time determines them. The two stand to one another, not in the relation of cause and effect, but in that of reciprocity.[25]

Bandura had three components (B, P, and E) in interaction, and Haldane only had two; but in matters of principle they were in full agreement.

Twelve years after the appearance of Haldane's paper, John Dewey—who in 1896 was still very much under the influence of Hegelianism—published "The Reflex Arc Concept in Psychology", a paper which became influential in the development of functional psychology.[26] Dewey attacked the dualism of stimulus and response, and argued that these were in internal relationship to each other; that is, they were in reciprocal interaction rather than being related in a unidirectional way. He expressed this by using the term "coordination". The elements of the reflex arc are coordinated, and "what we have is a circuit, not an arc or broken segment of a circle. This circuit is more truly termed organic than reflex."[27] The point was that the stimulus interacted and coordinated with the response; in fact, the stimulus was only made a stimulus by the response. On the other hand, the response was only made a response by its coordination with the stimulus. (The "husband and wife" parody of William James comes to mind here.)

The core problem

The fact that thinkers as diverse as John Dewey, J. S. Haldane, Ludwig von Bertalanffy, and Albert Bandura have been perplexed enough by complex relationships within integrated systems to flirt with the principle of internal relations (or its surrogate, the principle of reciprocal determinism[28]) is a testament to how difficult and important are the issues here. Nevertheless, there is good reason to believe—apart from the ones already indicated—that the principle of internal relations is flawed when used in a blanket way across the social and behavioral sciences.

As was indicated earlier, the central supposition of the principle of internal relations is that an entity—for Hegel himself, it was *any* entity—is changed if any of its relationships are changed; in other words, relationally determined properties are among the defining properties of an entity. And this, it turns out, is not as compelling as it sometimes appears.

Every entity has an indefinitely large number of characteristics, and those characteristics without which the entity would not be designated by a particular term are the characteristics that define that term. Characteristics that the entity possesses but which are not considered when deciding whether to apply the term to it, are accompanying characteristics. Interpreted in this light, Hegel and his fellow travellers seem to have been maintaining that as a result of its internal interaction with entities B and C, an entity A would have acquired some relational property P, and furthermore this property would be one of the defining characteristics of A. Without A's relationship with B or C, this defining characteristic P would not exist, and so A would really be not-A; in McTaggart's words, "if any part of the nature of A goes, the nature of A as a whole goes. . ."[29] Every relationship into which A entered, no matter what sort of relationship, would determine a defining characteristic of A. (This is why Hegel regarded everything that exists as forming a whole, a super system.)[30]

The main problem here is that not all of the characteristics of an entity are defining properties; many are accompanying characteristics. Thus, even if it is admitted that every relationship into which A ˙enters determines some property or characteristic of A, it may be the case that the characteristic is not defining, so that the characteristic can be removed without altering the way A would be labeled or identified. It follows from this that A can be removed from a system without it *necessarily* becoming not-A. And if this is granted, then the objection *in principle* to the naturalistic analytic or mechanistic or atomistic method disappears. A second difficulty is that the theory of internal relations makes the attainment of knowledge impossible, in principle. For to have knowledge of A, in the sense of knowing the defining features of A, all of A's relationships would have to be known; but since A is dynamically or reciprocally related to everything else in the whole of which it is a part, this whole must be known before A can be known. This is what William James had in mind when he wrote his parody, and called Hegelianism a "through-and-through" system whereby "if any Member, then the Whole System; if not the Whole System, then Nothing". Bertrand Russell, too, was scathing, and he stated: "If all knowledge were knowledge of the universe as a whole (as it was for Hegel, Bradley, and the more consistent systems theorists), there would be no knowledge."[31]

But there *is* knowledge. We build it up in a tentative and piecemeal way, and no doubt when faced with complex situations we make many mistakes and at first we tend to oversimplify. But as Popper said, we can learn from our mistakes, and with effort we can approach nearer the truth. Systems of interrelated parts offer special complexities, but there is no reason to believe they force us into radical departure from traditional modes of inquiry and into the realms of Hegelian logic.[32]

Notes and References

1. J. McTaggart, *The Nature of Existence*. Cambridge: Cambridge University Press, 1921, **1**, pp. 112–13.
2. See this spelled-out fully in D. C. Phillips, *Holistic Thought in Social Science*. Stanford, Ca.: Stanford University Press, 1976.

3. R. Harre, "Accounts, Actions and Meanings", in M. Brenner *et al.*, *The Social Context of Method*. NY: St. Martins Press, 1978, p. 44.

4. W. James, "Absolutism and Empiricism", *Mind*, IX, 1884, pp. 282–83. (My emphasis.)

5. Lincoln and Guba, op. cit., p. 39.

6. T. H. Allen, *New Methods in Social Science Research*. NY: Praeger, 1978, p. 17.

7. L. von Bertalanffy, *Modern Theories of Development*. NY: Harper Torchbooks, 1962, tr. J. H. Woodger, p. 46.

8. L. von Bertalanffy, *Problems of Life*. NY: Harper Torchbooks, 1960, p. 199.

9. A. Koestler, *The Ghost in the Machine*. London: Hutchinson, 1967.

10. A. Angyal, *Foundations for a Science of Personality*. NY: The Commonwealth Fund, 1941, pp. 2–4.

11. E. H. Madden, *Philosophical Problems of Psychology*. NY: The Odyssey Press, 1962, ch. 1.

12. A. Bandura, "The Self System in Reciprocal Determinism", *American Psychologist*, 1978, **33**, p. 356.

13. Ibid., p. 345.

14. Ibid., p. 346.

15. Ibid., p. 351.

16. Ibid., p. 352.

17. Ibid., p. 345.

18. B. Russell, *Mysticism and Logic*. Middlesex, England: Penguin Books, 1953, pp. 183–4.

19. A. Bandura, "Temporal Dynamics and Decomposition of Reciprocal Determinism", *Psychological Review*, 1983, **90**, no. 2.

20. A. Bandura, *Social Learning Theory*. NJ: Prentice-Hall, 1977, pp. 197–8. My emphasis.

21. Ibid., p. 198.

22. Ibid., p. 203.

23. See D. C. Phillips, op. cit.

24. J. S. Haldane, "Life and Mechanism", *Mind*, 1884, **9**, p. 35.

25. Ibid., pp. 32–3.

26. See D. C. Phillips, "James, Dewey, and the Reflex Arc", *Journal of the History of Ideas*, 1971, **32**, pp. 555–68.

27. J. Dewey, "The Reflex Arc Concept in Psychology", *Psychological Review*, 1896, **3**, p. 363.

28. This principle, and numbers of other organismic principles, are corollaries of Hegel's principle: see D. C. Phillips, *Holistic Thought in Social Science*, op. cit.

29. McTaggart, op. cit., **1**, p. 113.

30. More accessible than Hegel's account is that of the turn-of-the-century philosopher F. H. Bradley, *Appearance and Reality*. Oxford: Oxford University Press, 1962.

31. B. Russell, *A History of Western Philosophy*. London: Allen & Unwin, 1948, p. 772.

32. In replying to these criticisms, Bandura denies that he is Hegelian; reciprocal factors do not influence each other at the same time, he says! See his "Temporal Dynamics . . .", op. cit.

8

The New Philosophy of Science Run Rampant

In modern warfare it is often difficult to clearly delineate the opposing parties—each side is an uneasy coalition rather than a tightly-knit force. Cooperating groups may have a common enemy, yet remain uneasy with each other. And groups that share the same general ideology may also share hostility. Confusion is the watch-word of the day, as the troubles in and around the Middle-East amply illustrate.

A parallel situation exists in Academe. In the domains of social science and educational research, epistemological confusion reigns. It is widely (but not universally) recognized that old accounts of methodology, old accounts of the nature of science, have been thrown into doubt by the developments described earlier—by the rise of the new historically-sensitive philosophy of science, and by the apparent demise of positivism. Social scientists Mitroff and Kilmann have commented that "the tension between different views of science and the scientific method in Western cultures have reached the point at which it can no longer be ignored."[1] Richard Shweder and Donald Fiske express a similar view in an essay with the revealing title "Uneasy Social Science":

> Social science research institutions are hotbeds of pluralistic activity, each scientist holding that "progress is being made on the problem on which I am working". At the same time, and perhaps paradoxically, there has been in the social sciences, at least in recent years, a vague sense of unease.... A small, but visible, iconoclastic literature has emerged either challenging the scientific status of social research or expressing concern about the accomplishments of the social sciences. Some have even talked of a "crisis" in social inquiry.[2]

But those who share this unease may be in little agreement about anything else, and there have been some startling flights of fancy that have been defended in the name of these new developments. However, it is far from clear that the more radical departures from traditional viewpoints are, indeed, fully warranted. As philosopher David Thomas has commented,

> It is a sad fact that the philosophy of social science seems to invite garrulous and vacuous contributions on subjects which are not yet well understood; it is an exciting fact that there is so much left to investigate in this area.[3]

Before detailing how the lessons of the new philosophy of science have been mislearned, it will be as well to start by sketching the big picture.

In the field of research methodology in the social sciences and applied areas such as educational research and nursing research there are two warring sides.[4] However, as indicated, within each camp there is a great deal of uneasiness, and the knife in the back seems to be an occupational hazard. On one side, what might be called the "hard road" to scientism (or, in Popper's terminology, to naturalism) is being followed. Many in this camp hold a fairly traditional view of science, and argue that, in these terms, social science is indeed a scientific domain. Thus, Skinner is unrepentant, and so is James Popham; Fred Kerlinger regards behavioral research as, at its best, exemplifying a strong application of scientific method; so too does Nathaniel Gage. Testing, measurement, behavioral objectives, operational definitions, statistical inference, path analysis, and the rotation of axes are stock tools. The true experiment is still seen, in many quarters, as blazing the path to glory. Furthermore, it is not just empirical researchers who adopt a strong approach—a few philosophers remain closet Hempelians, and quixotically believe in the quest for "covering laws" which will explain human action.

Some in this very same camp, however, recognize that this is a difficult road to take, and they opt instead for an "easier road" to naturalism—they, too, hold that there is no epistemological difference between the natural and the social sciences, but (crucially) they hold a "softer" view of the nature of science, a view influenced by the "new philosophy of science". They can cite Popper as an ally, for he has never recanted his faith that there is no difference in principle between the physical and the social sciences, but of course he has been able to maintain this because his view of science is non-positivistic. It is also reasonable to construe John Dewey as being in this camp; he regarded scientific thinking as effective thinking, and because effective thinking can occur in all sorts of realms, all realms are potentially scientific. In 1916 Dewey wrote:

> Experimental science means the possibility of using past experience as the servant, not the master, of mind. It means that reason operates within experience, not beyond it, to give it an intelligent or reasonable quality. Science is experience becoming rational. The effect of science is thus to change men's idea of the nature and inherent possibilities of experience. By the same token, it changes the idea and the operation of reason.[5]

The rival camp is even more difficult to characterize. There is considerable disorder, disunity, and mutual disrespect. Perhaps the strongest thing that the members of this camp have in common is their dislike of the other (supposedly "scientific/naturalistic/positivistic") camp. Finn Collin notes that "we have seen that anti-positivistic views are legion and highly diverse, as is to be expected with a group of positions that is only negatively defined."[6] Many, if not all, in this camp would also assent to the argument put forward more than two decades ago by Peter Winch (and much earlier by Continental writers such as Dilthey) to the effect that the social sciences are more like philosophy than science; an argument with which many other philosophers concur (as will be seen in more detail in the following chapter). Recently Graham Macdonald and Philip Pettit put it this way:

> Social science, insofar as its concern is the explanation of human behavior, begins to look like a discipline which belongs with the humanities rather than the sciences. Social history, social anthropology, and social psychology, are attempts to do with art what is done crassly by common sense. . .[7]

A loud "Amen" would come from the many non-philosophers in the camp. They would be joined by latter-day supporters of action research; nowadays it is often touted that action research should become the model for all of social science, rather than social science being the model for action research (Michael Scriven has made a similar suggestion about evaluation research). Michael Apple rejects the strict determinism that typifies both traditional social science and "vulgar Marxism", and he stresses instead human autonomy and social contradiction. There are books with fighting titles like *Beyond the Numbers Game, Human Inquiry: A Sourcebook of New Paradigm Research, Positivism and Sociology, Toward Transformation in Social Knowledge, Rethinking Educational Research, The Nursing Profession: A Time to Speak,* and *Systematic Empiricism: Critique of a Pseudoscience.* To round things off, Lindblom and Cohen have scathing things to say in their *Usable Knowledge* about the practical sterility of PSI (professional social inquiry).

To confuse the battlefield even further, some of the central figures of the "scientistic" camp have shown signs of defection. Donald Campbell has softened his views on experimentation, and he has stressed that quantitative research is always based upon a foundation of qualitative knowledge (his argument will be examined in the following chapter); whilst, as we have seen, Lee Cronbach now thinks that the attainment of law-like knowledge in the social sciences is an unrealistic ideal. Furthermore, some in this anti-naturalistic camp use arguments and ideas from the "new philosophy of science" to bolster their case—a phenomenon that will be examined shortly. Finally, and as if all this wasn't enough, Derrida and Gadamer—despite their often difficult Continental prose—have become bedtime reading within this camp; and there are the usual Marxist and Hegelian variations.

What is the significance of this open if somewhat confusing warfare? Is it a war of liberation, or of oppression? Will it result in the end of social science as it is currently known?

Diagnoses From An Earlier Age

It is a truism that history repeats itself, but in this case the truism actually is true. Controversies about the nature of the social sciences, about how understanding of human society may best be achieved, are not new. Something may be learned from studying the way in which those of earlier times saw the issues; warfare, after all, is sometimes clearer when seen in historical context.

Some points made by the philosophers Morton White and William James will be revived, and it will be argued that these provide enlightenment about what is at stake in the current disputes. (Many other frameworks could have been selected, of course, but for the moment the work of these two Harvard men will have to suffice.)

(i) Anti-Formalism

Consider the following passage:

> It is not surprising, therefore, to find American intellectuals ranging themselves . . . against formalism, since they have been convinced that logic, abstraction, deduction, mathematics, and mechanics are inadequate to social research and incapable of containing the rich, moving, living current of social life.[8]

It is something of a surprise to learn that this passage was not written by a commentator on the state of the contemporary debate about the methodology of educational and social science research. Instead, it was written by Morton White in 1949, and he was looking back and commenting upon intellectuals working around the turn of the century—notably Justice Homes, Thorstein Veblen, and John Dewey. But he *could* have been writing about the present scene. (To mislead the reader here, the tenses of some of White's verbs were changed from past to present.)

According to White's analysis, the revolt against formalism (that is, against "logic, abstraction, deduction, mathematics and mechanics") in the United States at the turn of the century was inspired by such factors as the following: belief in the need for creativity and intelligence in producing new directions for social improvement; a belief in historicism—a belief that the world, including human thought, is changing, developing, evolving, and that present problems can be understood only when seen as growing out of conditions in the past (it was here that the influence of Hegel, Marx and Darwin was important); an anti-mechanistic attitude (for mechanism denegrates human creativity); a belief in organicism, especially a belief that social problems are interrelated and that knowledge cannot be successfully categorized in a watertight way into economics, politics, psychology, and so on; and a faith in democracy as a form of social organization that allows human action freedom to develop, and seek in an unfettered way solutions to social problems. It would seem that there are no themes here that could not be found in work of members of the second present-day warring camp (the anti-naturalistic or anti-scientistic group).

Now, it must be acknowledged at the outset that there is much to be said for the anti-formalist position, both for what it opposes and what it positively advocates. "Logic, mathematics, and abstraction" often yield unrealistic models of human affairs—think of economic models that assume perfect competition, full knowledge on the part of those in the marketplace, and games-theoretic rationality. David and Judith Willer wrote, in their 1973 attack on "pseudoscience" in the social sciences, that the "methods of achieving scientific sociology, however, can not include either new statistical procedures or scaling methods. . . . A scientific sociology implies a completely different method."[9] Contemporary anti-formalists, too, have rediscovered the insights of Dilthey and others from the earlier age, namely,

> We explain nature, but we understand mental life. . . . This means that the methods of studying mental life, history and society differ greatly from those used to acquire knowledge of nature . . .[10]

And one thing is clear—the methods of "understanding" that Dilthey pointed to are not formal, naturalistic ones.

The entries in anti-formalism's ledger are not all credits, however. But before turning critical, there are the insights of the second Harvard man to consider.

(ii) Tenderness

In the first chapter of his *Pragmatism* (1907), William James pointed out that Western intellectual history has been marked by a clash of temperaments. On one side have been the tender-minded, whom James depicted *inter alia* as rationalistic, intellectualistic, idealistic and free-willist. On the other side are the tough-minded, who are empiricist, sensationalistic, materialistic, fatalistic, and skeptical. The members of these two groups:

> have a low opinion of each other. . . . The tough think of the tender as sentimentalists and soft heads. The tender feel the tough to be unrefined, callous, or brutal. Their mutual reaction is very much like that that takes place when Bostonian tourists mingle with a population like that of Cripple Creek. Each type believes the other to be inferior to itself; but disdain in the one case is mingled with amusement, in the other it has a dash of fear.[11]

Who can doubt that James's words are applicable to the contemporary scene? Kerlinger, Gage, Skinner, and Hempel are indeed seen as unrefined and brutal by their critics; while Stake, Eisner, and practitioners of hermeneutical social science are viewed as sentimentalists, and many Continental writers are regarded as soft-in-the-head. Furthermore, Cronbach and Campbell are regarded in some quarters as becoming more addled with each passing day.

Some of the descriptors James appended to his two main categories need some updating, of course. To the tender-minded list there could be added such items as "anti-naturalistic", "anti-realist", "relativist", "hermeneutical/inter-pretive", "qualitative", and "epistemologically charitable"; while on the tough-minded side there could be put "naturalistic", "fallibilist", "epistemologically uncharitable", and "pro-scientific rationality".

By way of illustration, and also by way of showing that the insights of White and James overlap, consider the following three extracts from a recent paper by Elliot Eisner in the house journal of the American Educational Research Association, the *Educational Researcher*. The rationalism (that is, the stressing of the role of ideas or thought in inquiry, and the relegation of empirical matters to a minor role), the relativism, and the charity about what is to count as knowledge, are so apparent as to require little highlighting:

> (a) I gladly accept the label relativist if the term refers to someone who recognizes that different theoretical systems regard different phenomena as data, that what constitutes evidence is determined by the theoretical system within which one operates, and that conclusions about reality cannot be dissected from the theoretical and methodological procedures used to generate those conclusions.
> (b) I also accept the label *eclecticist* if the term refers to the belief that there is not now, nor is there likely to be, any single theoretical view that will encompass the whole of reality . . . the best we are likely to do is draw from a variety of theoretical systems . . .
> (c) . . . skilled physicians and teachers have knowledge in their craft or practice: they know what they need to do and they know how to do it. But what they know they often cannot articulate. Because they cannot produce the propositions that account for their actions and their consequences, do we conclude that they have beliefs but not knowledge? . . . I find such a view of knowledge bizarre.[12]

Another example is provided by the work of Yvonna Lincoln and Egon Guba. There is a slight terminological problem here, for they call the view they are explicating "naturalistic", although in the Popperian terminology that has been adopted in the present volume their view is "anti-naturalistic". They point out that the position they are supporting is "postpositivistic", and they comment that, according to this perspective, "Objective reality has become very relative indeed!"[13] They list the "axioms" of this position as follows:

> Realities are multiple, constructed, and holistic.
> Knower and known are interactive, inseparable.
> Only time- and context-bound working hypotheses (ideographic statements) are possible.
> All entities are in a state of mutual simultaneous shaping, so that it is impossible to distinguish causes from effects.
> Inquiry is value-bound.[14]

They amplify the first of these axioms with these words:

> There are multiple constructed realities that can be studied only holistically; inquiry into these multiple realities will inevitably diverge (each inquiry raises more questions than it answers) so that prediction and control are unlikely outcomes although some level of understanding (*verstehen*) can be achieved.[15]

Social scientist William Filstead supports this latter point; he writes that

> The qualitative paradigm does not conceive of the world as an external force, objectively identifiable and independent of man. Rather, there are multiple realities. In this paradigm individuals are conceptualized as active agents . . . rather than responding in a robotlike fashion. . . .[16]

In 1967 Israel Scheffler, another Harvard man, considered a set of views not far removed from those later espoused by Eisner, and Lincoln and Guba. He referred to these views as offering a "bleak picture", which represented an

"extravagant idealism".[17] In what follows, this tender-minded, anti-formalis-
tic, anti-naturalistic idealism will be called, to non-pejoratively, "the
Position". And now that the cards are on the table, it is time to enter the fray.

Misreadings of Philosophy

Supporters of the Position have put forward a variety of arguments, many of
which are bad ones. It is interesting that Macdonald and Pettit, in *Semantics
and Social Science* (1981), actually reject most of the arguments they report,
although they are, in fact, supporters of the Position themselves. In the
following discussion, only arguments drawn from philosophy of science on
behalf of the Position will be discussed and assessed.

As indicated earlier, some of the vocal adherents of the Position in the social
science and educational research communities have been strongly influenced
in their thinking by recent developments in epistemology and philosophy of
science. As reported in Part A, the last few decades have been exciting ones in
philosophy, and a number of controversial theses have been advanced, and
these have met with vigorous discussion, opposition, and even refutation.
Those writers who are enamored of the Position, however, have adopted
theses from one side of these hotly contested debates, and they have boldly
extrapolated them; they have rarely discussed or evaluated the strong
criticisms that have been directed at the views that they have taken as
foundational. Thus they owe their readers an explanation—one cannot, in
seriously contested matters, simply pluck out one viewpoint as being worthy,
and pass over the rest in silence.

The controversial theses adopted by these supporters of the Position can be
discussed under four headings: (1) Rampant Hansonism; (2) Rampant
Kuhnism; (3) Rampant pseudo-Polanyism; (4) Rampant anti-Positivism.

(1) Rampant Hansonism

Hanson's work was discussed in Chapter 2, where his basic thesis was
reduced to one sentence: "The theory, hypothesis, framework, or background
knowledge held by an investigator can strongly influence what is observed".
There is a great deal of evidence that this is correct; psychological research
supports the theory-ladenness of observation, and the point is willingly
granted even by opponents of the Position (see, for instance, the discussion in
Scheffler's *Science and Subjectivity*, or the works of Hempel). Popper not only
accepted the thesis, he insisted upon it:

> The belief that science proceeds from observation to theory is still so widely and so firmly held
> that my denial of it is often met with incredulity. . . . But in fact the belief that we can start
> with pure observations alone, without anything in the nature of a theory, is absurd. . . .
> Observation is always selective. It needs a chosen object, a definite task, an interest, a point of
> view, a problem. And its description presupposes a descriptive language, with property

words; it presupposes similarity and classification, which in its turn presupposes interests, points of view, and problems.[18]

Supporters of the Position do not seem to recognize this widespread acceptance, and they write as if a major issue is the *truth* of Hanson's thesis, whereas the real problem concerns its *significance*. What seems to have been happening is this: Supporters of the Position have been overstimulated and have exaggerated the significance of Hanson's thesis; from that perspective it no doubt has appeared that others, who have not overreacted, have not seen Hanson's point at all!

As discussed in the earlier chapter, often the moral has been drawn that Hanson has destroyed empiricism, whereas according to a more balanced view he only destroyed naive empiricism (which, indeed, was well-destroyed long before Hanson's time). But it is a mistake to suppose—as the adherents of the Position do—that Hanson also destroyed the credibility of notions like objectivity and testing (which are important for non-naive empiricism which focusses not on the origin but on the status and warrant for our beliefs). Just because the categories within a theory dictate the sort of data that have to be collected—the way the world has to be looked at—it does not follow that the theory is not open to objective test. For if a severe test is devised, using the theory's own terms, it still is on the cards that the theory will run into difficulty. This is a point that Scheffler makes much of in his sadly-neglected *Science and Subjectivity*—sadly neglected, that is, by those sons and daughters of the Position who could most profit from it. To take an example from contemporary physics, just because a scientist holds the view—supported by his or her theory—that magnetic monopoles exist, it does not follow that he or she will detect such contentious objects. And if some are detected, almost certainly those scientists who previously did not believe in monopoles will be won over.

In the light of this discussion, consider again Elliot Eisner, who, apparently suffering a severe dose of Hansonism, wrote (in a passage quoted more fully earlier) that because each theoretical system determines what will count as its own data, "conclusions about reality cannot be dissected from the theoretical procedures used to generate those conclusions".[19] But indeed they can! Conclusions *can* be dissected and put to a severe test, but a test that is fair in the theory's own terms. Failing a test is not necessarily fatal—another lesson of recent philosophy—but as failures mount the theory becomes less and less credible. It is not clear how typical Eisner is, in this respect, of the mainstream of those who adhere to the Position, but testing and validating form no part of his philosophy. In the same article quoted above, he spells out six ways of "appraising a view", but the fact that a theory may fail tests is not one of them. After all, he cannot include it, for the Position would start to crumble. (Eisner seems to hold a "coherence" view; and he places some reliance on the fact that if other people can see the world the way the theory in question suggests, then it is true. But the fact that our observation is theory laden, and that we can look at the world in the same way as Hitler or Freud, does not offer sufficient grounds for judging their views to be well-warranted.) Scheffler's words, quoted fully earlier, are worth recalling:

> What is the upshot? There is here no evidence for a general incapacity to learn from contrary observations, no proof of a pre-established harmony between what we believe and what we see . . . [20]

Supporters of the Position often draw another—and quite relativistic—conclusion from Hanson. The reasoning goes something like this: All observation is theory-laden; hence no observation is made "objectively"; hence no observation has an unchallengeable status; any observation can be discounted by an observer who is working from the vantage point of a rival theoretical position; hence the "observed world" is constructed by the observer rather than discovered by him or her, and different observers will construct different worlds. It was probably this reasoning that Lincoln and Guba had in mind when they stressed the existence of "multiple realities". To cite another example, the neo-Marxist writer Kevin Harris puts forward a view that tends in the same direction:

> There is no such thing as "given nontheoretical knowledge"; and since theory always mediates between the individual and the world, knowledge is never merely a discovery of what is out there in the existential world. [21]

Thus, if a scientist reports seeing a gene by means of an electron microscope, the report is theory laden. What counts as a gene is determined by current biological theories; furthermore, the skeptic can only be assured that what is being seen is not an artifact of the instrument by relying upon the physical theories that explain the workings of the electron microscope. If the relevant parts of either biology or physics were challenged successfully, the claim to have seen a gene would be overthrown. Similarly, an educational researcher observing a child of low intelligence trying to solve a difficult problem can have his or her judgment revised if another researcher with a rival theory were to attack the notion of intelligence that was being used; it might be decided that, in fact, a highly intelligent but culturally deprived child was being seen.

Now, while this line of attack on theory-free observation is well founded, the conclusions that are drawn from it (via the chain of reasoning described above) are too extreme. From the fact that all observation statements are *potentially* challengeable by refuting the theories on which they are based, it does not follow that all face such challenges *at present*. It does not follow that all observation statements are so little tested and supported that there is nothing that is not in imminent danger of being overthrown. It does not follow that all positions are so insulated from criticism and debate that they must be regarded as "unobjective" (it will be recalled that, for Popperians, objectivity is related to openness to criticism and refutation). It does not follow that all conceivable knowledge claims are on an equal footing in that they all are equally risky. And it does not follow that all "alternative realities" are equally viable as alternatives.

The point is that if a well-tried observation statement, based on a long-successful theory, is to be challenged credibly, the challenge has to come from a better tested and more trustworthy theory. It can be added, too, that a great many "low level" observation reports, which provide the bases for our dealings with the world, are so well attested and have been successfully relied upon for such long periods of time that it is not irrational to continue to count on them. The argument summarized earlier serves only as a salutory reminder that no such reports can be relied upon absolutely.

Newton-Smith assesses the situation well. He asks: How "do I know that the particular reports which I rely on in making my theory choices now will not in fact need revising?" And he replies:

> while we cannot have absolute faith in any particular reports or a particular range of reports, we are entitled to have a general faith in the low-level O-reports we are inclined to make. Our success in coping with the world gives us grounds for this general confidence. If such judgments were not by and large reliable, we should not be still here to make judgments.[22]

The work of the educational theorist Elliot Eisner provides a good example of what happens when too extreme a conclusion is drawn from the attack on theory-neutral observation. He writes:

> Does objective mean that one has discovered reality in its raw, unadulterated form? If so, this conception of objectivity is naive. All of us construct our conception of reality by interacting with the environment. . . . And that construction is influenced by our previous experience, including our expectations, our existing beliefs, and the conceptual tools through which the objective conditions are defined.[23]

So far, so good. But Eisner erroneously supposes that this argument entitles him to adopt—indeed, he constructed the argument to be able to adopt—what can be called "extreme tolerance of belief". As documented earlier, he sees no way to choose, using evidence, between rival theories or paradigms, for each theory will determine what kinds of observations will count in its own favor. There is "no critical test", he says, that "will resolve the truth or falsity" of rival belief systems.[24] Eisner suggests that so long as members of a group of believers maintain their agreement, and so long as they can point (to their own satisfaction) to things that they would count as instantiating their theories, the views they hold are true, for them. This is an extremely tolerant position; Nazis, flat-earthers, astrologers, paranoics, Freudians, Skinnerians, and anyone else who ever strongly believed in a theory, in principle could satisfy Eisner's criteria. However, if belief systems could be accredited so cheaply, they would be worth very little.

It should be noted in passing that Eisner was right to say that there is no critical test (i.e. no *single* test) that can be used to decide between rival positions. But Eisner seems to overlook the historical evidence showing that the settling of a theoretical dispute *can* take place; usually, however, it is a long-drawn-out business, a battle of attrition. Nevertheless such disputes eventually are settled. Gradually a case is built up that favors one position rather than another. (There is no serious dispute these days that "the earth is flat" is a discredited view, despite the fact that some folk still hold it and adduce evidence that they are right; but Eisner's criteria cannot account for discreditation.)

Perhaps, in all this, Eisner and the others have been unduly accepting, not only of Hanson, but of Kuhn's views that also tend in the same direction. So it is appropriate for the discussion to move on.

(2) Rampant Kuhnism

As suggested above, there is a tendency for rampant Hansonians to drift and become rampant Kuhnians, unfortunately ending up on ground no less shaky than that from which they set out.

Perhaps Kuhn's most notorious thesis—and the one that blends most readily with Hansonism—concerns the incommensurability of paradigms: the supposed fact that two paradigms cannot be compared, nor one criticized in terms of the other, for each "carves the universe up" in different ways. (Many of the anti-positivistic sources cited earlier make heavy use of the notion of paradigms.) Even if the same word is used in the two paradigms ("space" in Newtonian and Einsteinian physics, for example), it has quite a different meaning in each case; meaning is determined by the theoretical network in which a term is embedded (the doctrine of semantic holism). Kuhn wrote that "the proponents of competing paradigms practise their trades in different worlds".[25]

The point to be recalled here (it was discussed more fully in Chapter 3) is that Kuhn's radical position has come under intense criticism; the literature has grown to mammoth proportions. And the criticisms have come from all philosophical quarters: from Popper and Lakatos and their colleagues and students, from Wittgensteinians like Toulmin, from Scheffler and Siegel and Shapere, from Newton-Smith. . . . It is pointless to continue. The fact of the matter is that many of the social science and educational researchers who hold the Position have been selective in their philosophical reading. They have not done their homework, and they naively suppose that because a well-known author (like Kuhn) asserts something, then that makes it true. (An added complexity which they also overlook is that there are tensions in Kuhn's work, if not inconsistencies, and he sometimes takes back with one hand what he has given with the other. It was perhaps a Freudian slip that Kuhn titled a collection of his essays that appeared some years after his classic work on scientific revolutions, *The Essential Tension*.)

Even the staunchest admirers of Kuhn's work have acknowledged that it was misunderstood by some of those who were positively influenced by it. Thus Barry Barnes noted recently that

> Given the general acceptance of liberal-rationalist modes of thought in our society, it is not altogether surprising that Kuhn's work has occasionally been interpreted as anti-scientific polemic, and that it attained a certain celebrity amongst radical critics of science when it first appeared in the 1960s.[26]

Not only in the 1960s! Barnes also points out that here and there a reader can find a remark in Kuhn—like the remark that, with respect to how choices about theoretical concepts can be made, "What better criterion than the decision of the scientific group could there be?"—that

> appears to imply that whatever a scientific community has a fancy to assert must *ipso facto* be accepted, that scientists can, as it were, pick and choose what is to count as knowledge. Needless to say, this is not Kuhn's view at all.[27]

What was "needless to say" needs to be said, and argued, for there certainly *are* remarks in Kuhn that give this impression; but the main point—which Barnes evidently agrees with—is that at least some people interpreted Kuhn to be saying this. Some, like Eisner, even went so far as to actually *accept* what they took to be Kuhn's position.

There is no need to repeat here the other points about Kuhn's work that were made in the earlier chapters. But one further matter does need to be raised. It seems to have been Kuhn's influence (whether justified or not), even more than Hanson's, that inspired the remarks about "multiple realities" that are to be found in the literature of the Position. Consider the view held by Lincoln and Guba:

> There is, in this ontological position, always an infinite number of constructions that might be made and hence there are multiple realities. Any given construction may not be (and almost certainly is not) in a one-to-one relation to (or isomorphic with) other constructions of the same (by definition only) entity. The definition is implied by the use of some common referent term, which is nevertheless understood (or constructed) differently by different individuals (or constructors).[28]

What is going on in this difficult passage is, one can guess, based upon two Kuhnian notions—incommensurability of paradigms, together with the idea that researchers in different paradigms inhabit different worlds. Elliot Eisner's Kuhnianism is even more easily detected:

> (s)cientists themselves hold beliefs, even within science, that cannot be warranted by scientific methods. In the social sciences, this most clearly is the case. The differences in basic assumptions among Freudians, Rogerians, Skinnerians, Heiderians, Ericksonians, Piagetians, and the like are not resolvable through science. The fundamental theoretical structures through which each defines psychological reality differ. . . .[29]

The issues here are complex, and it would not be wise to reject the notion of "alternative realities" out-of-hand. A naive or uncritical use of Kuhnian notions, however, is unlikely to produce a credible case; it was shown in Chapter 3 that Kuhn's semantic holism can be questioned, and the relativism to which it leads has implausible consequences. It should be noted, too, that the arguments of Eisner, and of Lincoln and Guba, pale in comparison to the much lengthier and much more detailed discussions of the issues surrounding the "multiplicity of worlds" given by the philosopher Nelson Goodman.[30] Goodman calls himself a "radical relativist", and he argues that there are "countless alternative true or right world-versions". Nevertheless, he tries to impose "severe restraints", for he does not want to allow that "everything goes" or that "tall stories are as good as short ones, that truths are no longer distinguishable from falsehoods."[31] It is far from clear, however, as Harvey Siegel has shown,[32] that Goodman can at the one time hold all these positions; for his (sometime) belief in standards or criteria by use of which he wants to prevent all tall stories from being acceptable, is fundamentally incompatible with his relativism.

(3) Rampant pseudo-Polanyism

In the writings of many who hold the Position, there is a pronounced leaning towards the notion of "tacit knowledge" developed by Michael Polanyi. According to Polanyi's notion, people often know more than they can tell—their knowledge cannot be put into words. Thus, a chicken-sexer is able to succeed in sorting chickens by sex, and yet is not able to say how it was done; and a champagne-maker knows how much to twist the bottles during a tour of the cellars, but is not able to describe how he knows the degree to which each needs to be turned. In the opening pages of one of his books, Polanyi wrote that his thinking about human knowledge started from the fact that

> we can know more than we can tell. This fact seems obvious enough; but it is not easy to say exactly what it means. Take an example. We know a person's face, and can recognize it among a thousand, indeed among a million. Yet we usually cannot tell how we recognize a face we know. So most of this knowledge cannot be put into words.[33]

Eisner often attacks what he takes to be a positivist or scientific view of knowledge by arguing, for example, that he recognizes his mother's face but cannot describe in words how he does this. Lincoln and Guba state that the adherent of the methodology they wish to support

> argues for the legitimation of tacit (intuitive, felt) knowledge in addition to propositional knowledge (knowledge expressible in language form) because often the nuances of the multiple realities can be appreciated only in this way; because much of the interaction between investigator and respondent or object occurs at this level; and because tacit knowledge mirrors more fairly and accurately the value patterns of the investigator.[34]

Nevertheless, they are a little uncomfortable, and seem to realize the obscurantism that is lurking here—for later they let slip a remark that effectively cancels the concession they have made to Polanyi: "Of course", they say, the inquirer "cannot be content to leave his or her knowledge at the tacit level. That tacit knowledge must be converted to propositional knowledge so that the inquirer can both think about it explicitly and communicate it to others."[35] The trouble is, tacit knowledge that is communicable in words is *no longer* tacit knowledge; and if this verbal translation really has to be possible in order to justify an inquirer in using it, then proper, Polanyian tacit knowledge can *never* be used.

Robert Stake is another well-known educational researcher who has been strongly influenced by Polanyi; in fact, from their citations it seems that Lincoln and Guba were sensitized to Polanyi in part via Stake's writings. If a qualitative researcher believes that he or she has achieved "understanding", according to Stake, then this claim must be accepted—it is as simple as that! Stake writes that

> Naturalistic (sic) generalizations develop within a person as a product of experience. They derive from the tacit knowledge of how things are . . .[36]

Stake accepts these as genuine, valid generalizations, and he states that action is quite properly based upon them. It seems to be of little concern to him that such generalizations have not "yet passed the empirical and logical tests that characterize formal (scholarly, scientific) generalizations." But then, if they have not passed *these* tests, how have such generalizations been validated or warranted? Stake does not face up to this issue, but instead merely restates his faith: "It is foolish to presume that a more scholarly report will be the more effective".[37]

Elliott Eisner fares no better. Recall his examples, from earlier in the chapter, of "skilled physicians and teachers" who have knowledge of their crafts that they cannot articulate. He continues his discussion in these terms:

> because they cannot produce the propositions that account for their actions and their consequences, do we conclude that they have beliefs but not knowledge? Do we believe that an excellent teacher or school administrator who cannot provide a theoretical explanation of what he or she has done knows nothing about teaching or school administration?[38]

He concludes that it is "wrong" to "claim that all knowledge is scientific knowledge". Here Eisner has confused, in a pernicious way, the *stating* of a knowledge claim with its *justification*. Polanyi's work has shown, at best, that people sometimes know how to perform skilled tasks without being able to explain how they are able to do them. (The philosopher Gilbert Ryle, writing in his classic *The Concept of Mind* (1949), advanced a similar thesis; he used as one of his examples the fact that people before Aristotle were able to argue well, although the theory of logical discourse had not yet been formulated.) Polanyi did *not* argue that *any* claim a person made had to be accepted.

The "tacit knowledge" thesis, then, involves two things: first, a person need not be able to articulate the theory behind his or her skill; and second, others recognize that this person is skilled by *judging the performance* against explicit standards. Thus Polanyi's "chicken sexer" and "champagne cellar master" are recognized as having tacit knowledge because they can be put to the test—the chickens all grow up having the predicted sex, and the wine matures perfectly. Furthermore, it is apparent that some sort of test or warrant is needed *even if* the person can articulate a theory. Thus, to return to one of Eisner's examples, if a school administrator were to claim she was good merely on the basis of her being able to articulate a theory, this would not normally be enough for others to judge her as being good. She would have to perform up to some standard. In this minimal sense of "scientific", all knowledge *is* scientific—it is warranted or tested belief. Behind Stake's and Eisner's rhetoric lurks an epistemology that is scandalously charitable, for it lacks an explicit recognition of the need to put knowledge-claims to the test. And this is why it is *pseudo* and not genuine Polanyism. (Eisner, of course, does talk of "*skilled* teachers and administrators", but he does not see that this key term begs the whole question. As is implicit in Polanyi's examples, the skill has to be publicly displayed, and it is this that warrants the claim that it is possessed. Eisner's talk of "articulating" is a red-herring.)

(4) Rampant anti-Positivism

In Chapter 4 it was suggested that there have been many exaggerated claims about the evils of positivism, and about the beneficial effects of its demise. It was, to be sure, a badly-blemished set of doctrines, but it is far from clear that it possessed all the monstrous qualities depicted by the adherents of the Position. Of these latter, Lincoln and Guba have been among the most moderate and fair-minded. "Positivism is passe", they report;[39] and

> Perhaps the *most* unexpected aspect of postpositivism [i.e. what has, in the present volume, been called the Position] is that its basic tenets are virtually the reverse of those that characterized positivism—perhaps not so surprising, after all, when one contemplates that postpositivism is as much a reaction to the failings of positivism as it is a proactive set of new formulations; reaction, too, is a form of "standing on the shoulders of giants".[40]

The simplest way to proceed is to catalogue some of the misinterpretations and problems in the work of those who hold the Position.

(i) First, many factual errors are made when researchers refer to positivism. Indeed, without suggesting that those who make the errors are deliberately dishonest, it seems as if the word "positivism" arouses such negative feelings that it is often used in a blanket way to condemn any position at all that the writer in question disagrees with, irrespective of how positivistic that position really is. Peter Halfpenny pointed out that anti-positivists "use the term loosely to describe all sorts of disfavored forms of inquiry."[41] Lincoln and Guba point out that

> positivism can be reshaped, apparently, to suit the definer's purpose. . . . One might venture to say that the particular form of definition offered by any commentator depends heavily upon the counterpoints he or she wishes to make.[42]

Henry Giroux is guilty of using the term in this way, and according to his account the positivists commit a variety of heinous sins: they are not future oriented but they celebrate the present; they hold a passive model of man; they adopt theories to serve as foundations for "technical control and coordination" (a point also stressed by Habermas); they are interested in prediction and explanation; and they hold that the "principle of rationality in the natural sciences" is superior to the hermeneutic principles underlying the "speculative social sciences".[43] It is not surprising that Giroux sees positivists (*his* positivists) everywhere.

There are less extreme cases. Robert Stake, for example, makes several slips about positivism in the course of one long sentence in an article in the *Educational Researcher* in 1978, but he seems to be using the word in the standard way:

> Philosophers of the positivist school, Carl Hempel and Karl Popper particularly, have posited that propositional statements of lawful relationship are the closest approximations of Truth—whether we are talking about physical matter or human.[44]

Popper, of course, was not in the "positivist school" at all, and even if his claim to be the executioner of positivism is not credited, he certainly was always a staunch opponent. Furthermore, as discussed earlier, philosophers of positivistic bent tended to adopt a non-realist view of science, and they did *not* regard "lawful relationships" as the nearest approximation to "Truth"; as reported in Chapter 4, for the positivists there was a well-recognized problem about how the universal claims of scientific laws could ever be verified, and therefore there was a problem about the meaning of these laws ("all particles of matter in the universe attract all others" cannot be verified in part because not every particle can be investigated).

Consider another but related example. Elliott Eisner has written that

> The behavioristic-positivistic tradition in American educational research tended to regard experience as unknowable and focused therefore on what children did.[45]

Despite his linking of behaviorism and positivism, it is not clear that Eisner could mean either of them. For in a sense, both of these positions postulate experience as the only thing that can be known, or as the only thing that can be the source of knowledge. What Eisner probably means is that there is a widely held view among researchers that what an individual has gained from an experience can only be gauged by studying what that person does; that is, by studying behavior. But a person certainly does not have to be a behaviorist or a positivist to hold this view; even Polanyi, whom Eisner is fond of citing, holds it. (It has been shown that Polanyi's theory of tacit knowledge—that a person can know more than he or she can tell—implies that such a person displays the knowledge in behavior; after all, this is how the outsider comes to realize that the person—the champagne-maker or the chicken-sexer—does have tacit knowledge).

Finally, the mistake is sometimes made of identifying positivism with particular scientific research methods, namely the use of experimental designs and the use of statistics. Thus, Stake writes:

In American research circles most methodologists have been of positivistic persuasion. The more episodic, subjective procedures, common to the case study, have been considered weaker than the experimental or correlational studies for explaining things.[46]

There are a number of things wrong here. First, a positivist, *qua* positivist, is not committed to any particular research design. There is nothing in the doctrines or positivism that necessitates a love of statistics or a distaste for case studies. Second, it is widely recognized, even by those who use experimental designs and correlational techniques, that there is a difference between establishing that there is a relationship between two variables and explaining that relationship (correlational studies are not always seen as "explaining things"). Third, subjective procedures are regarded as weak by more than the positivists (though, of course, a lot hinges on the sense of "subjective" here, and case study methods, ethnography, and so on, are not necessarily subjective in any weak and pejorative sense; indeed, many anthropologists join in the attack on subjectivity).

(ii) It is evident that positivists are often depicted as believing in an "absolute reality" to which their research methods give them privileged access. Positivists attempt to discover "Truth"; they "dig up" the laws of nature. Robert Stake's slip on this issue has already been cited; here is a different example from the pages of the *British Journal of Educational Studies*: "A positivist perspective" makes the assumption "that there is a fixed and unchanging reality based on constant relationships which is amenable to scientifically-modelled, objective research."[47]

It is interesting to contrast these misinterpretations of positivism with what L. J. Cronbach has written about construct validation in the domain of educational and psychological measurement. Cronbach and Meehl pioneered the notion of construct validation in a classic paper in 1955, and Cronbach has acknowledged the influence of logical positivist philosophers on science. Looking back later, he referred to papers written by Hempel in the 1960s as being the best elucidations of the formal philosophical bases of construct validation.[48] Cronbach also recognized that the arguments over what it is that tests measure involve "issues long-argued among philosophers on science",[49] and he wrote that Ernest Nagel "classifies views (about the nature of theoretical entities or contructs) as descriptive, realist, or instrumentalist." Then Cronbach quoted Nagel's discussion of instrumentalism:

Theories are intellectual tools . . . conceptual frameworks deliberately devised for effectively directing experimental inquiry, and for exhibiting connections between matters of observation that would otherwise be regarded as unrelated.[50]

Significantly, Cronbach continued: "This is essentially the position taken by Cronbach and Meehl (1955) in advocating construct validation of tests."

Here, then, there was no misunderstanding. Cronbach was perfectly clear that to be consistent with the logical positivistic approach that, he said, Meehl and he had acquired from the philosophers of science, an instrumentalist rather than a realist view of the nature of constructs was appropriate. Indeed, he identified some of the earlier *critics* of construct validation as being "realists at heart".[51] There is little ground, then, for the claim that, in general, logical positivists and their fellow travellers believed they were discovering the nature of "absolute reality".

(iii) All this leads to a significant point. Rather than logical positivism being an enemy, the diverse group made up of Lincoln and Guba, Eisner, Stake, and others who were influenced to move in the direction of the Position by the "new philosophy of science", should regard it as an ally in at least one central respect. For these writers have, as one of their main targets, the realist interpretation of science, and instrumentalists—among whom have been many positivists—oppose this as well. (The positivists, of course, came to this stand somewhat reluctantly, but come some of them did; and the path that led them to their antirealism was quite different from the one followed by holders of the Position.)

It should be clear that anyone who holds that there are multiple realities, or that there are incommensurable paradigms between which it is impossible to decide on the basis of evidence, is both a relativist and an anti-realist. Indeed, Lincoln and Guba make this abundantly clear; the position they advocate is opposed to the view that "there is a single tangible reality 'out there'", upon which "inquiry can converge ... until, finally, it can be predicted and controlled."[52]

Related to this, supporters of the Position often regard truth as being relative to the framework or paradigm of the investigator, and this sometimes leads directly to them holding an instrumental view:

> My point here is simply this: objectivity is a function of intersubjective agreement among a community of believers. What we can productively ask of a set of ideas is not whether it is *really* true but whether it is useful, whether it allows one to do one's work more effectively.[53]

Here it is apparent that Eisner has an instrumental criterion (whether a theory is "useful" rather than "really true"); although in much of his writing—some of the relevant passages were quoted earlier—he also was toying with relativism (the view that what is true depends upon the framework or paradigm being adopted). These two views are somewhat similar, though they are not identical; but in many contexts they overlap. At any rate, it is clear that with respect to anti-realism Eisner is (unknowingly) united with the logical positivists, and also with the other group of instrumentalists—the American pragmatists. (John Dewey had adopted C. S. Peirce's criterion of meaning which was parallel to the one later adopted by the logical positivists, and he much preferred to be identified as an "instrumentalist" than as a "pragmatist".)

Now, in arguing that Eisner and other upholders of the Position who followed Kuhn into relativism (or the neighboring instrumentalism) should be allies with the logical positivists, the point has not been to suggest that this powerful junta is correct, or even that it is united in all the doctrines the members accept. In fact, as was suggested at various places throughout the earlier discussions, the anti-realist position they all adopt is flawed—or, more accurately, the arguments they adduce in support of their position are flawed. Matters of such "pith and moment" are not to be settled as easily as they have supposed.[54]

(iv) Some of the more outspoken critics of positivism in the fields of education and the social sciences have not been as careful as those they criticize in maintaining a critical distinction. Positivistic philosophers, as well as others, have been clear about the difference between meaning and truth. Consider the words of the philosopher of science Arthur Pap:

> The question of *meaning* is prior to the question of *truth*. That is, we cannot assess the degree to which the known facts warrant belief in a proposition unless we are fairly clear about the meaning of that proposition.[55]

As far as the logical positivists were concerned, for a proposition to be meaningful (i.e. for it to be a proposition at all) it had to be testable or verifiable in principle (unless it was a logical truism); but another crucial point is that a meaningful proposition need not be true. In order to be judged as true, the meaningful proposition actually had to have undergone—successfully—some relevant test. If an untested (but testable) proposition were accepted, the person concerned could claim to have belief but not knowledge; for knowledge is *justified true belief*.

Since the work of Gettier in the early 1960s this analysis of knowledge has undergone critical scrutiny, largely in the attempt to strengthen it; none of the positions currently espoused suggests that any or all beliefs that are held can be regarded as knowledge. The philosophical community at large is united behind the view that to be regarded as knowledge, the belief in question has to be justified in some way, and in essence the current disputes focus upon what constitutes a satisfactory justification.[56] There is nothing that has happened since the demise of logical positivism, in other words, that legitimizes blurring the distinctions between meaning, truth, belief, and knowledge.

Some of the more exuberant critics of logical positivism in educational and social science arenas do ignore these distinctions. Throughout his writings Eisner, for example, uses the words "experience", "meaning", and "knowledge" interchangeably. The sciences and the arts are alternative forms of cognition, they are alternative ways of experiencing the world, they are alternative sets of meanings, they are alternative forms of representations, they are alternative ways of knowing. "It is not possible", he says, "to represent or know everything in one form."[57] For Eisner, Miller's *Death of a Salesman*, his memory of his own mother's face, a Bach fugue, a portrait by Velasquez, and a poem by Dylan Thomas or e. e. cummings, are all statements of knowledge. But he gives no indication of how the prior question of the meaning of these various statements is to be settled (is it not possible for me to claim to understand the meaning of any of these, but nevertheless to get it wrong—how would anyone ever know?); and he does not say how these knowledge claims are to be investigated. After all, not everyone who claims to know actually does so; I may claim to know that my mother had purple hair, or that I know Mozart wrote *Oliver Twist*, or that I know the meaning of Tchaikovsky's Fourth Symphony, but it is conceivable that I am mistaken, so there has to be some way of validating or refuting these claims. To deny this is to do away with the concept of a mistake—a heavy price to pay in support of anti-positivism. Dewey, whose views on many matters Eisner admires, replaced "truth" with "warranted assertibility", and he recognized that sometimes the warrant had to be produced, and that it could be challenged. Perhaps the words of another Harvard man will be authoritative. The philosopher Hilary Putnam had met ideas similar to those of Eisner in the realm of literary theory, and he wrote:

> The Greek dramatists, Freudian psychology, and the Russian novel are all supposed by these thinkers to embody *knowledge—knowledge about man.* . . . They conflict with science in the sense of representing a rival kind of knowledge, and thereby contest the claim of science to monopolize reliable knowledge. But it is a rival *kind* of knowledge, and hence inaccessible to scientific testing.

Putnam calls this "a full-blown obscurantist position", and he adds:

> No matter how profound the psychological insights of a novelist may seem to be, they cannot be called *knowledge* if they have not been tested.[58]

Conclusion

The supporters of the Position have been right, of course, to oppose narrow-minded scientism. But they go too far; not *everyone* is narrow-minded. They draw inspiration from Kuhn and from the demise of positivism, and they take some interesting ideas from Hanson and Polanyi. But they play with these ingredients so that they become half-truths. A little more attention to the philosophical controversies would have sensitized them to the dangers.

It is fitting to allow one of our early Harvard men to have the last word. William James wrote:

> . . . you will doubtless have felt my discourse so far to have been crude in an unpardonable, nay, in an almost incredible degree. Tender-minded and tough-minded, what a barbaric disjunction! . . . The picture I have given is indeed monstrously oversimplified and rude. But like all abstractions, it will prove to have its use. . . . In point of fact the picture I have given is, however coarse and sketchy, literally true.[59]

Notes and References

1. I. Mitroff and R. Kilmann, *Methodological Approaches to Social Science.* SF: Jossey-Bass, 1978, p. vii.
2. R. Shweder and D. Fiske, "Introduction: Uneasy Social Science", in Shweder and Fiske, eds., (Metatheory in Social Science.) Chicago: University of Chicago Press, 1986, p. 1.
3. David Thomas, op. cit., p. 196.
4. See, on this last point, Mary C. Silva and Daniel Rothbart, "An Analysis of Changing Trends

100 Philosophy, Science and Social Inquiry

in Philosophies of Science on Nursing Theory Development and Testing", *Advances in Nursing Science*, January 1984.

5. J. Dewey, *Democracy and Education*. NY: Free Press, 1966, p. 225.
6. Finn Collin, *Theory and Understanding: A Critique of Interpretive Social Science*. Oxford: Blackwell, 1985, p. xiv.
7. G. Macdonald and P. Pettit, *Semantics and Social Science*. London: Routledge, 1981, p. 104.
8. Taken, with some grammatical liberties, from Morton White, *Social Thought in America: The Revolt Against Formalism*. Boston: Beacon Press, 1957, p. 11.
9. D. Willer and J. Willer, *Systematic Empiricism: Critique of a Pseudoscience*. Englewood Cliffs, NJ: Prentice-Hall, 1973, p. 137.
10. W. Dilthey, in H. P. Rickman, ed., *Dilthey: Selected Writings*. Cambridge: Cambridge University Press, 1976, p. 89.
11. William James, *Pragmatism, and Four Essays from The Meaning of Truth*. New York: Meridian, 1955, pp. 22–3.
12. E. Eisner, "Anastasia Might Still be Alive, But the Monarchy is Dead", *Educational Researcher*. **12**, no. 5, May 1983. The first and second extracts are from p. 14, the third from p. 23.
13. Yvonna Lincoln and Egon Guba, op. cit., p. 30.
14. Ibid., p. 37.
15. Ibid.
16. W. Filstead, "Qualitative Methods: A Needed Perspective in Evaluation Research", in Thomas Cook and Charles Reichardt, eds., *Qualitative and Quantitative methods in Evaluation Research*. Beverley Hills: Sage, 1979, pp. 35–6.
17. Israel Scheffler, *Science and Subjectivity*. New York: Bobbs-Merrill, 1967, p. 19.
18. K. Popper, *Conjectures and Refutations*, op. cit., p. 46.
19. E. Eisner, op. cit., p. 14.
20. I. Scheffler, op. cit., p. 44.
21. K. Harris, op. cit., p. 7.
22. Newton-Smith, op. cit., p. 281.
23. E. Eisner, *The Educational Imagination*. NY: Macmillan, 1979, p. 214.
24. Ibid.
25. Thomas Kuhn, op. cit., p. 150.
26. B. Barnes, "Thomas Kuhn", in Quentin Skinner, ed., *The Return of Grand Theory in the Human Sciences*. Cambridge: Cambridge University Press, 1985, p. 94.
27. Ibid., p. 97.
28. Y. Lincoln and E. Guba, op. cit., pp. 83–4.
29. E. Eisner, *The Educational Imagination*, op. cit., p. 214.
30. Nelson Goodman, *Ways of Worldmaking*. Indianapolis: Hackett, 1978.
31. Ibid., p. 94.
32. H. Siegel, "Goodmanian Relativism", *The Monist*, **67**, 3 July 1984, pp. 359–75.
33. Michael Ponayi, *The Tacit Dimension*. Garden City, NY: Anchor, 1967, p. 4.
34. Y. Lincoln and E. Guba, op. cit., p. 40.
35. Ibid., p. 198.
36. Robert Stake, "The Case Study Method in Social Inquiry", *Educational Researcher*, **7**, no. 2, 1978, p. 6.
37. Ibid.
38. E. Eisner, "Anastasia Might Still Be Alive . . .", op. cit., p. 23.
39. Lincoln and Guba, op. cit., p. 24.
40. Ibid., p. 29.
41. Peter Halfpenny, op. cit., p. 11.
42. Lincoln and Guba, op. cit., p. 24.
43. H. Giroux, *Ideology, Culture, and the Process of Schooling*. Philadelphia: Temple University Press, 1981, pp. 42–6.
44. R. Stake, op. cit., p. 6.
45. E. Eisner, *The Educational Imagination*, op. cit., p. 18.
46. R. Stake, op. cit., p. 6.
47. Quoted by P. Broadfoot and J. Nisbet, "The Impact of Research on Educational Studies," in *British Journal of Educational Studies*, 1981, **29** (2), p. 119.

48. L. J. Cronbach, "Test Validation," in R. L. Thorndike (ed.), *Educational Measurement*. Washington, DC: American Council on Education, 2nd ed., 1971, p. 475.
49. Ibid., p. 481.
50. Ibid., p. 481.
51. Ibid., p. 481.
52. Lincoln and Guba, op. cit., p. 37.
53. E. Eisner, *The Educational Imagination*, op. cit., p. 214.
54. But see the simple argument for realism in Ian Hacking, *Representing and Intervening*. Cambridge: Cambridge University Press, 1983, ch. 1. He later backs this up with further discussion.
55. Arthur Pap, *An Introduction to the Philosophy of Science*. London: Eyre and Spottiswoode, 1963, p. 4.
56. G. Pappas and M. Swain, eds., *Essays on Knowledge and Justification*. Ithaca: Cornell University Press, 1978.
57. E. Eisner, "The Role of the Arts in Cognition and Curriculum", *Phi Delta Kappa*, **63**, 1, 1981, p. 52.
58. Hilary Putnam, *Meaning and the Moral Sciences*. Boston: Routledge, 1978, p. 89.
59. William James, op. cit., pp. 34–5.

9

The Hermeneutical Case Against Naturalistic Social Science

The criticisms of mainstream naturalistic research in the social sciences and applied areas such as education and nursing are noteworthy for their variety, as has been seen in the preceding chapters. There is a burgeoning literature; and at the philosophical heart of these swelling criticisms is a set of arguments deriving from the broad hermeneutical or interpretive movement. Handbooks and collections have appeared—for example, Rabinow's and Sullivan's *Interpretive Social Science: A Reader*, and Peter Reason's *Human Inquiry: A Sourcebook of New Paradigm Research*. Representative philosophical authors are Dilthey, Gadamer, Macdonald and Pettit, Ricoeur, Taylor, Winch and, to some extent, Rorty and Habermas[1]—though it must be stressed at the outset that these men are not in full agreement and some may even object to the descriptive label "hermeneutical". (In response to this latter point, it is worth recalling that the Bard of Avon noted that "a rose by any other name would smell as sweet".) At any rate, this rough initial characterization will suffice to indicate the scope of the present discussion, the focus of which will be the strengths but more particularly the weaknesses of the core hermeneutical case against naturalistic research.

Almost every book or article that has been written about hermeneutics contains a brief genealogical statement, so, in keeping with this tradition, that is where the present chapter will begin. This first section will be expository, and assessment and criticism will be held over until later.

The term "hermeneutics" itself is taken from the name of the messenger of the gods in Greek mythology, Hermes, whose job it was to interpret or communicate the desires of the deities to mortals. Aristotle engaged in forms of hermeneutical inquiry; but for the present purposes it is sufficient to note that hermeneutics as a discipline was largely driven in its early days by the necessity to interpret Biblical sources—the word of God, recorded in terminology suitable for cultures and conditions long since gone, needed interpretation in order for the meaning to become apparent. St. Augustine, for example, struggled with the meaning of Old Testament passages, apparently realizing that his problems were due to the distance in time that separated him from when they were written. A similar situation arose in the legal field, where the import of laws enacted in byegone days needed to be ascertained. But by the late nineteenth century, due to the work of scholars such as Schleiermacher and Dilthey, hermeneutics underwent broadening.[2] As Hans-Georg Gadamer has noted,

> But even Schleiermacher, the founder of the more recent development of hermeneutics into a general methodological doctrine of the *Geisteswissenschaften*, appeals emphatically to the idea that the art of understanding is required not only with respect to texts but also in one's intercourse with one's fellow human beings.[3]

The import of this passage is heightened if it is realized (in itself a type of hermeneutical act) that the term "Geisteswissenschaften" is the German translation of John Stuart Mill's expression "moral sciences", which in turn was his way of referring to what these days would be called the "social sciences". In short, then, hermeneutics came to be seen as the study of the interpretation and understanding not only of texts, but also of human actions and customs and social practices. In Dilthey's words,

> We explain nature, but we understand mental life. . . . This means that the methods of studying mental life, history and society differ greatly from those used to acquire knowledge of nature. . . .[4]

In the twentieth century this line of thinking about hermeneutics developed apace on the Continent—witness the conclusions that Gadamer arrived at:

> hermeneutics reaches into all the contexts that determine and condition the linguisticality of the human experience of the world. . . . In the social sciences, one finds linguisticality deeply woven into the sociality of human existence, so that the theorists of the social sciences are now becoming interested in the hermeneutical approach.[5]

However, it was only about two decades ago that the English-speaking world fully caught on—although with the gift of hindsight it can be seen that the later Wittgenstein and Peter Winch were saying somewhat similar things to their Anglo-American audiences in works published in the 1950s.

Winch, in his *The Idea of a Social Science* (1958) argued a theme that, as we have seen, was soon to become commonplace, namely, that the social sciences are more like philosophy than they are like the natural sciences. In the latter, understanding—and more precisely explanation—proceeds by bringing a puzzling phenomenon under the rubric of a law of nature, but the way human actions are accounted for is quite different. Winch was much taken with Wittgenstein's notions of a "rule" and a "form of life", and he held that to understand a social activity the rules which were constitutive of it had to be comprehended, and this involved understanding the form of life in which the activity in question was imbedded. In general this understanding was not unproblematical even when our own, or similar Western, societies were under investigation, but even more severe problems emerged when exotic cultures were concerned. The understanding of primitive religion became a topic of controversy, and there were lively disputes between Winch and his critics (such as the Popperians) about how the rationality of other cultures was to be judged.[6] The Azande became famous as a test case, and their beliefs and practices were dissected even by those who never had been within thousands of miles of them.

Gadamer's major work *Truth and Method* was published in 1960, not long after Winch's, but it was not translated into English until 1975; and Richard Palmer's introductory exposition of the issues in hermeneutics for an English reading audience appeared in 1969 and went through six printings in about thirteen years. In 1983 Richard J. Bernstein published *Beyond Objectivism and Relativism: Science, Hermeneutics, and Praxis*. Although these are all worthy of discussion, this "potted history" will focus briefly upon two papers published in 1971. Paul Ricoeur, who had written on psychoanalysis, argued in his "The Model of the Text: Meaningful Action Considered as a Text" that although hermeneutics had developed as the study of interpretation of written texts, it could validly be extended to the study of human action:

> Now my hypothesis is this: if there are specific problems which are raised by the interpretation of texts because they are texts and not spoken language, and if these problems are the ones which constitute hermeneutics as such, then the human sciences may be said to be hermeneutical (1) inasmuch as their *object* displays some of the features constitutive of a text as text, and (2) inasmuch as their *methodology* develops the same kind of procedures as those of . . . text-interpretation.[7]

As an aside, it can be pointed out that to some hermeneuticists spoken language presents less interpretive problems than written texts, because the spoken word is directed at a contemporaneous listener who is dialectically engaged with the speaker, and the meaning can be underscored by such devices an intonation and gestures. Be that as it may, Ricoeur's article argued that the human sciences *did* have enough in common with texts to warrant the extension of hermeneutics in this direction.

Ricoeur's argument had a simple structure; he distinguished four characteristics that discourse (written or spoken) possesses, and which human actions must also be shown to possess if they were to be subject to hermeneutical scrutiny. Briefly, these were as follows: (i) To become an "object of science", discourse (including human action) must be objectified or fixated in the way that speech becomes fixated in writing. He was satisfied that this happens with actions, for the *meaning* of an action can be "detached" from the *event* of the act. "We say that such and such event *left its mark* on its time"[8]. Here, as elsewhere in his paper, Ricoeur was indebted to the "speech act theory" developed by the philosopher John Searle. (ii) Discourse, and action, must become "autonimized", that is, just as a text is detached from its author and becomes a separate entity, so "an action is detached from its agent and develops consequences of its own."[9] He pointed out that this autonomization of action "constitutes the *social* dimension of action." (iii) Like a text, a meaningful action has an importance that transcends its relevance to the situation in which it originally occurred. (iv) Just as texts are "open works", addressed to an indefinite range of potential readers, so it is that human actions are open "to anybody who can read."[10] Ricoeur must be understood as arguing not that all human actions have these characteristics (after all, most of our actions are ephemeral and have little later significance even to the actor, and indeed all trace of them may rapidly fade), but that all actions *potentially* have these characteristics.

At the same time, in 1971, the philosopher Charles Taylor writing in *The Review of Metaphysics*, made much the same case in what was to become a very well-known essay, "Interpretation and the Sciences of Man". His argument, too, had the same structure, but he reduced the conditions that must be met by the object of any "hermeneutical science" to three:

> The object of a science of interpretation must thus have: sense, distinguishable from its expression, which is by or for a subject.[11]

Having shown that, indeed, human actions meet these conditions, he illustrated the fruitfulness of the hermeneutical approach with a brief discussion of some examples from the field of political science. Taylor's final conclusion was straightforward:

> There are thus good grounds both in epistemological arguments and in their greater fruitfulness for opting for hermeneutical sciences of man. But we cannot hide from ourselves how greatly this option breaks with certain commonly held notions about our scientific tradition.[12]

Within a few years this general position was orthodox. As quoted in the previous chapter, Macdonald and Pettit, two British philosophers of social science, wrote in 1981 that

> Social science, insofar as its concern is the explanation of social behaviour, begins to look like a discipline which belongs with the humanities rather than the sciences.[13]

Rom Harre put forward a similar anti-naturalistic view; the study of social life requires skills that "are more like the skills of literary and dramatic criticism and of poetics than the skills of physical scientists."[14] The underlying point in all this is that the physical sciences, with their emphasis on uncovering the causes that produce effects, are not a relevant model for the social sciences for a simple reason: people act because they are swayed by reasons, or because they decide to follow rules, *not* because their actions are causally determined by forces. Thus, when one person manages to persuade another to act in a certain way, what is going on is quite different from the situation that exists when one physical particle interacts causally with another. The philosopher Michael Simon put the point pithily: "Effective persuasion makes people act: not by supplying causally sufficient conditions but rather by providing conditions that give them reasons to act."[15]

Hermeneutical methods have found their way into areas of applied social science research. Nursing researcher Patricia Benner has written:

> The model of study of practical knowledge resembles the interpretation of a text. A sentence,

for example, cannot be understood by analyzing the words as constituent elements alone. Rather one understands a sentence as part of a larger whole and interprets its meaning from the context of the text in which it is found. Similarly, behavior can be seen as having potentially multiple rather than single meanings. To understand behavior, therefore, one must look at it in its larger context. . . . Interpretive methods offer one strategy. . . .[16]

In 1983 Wilfred Carr, writing in the *Journal of Philosophy of Education*, noted that the hermeneutical position had become a well-established research tradition in education and the social sciences; he pointed out that many now adhere to the "interpretive view",

which holds that because social action is intentional and rule-governed it cannot be studied "scientifically". . . . In contrast to naturalism . . . interpretive approaches to educational research insist that their principal task is not to construct scientific theories that can be experimentally tested, but to construct interpretive accounts which grasp the intelligibility and coherence of social action by revealing the meaning it has to those who perform it.[17]

Carr's main point is sound, although it should be noted in passing that his exposition is not faultless; hermeneuticists, as we have seen, are not unduly concerned with what an action may mean to the person who acted. But there can be little argument with the judgment that the "interpretive approach" is now a flourishing one, and that it stands as a major rival to what Carr has called the "scientistic approach" (and what others have labeled the "naturalistic approach", or even more uncharitably the "positivistic approach").

Perhaps even more startling has been the way hermeneutics has been incorporated into the thought of Richard Rorty, as expounded in his much discussed *Philosophy and the Mirror of Nature*. Rorty regards hermeneutics as being related to the quest for "edification", which he views as replacing the quixotic quest for knowledge that "mirrors" nature: "Hermeneutics is not 'another way of knowing'—'understanding' as opposed to (predictive) 'explanation'. It is better seen as another way of coping."[18]

Finally, in the last decade or so another noteworthy development has taken place. Researchers and methodologists of a more "traditional" mold have started to shift ground, adopting some of the insights of the interpretive school. Perhaps one of the most important has been Donald Campbell. Well-known in educational and social science circles for his standard work on experimental and quasi-experimental designs (written with Julian Stanley), Campbell also has been an important figure in the emerging field of evaluation, and he is no mean philosopher of science. Reading a paper in response to receiving an award at the 1974 convention of the American Psychological Association, Campbell argued that quantitative understanding in the sciences is built upon a foundation of qualitative understanding—a base that scientists take for granted and rarely if ever discuss or examine.

Most of this underpinning of common-sense knowing is so ubiquitous and so dependable that we fail to notice it. But I believe that such a base underlies all quantitative knowing in the social sciences. . . .[19]

In essence, Campbell was pointing out that the interpretive process very often takes place unconsciously, but nevertheless it occurs—indeed, it *must* occur.

Too much of a good thing

It must be made clear, at the outset of the somewhat critical discussion that will ensue, that there is much merit in the core hermeneutical case. Just what merit, and what the implications of it are for naturalistic social science and applied research, are matters to be determined. But the discussion must not be interpreted as a wholesale attack on the hermeneutical approach to human affairs.

(1)(A). While the argument of Ricoeur and others—that human action closely resembles textual material—is strained, it nevertheless seems incontrovertible that much action (whether text-like or not) requires explicit interpretation. In the first place, there is the problem of simple ambiguity, amply illustrated in the well-known case of a person raising her arm. It may not be clear, even taking the context into account, whether she is stretching, hailing a friend, seeking attention, wanting to ask a question, and so forth. So interpretation is called-for. More substantial are the problems of understanding that arise when the person being observed (or interacted with) comes from a foreign culture. A figure of speech, a gesture, even the use of words that to us are everyday terms, may be fraught with difficulty. (The present writer, in the first few months following his immigration to the USA from Australia, found that his style of joke-telling was not understood by American students, and he learned to signal an up-coming witticism; but at first the behavior of the students—or rather their lack of it—had to be interpreted for him, and vice versa.) Finally, there are hosts of actions that are unabashedly symbolic; behaviors at worship, in school, at dinner, at college Commencement, at an auction, at the Masonic Lodge, at a military parade, may all be unintelligible to the uninitiated and require interpretation. In many cases, too, the meaning is constitutive of the action—the action cannot even be *identified* unless its meaning is understood ("ah, that's what he is doing" we sometimes say as a puzzling situation is resolved). Sometimes it is even the case that when an action has been identified—when its meaning has been interpreted—then that action has also been explained. (We often ask for explanations when the meaning of what we see is not apparent.)

In the field of education all of these problems can be located. In a culturally diverse classroom, for example, the behavior of individual students may require sensitive interpretation even to be identified. Is this boy's refusal to make eye contact a sign of defiance, or is it a reflection of his culture's way of showing respect to an authority-figure? Is that girl distracting her partner by gossiping, or is she talking about the work they are supposed to be doing? And when an observer seeks an explanation for a child's puzzling behavior ("why is she behaving like that?"), to provide the meaning may also be to provide the explanation ("she is rehearsing a classroom presentation she has to give later in the day").

(B). Although human actions may require interpretation, then, it does not thereby follow that Ricoeur, Taylor and the others were right in treating them as being on a par with texts. Their form of argument, it should be noted, is risky, although it is a venerable one in philosophical circles. Any two things can *always* be shown to be similar in at least some respects, so it is no surprise that Ricoeur and Taylor were able to show that social action and textual material have some similarities—indeed, the surprise would have come if they were not able to do so! The risk enters because any two things also can be shown to have some differences, and there are plenty that come to mind in the cases in question here. Textual material is produced by an author, and the author had some meaning in mind. (There are two trivial exceptions: the first is when an author deliberately constructs an ambiguous or "open" passage—as did the Delphic Oracle; and the second is when the author was a successful one of those proverbial million monkeys that were set in front of typewriters to see if any of their random tappings could produce Hamlet's soliloquy.)

Now, it is a controversial issue in literary hermeneutics whether or not an author's meaning has any special significance (or whether there is any such meaning at all), and while the views of Stanley Fish will be touched upon later, it is sufficient to point out here that unless the author of a text is held to have some meaning that he or she is attempting to convey, hermeneutics is a forlorn endeavour. (This, of course, seems to be denied by Gadamer, who has insisted that "the hermeneutical problem is universal and basic for all interhuman experience, both of history and of the present moment, precisely because meaning can be experienced even when it is not actually intended."[20]) As E. D. Hirsch, Jr., has put it, the doctrine of "authorial irrelevance" "has frequently encouraged willful arbitrariness and extravagance in academic criticism", and has led to "skepticism and disarray".[21]

> Thus, when critics deliberately banished the original author, they themselves usurped his place, and this led unerringly to some of our present-day theoretical confusions. Where before there had been but one author, there now arose a multiplicity of them, each carrying as much authority as the next.[22]

Wherever one stands on the issue of "authorial irrelevance", it should be apparent that social practices, traditions, ceremonies, customs, and the like, only rarely have *an* author, and only rarely were designed specifically to convey *a* meaning. Usually these practices evolved over a period of time, and different contributors to the evolution of a particular practice probably had different things in mind, and the innovations caught on ("diffused" is the current popular term) for a variety of reasons. (Think of the following rich example: the evolution and spread of games such as rugby in the English public schools over the past two hundred years or so.)

There is a major ambiguity here. Such social traditions and practices have *significance*, but it is far from clear that they have a *meaning* in the same sense that Hamlet's solitary musings have a meaning (whatever it may be). To seek—or to make or impose—a meaning in the hermeneutical sense, can be "edifying" (as Rorty put it), but it is not clear *what else* it is.

(2) There is, then, an important ambiguity that surfaces in our customary way of giving voice to some of the difficulties we experience in cases requiring interpretation, like those above involving the student who does not make eye-contact. Often we ask "What is the meaning of this behavior?" And, in these cases, this may well be a straightforward request for interpretation or hermeneutical understanding, on a par with St. Augustine asking himself "What is the meaning of this Old Testament passage?" The ambiguity arises from the fact that a request for meaning often can be a query about *significance*, as when we ask "What was the meaning of President Nixon's resignation?" Asking about the effect or significance or consequences of an action is *not* a hermeneutical question, but it very often can be a straightforward social science question. ("What is the effect of the recent election results in New Zealand?"—a political science or international relations issue if ever there was one, and it retains this status even if misleadingly phrased "What is the meaning of the recent election results in New Zealand?")

David Thomas, in his book *Naturalism and Social Science* (1979), very effectively debunked the notion that this particular sense of "meaning" marks an important difference between the natural and the social sciences (i.e. the notion that social science deals with meanings and natural science doesn't, thus there is a fundamental difference between the two). Using as an example Levi-Strauss's remark that the meaning of the incest prohibition that exists in most societies is to establish social bonds between different biological groups, Thomas wrote:

> To label social scientific explanations "meaningful" or "interpretative" in a way which is meant to differentiate them from natural scientific explanations is mere confusion. . . . If we wish to use the rather quaint locution that the meaning of the incest prohibition is to create social bonds between different biological groups, then we are also entitled to say that the meaning of a thermostat is to control the temperature in the house.[23]

In other words, Levi-Strauss was talking about the *significance* of the incest prohibition (or its effect or consequence), and this was a perfectly reputable scientific undertaking that should not have been "dressed up" as a hermeneutical one.

(3) It can be imagined that an enthusiastic supporter of the hermeneutical approach, or perhaps a person who found Campbell's article pursuasive, might argue that even these latter questions about significance or consequences depend upon a hidden foundation of understanding. After all, it might be said, one cannot inquire about the significance of an action or event that

one has not understood. Gadamer put it nicely: "The hermeneutical experience is prior . . . because it is the matrix out of which arise the questions that it then directs to science."[24] Add to this the fact that meaning in the first sense remains unsullied by criticism (i.e. the sense in which the meaning of person raising her arm may need to be determined), and what results is a strong case that interpretive or hermeneutical activity is central in the social sciences.

To this argument, that goes to the heart of the issues, there are several lines of response.

(A) Campbell's paper makes an important point, the validity of which it is not intended to question. But it is noteworthy that although he argues that *all* science is based on a foundation of "qualitative understanding", he does not conclude that thereby *any* science is undercut or shaken. In Campbell's view, physics as well as social science is built on this foundation, and he does not regard this as a "blot on the escutcheon" of physics, and in no way does it challenge the status of physics as a science. He uses the example of a scientific paper on the quantum nature of light, and he argues that

> the few scientific terms have been imbedded in a discourse of pre-scientific ordinary language which the reader is presumed to (and presumes to) understand. This language is demonstrably incomplete, elliptical, metaphorical and equivocal. In addition, in the laboratory work of the original and replicating laboratory, a common-sense, pre-scientific perception of objects, solids and light was employed and trusted in coming to the conclusions that revise the ordinary understanding.[25]

Read carefully, there is little succour here for those who believe that the necessity for hermeneutical understanding undercuts the naturalistic scientific status of social science. Of course social phenomena need to be understood, and of course a scientific investigation of them, as thus understood, is still possible—and perhaps, as Campbell indicated, the scientific inquiry might lead to a "revision" of the "ordinary understanding".

This is such a central matter that it is worth giving another example, this time not one from physical science but a social activity where the norms or rules are centrally a part of the activity and where, without understanding, the activity cannot even be engaged in. (In Searle's terms, the rules are constitutive of the activity.) Baseball is played according to rules; indeed, the rules are constitutive, because if they are departed from then it is not baseball that is being played, but some other game (or no game at all). Nevertheless, knowing the rules is not the same as being able to play baseball; and coaching a Little League team involves much more than teaching the rules or helping team-members "understand" the game. One can coach the pitcher by showing him how to hold the ball for various types of pitch, and one can coach the batter and teach how to hold the bat and give him some insights into strategy (such as when to bunt). These matters transcend the rules, and though there is a sense in which the coach is helping the players to "understand" the game, it is not understanding in the hermeneutical sense that knowledge of the rules is. It takes little imagination to guess what the reaction of a coach would be if it were suggested to him that all he required to carry out his duties was hermeneutical understanding; translated into polite language, and with the expletives deleted, his reply might refer to the additional factual and theoretical and tactical knowledge that he used. Hermeneutical understanding no more exhausts what there is to know about baseball than it does for social science and educational research. (Similarly, to identify what the youngsters are doing as "playing Little League baseball", may be to explain all that was puzzling, but it may not. There are lots of questions that can be asked here, and the hermeneutical activity does not exhaust the inquiries that can be pursued.)

(B) Social science can transcend or go beyond the level of ordinary understanding in a variety of ways. Or, to put it differently, there is much in social science that does not involve hermeneutical understanding in any central or significant way (any way that is different from the way that understanding is involved in the procedures of physics, for example). Thus the claim—that if the social sciences can be shown to involve hermeneutical understanding this is the end of social science as naturalistic—is nonsense. To cite a few examples: the issue of which of massed or distributed practice is more effective in influencing mathematical achievement, the issue of whether group work is more effective than individual work as a way of teaching mathematics, the optimum size for classroom groups in order to maximize learning, the most effective composition of groups by sex and ability (given some pre-set criterion measure), the issue of whether educational vouchers would cause a flight from the public schools, the issue of whether humans process information serially or in parallel, the issue of how innovations diffuse throughout a system—none of these (and literally thousands more could be cited) are centrally hermeneutical issues in the same way that determining the identity of the mysterious passenger in the fifth act of Ibsen's "Peer Gynt" is an hermeneutical or interpretive task.[26] (The aficionado will have noted that the present discussion skirts around the issue of whether or not the explanation of individual human action must make reference to general laws of some type. As a closet Popperian/Hempelian the author is inclined to argue "yes", but the arguments advanced in the present chapter do not depend upon taking a specific stand on this contentious issue.)

(C) Even *if* the understanding of the action of an individual is hermeneutical, it does not follow that the understanding of *groups* of individuals is necessarily hermeneutical (although understanding *some* group activities might be). Neither does the hermeneutical understanding of the individual or the group exhaust the inquiries that can be made, as the list of examples just given should amply illustrate. Thomas Schelling has an interesting example that can be used to put flesh on this point about understanding groups; individuals coming into an auditorium for a lecture pick their seats for a variety of reasons, and a social scientist could perhaps hope to come to hermeneutically understand why certain people chose to sit in certain locations, but there would be little hope of predicting where given individuals might sit. (Seating preferences are interactive, which is an added complexity.) Nevertheless, there is an overall pattern to the way the seats fill, and this pattern holds good over a variety of audiences made up of different individuals. This pattern can be discovered, and used to make predictions. Whatever the understanding of the seating decisions of individuals involves, the task of determining the overall pattern is clearly not a hermeneutical one.[27]

4. There is a final general issue to take up. The tone of the preceding discussion might be taken to concede that *in so far* as social science is hermeneutical (although it has been argued that this is *not* so far as has been supposed), then it is not "scientific". It is not the author's intent, however, to make such a concession, vague as it is.

One way for the discussion to proceed would be to enlarge upon the general account of the "nature" of science given in the chapters in Part A, and show that hermeneutical investigations fall under this rubric. This "easy road" to naturalism would not be difficult to take, especially in this age of the "new philosophy of science", when science is recognized to be a more open and speculative endeavor than had been believed in byegone positivistic days. Hermeneutics being somewhat open and speculative and non-positivistic, the case would fall into place. There are indications that Popper believed this to be a fruitful line to take; he wrote:

> Thus I oppose the attempt to proclaim the method of understanding as the characteristic of the humanities, the mark by which we may distinguish them from the natural sciences. And when its supporters denounce a view like mine as "positivistic" or "scientistic", then I may perhaps answer that they themselves seem to accept, *implicitly and uncritically*, that positivism or scientism is *the only philosophy appropriate to the natural sciences.*[28]

Life is short, however, so rather than arguing this an even quicker route will be taken. A few simple but hopefully suggestive points will be made, and the discussion will terminate.

(A) Although it seems to be a matter of controversy within hermeneutics itself, a good case can be made that extensive use is made of the hypothetico-deductive method. Hermeneuticists advance interpretations, ones they believe to be warranted by textual evidence. If a rival account is put forward, it is because it is felt that in some way the new one does more justice to the evidence at hand. If an interpretation is advanced quite spuriously, that is, if it does not withstand scrutiny in the light of the text in question, it will be dismissed as nonsense. Harre, in his *Social Being*[29] alludes to the importance of the HDM; and the classic hermeneutical work by E. D. Hirsch, Jr., *Validity in Interpretation*, makes the following important point:

> The identity of genre, pre-understanding, and hypothesis suggests that the much-advertised cleavage between thinking in the sciences and the humanities does not exist. The

hypothetico-deductive process is fundamental in both of them, as it is in all thinking that aspires to knowledge.[30]

Dagfinn Follesdal argues the same point at length.[31] And Popper, too, noted:

> Labouring the difference between science and the humanities has long been a fashion, and has become a bore. The method of problem solving, the method of conjecture and refutation, is practised by both. It is practised in reconstructing a damaged text as well as in reconstructing a theory of radioactivity.[32]

(B) There are some in the field of literary criticism who have a much more liberal (if not anarchistic) view. Stanley Fish, for example, denies that he uses a text in his class, for although all students read the one book it is not the *same* for different readers. He also tells the amusing story of leaving up on the blackboard notes and jottings from the lecture given to one class, and telling the next class (taking a different course) that it was a poem and they had to write interpretations of it. All members of the class succeeded in doing so. His point was not to show that the interpretations were spurious, but quite the reverse:

> Skilled reading is usually thought to be a matter of discerning what is there, but if the example of my students can be generalized, it is a matter of knowing how to *produce* what can thereafter be said to be there. Interpretation is not the art of construing but the art of constructing. Interpreters do not decode poems; they make them.[33]

This does seem quite antithetical to the scientific or naturalistic spirit, and is moving in the direction of a rampant relativism and subjectivism which is not readily applicable to the interpretation of social life. It is far from clear that Fish's controversial position is viable (Hirsch's contrary views have been alluded to); but if Fish is right about literary hermeneutics, it is indeed far from science—although there is the added complexity that a few folk would argue that on the new understanding of science that is emerging the two are very close! (Fish's position is somewhat more complex than this discussion has indicated, and it may not be fair to label him in an unqualified way as an adherent of these unpleasant "isms"; Fish—not unlike Kuhn—points to the directive role of the community of interpreters to which any individual interpreter belongs.) Leaving these complexities aside, it would seem that while social scientists may disagree about what is going on at some ceremonial event—say a Catholic mass—it is not the case that any and all interpretations are equally acceptable, and neither is it the case that the observers themselves construct what is happening. To pursue this line of discussion further would involve examining the contentious notions of "reality" and "truth", and this is too mammoth a task for the present chapter.

Notes and References

1. Others come close to this tradition, e.g. Harre and Secord. For Habermas—not discussed further here—see his "Interpretive Social Science vs. Hermeneutics" in N. Haan *et al.*, eds., *Social Science as Moral Inquiry*. NY: Columbia University Press, 1983.

2. See W. Dilthey, "The Development of Hermeneutics", in H. Rickman, ed., *Dilthey: Selected Writings*. Cambridge: Cambridge University Press, 1976.

3. H-G. Gadamer, *Reason in the Age of Science*. Cambridge, Mass.: MIT Press, 1981, tr. by F. G. Lawrence, p. 113.

4. W. Dilthey, in H. P. Rickman, ed., *Dilthey: Selected Writings*. Cambridge: Cambridge University Press, 1976, p. 89.

5. H-G. Gadamer, "On the Scope and Function of Hermeneutical Reflection", in his *Philosophical Hermeneutics*. Berkeley: University of California Press, 1977, tr. by E. Linge, pp. 19–20.

6. See papers by Jarvie, Agassi, and Winch, in B. Wilson, ed., *Rationality*. Oxford: Blackwell, 1970; and also R. Borger and F. Cioffi, eds., *Explanation in the Behavioral Sciences*. Cambridge: Cambridge University Press, 1970.

7. P. Ricoeur, "The Model of the Text", reprinted in F. Dallmayr and T. McCarthy, eds., *Understanding and Social Inquiry*. Notre Dame: University of Notre Dame Press, 1977, p. 316.

8. Ibid., p. 324.

9. Ibid., p. 324.

10. Ibid., p. 327.

11. Charles Taylor, "Interpretation and the Sciences of Man", reprinted in Dallmayr and McCarthy, op. cit., p. 102.

12. Ibid., p. 130.

13. G. Macdonald and P. Pettit, *Semantics and Social Science*. London: Routledge, 1981, p. 104.

14. R. Harre, "Accounts, Actions and Meanings", in M. Brenner et al., eds., *The Social Context of Method*. NY: St. Martin's Press, 1978, p. 52.

15. M. A. Simon, *Understanding Human Action*. Albany, NY: State University of New York Press, 1982, p. 130.

16. Patricia Benner, "Uncovering the Knowledge Embedded in Clinical Practice", *Image: the Journal of Nursing Scholarship*, XV, 2, Spring 1983, p. 41.

17. W. Carr, "Can Educational Research be Scientific?", *Journal of Philosophy of Education*, **17**, no. 1, 1983, p. 36. Carr's paper is mainly concerned to see how much attention is paid to the notion of "education" in educational research.

18. R. Rorty, *Philosophy and the Mirror of Nature*. Princeton, NJ: Princeton University Press, 1979, p. 356.

19. D. Campbell, "Qualitative Knowing in Action Research", reprinted in M. Brenner et al., eds., *The Social Context of Method*. New York: St. Martin's Press, 1978, p. 193.

20. Gadamer, "On the Scope and Nature of Hermeneutical Reflection", in his *Philosophical Hermeneutics*, op. cit., p. 30.

21. E. D. Hirsch, Jr., *Validity in Interpretation*. New Haven: Yale University Press, 1967, pp. 2, 3.

22. Ibid., p. 5.

23. David Thomas, *Naturalism and Social Science*. Cambridge: Cambridge University Press, 1979, pp. 83–4.

24. Gadamer, "On the Scope and Function of Hermeneutical Reflection", op. cit., p. 26.

25. D. Campbell, op. cit., p. 187.

26. This example was taken from an engaging paper by Dagfinn Follesdal, "Hermeneutics and the Hypothetico-Deductive Method", *Dialectica*, **33**, no. 3–4, 1979.

27. Thomas C. Schelling, *Micromotives and Macrobehavior*. NY: W. W. Norton, 1978, ch. 1.

28. K. Popper, *Objective Knowledge*. Oxford: Oxford/Clarendon Press, 1972, p. 185.

29. Rom Harre, *Social Being*. Totowa, NJ: Littlefield, Adams, 1980. It is noteworthy, too, that Harre and Secord think that their method of ethogeny is quite scientific. See their *The Explanation of Social Behavior*. Totowa, NJ: Littlefield, Adams, 1973.

30. E. D. Hirsch, Jr., op. cit., p. 264.

31. Follesdal, op. cit.

32. K. Popper, *Objective Knowledge*, op. cit., p. 185.

33. Stanley Fish, *Is There a Text in this Class?* Cambridge, Mass.: Harvard University Press, 1980, p. 327.

Part C
CRITICISMS
Evaluation of a Field of Theory and Research

10

Introduction

The preceding chapters contained expositions of some salient aspects of the new philosophy of science, and a number of misconceptions were exposed. The theme throughout was a mild Popperianism and naturalism: Knowledge progresses not by the absolute establishment of conclusions, but by the exposing of conjectures or hypotheses to criticism and to the possibility of refutation. However, not even this process yields certainty, for a position that is soundly criticizable today might undergo resuscitation tomorrow. Progress follows a tentative and meandering course. The quotation from Popper in the front of this volume summarizes matters well, as does David Krathwohl's happy expression "organized skepticism".

In the remaining chapters there will be something of a change of direction. The attempt is made to put flesh on to the bones of this general Popperian and naturalistic orientation, by subjecting an area of research to fairly sustained criticism. The area chosen as the butt of this organized skepticism is a broad one, and it is one that is marked throughout by lively debates, impressive empirical accomplishments, and sophisticated theory. There has been no way to responsibly avoid dealing with the complexities of the area, for criticism that is not faithful to the "state of the art" is worthless. On the whole, these complexities were not introduced maliciously, or with the intention to bamboozle; it is charitable to assume that they result from internal developments that those people working in the area believe to be crucial. There is no simple way to summarise what is going on, or to describe what points of criticism emerge—the chapters will have to speak for themselves. (It is hoped, nonetheless, that the discussions will be interesting and comprehensible to the non-expert.) Suffice it to say, by way of motivation, that many of the ideas of Popper, Quine, Lakatos and others will come home to roost in what follows.

The selection of any case study is heavily influenced by the interests and expertise of a particular author. But there are other factors at work in the present instance. In brief, the material to be discussed here focusses, in one way or another, upon what happens in the mind of a developing learner as he or she tries to master some body of knowledge (such as any of the subjects that are included in the school curriculum). There are major philosophical, theoretical, and empirical difficulties facing those who do research in this general area, but, to look for the silver lining, there are concomitant opportunities to show how "organized skepticism" can be applied in these different contexts. Often the warrants for claims that are made are not clear (nor is the status of the claims themselves), so there is scope to demonstrate the fruitfulness of the Popperian notions of testability and openness to refutation. The area is ever-changing, and there is much ongoing work, so the issues raised by Kuhn and Lakatos about the dynamics of science have obvious relevance. Finally, the authors who figure in the case study have been well aware of some, if not all, of the developments discussed in the first Parts of this book: Piaget was a longstanding critic of empiricism, and he claimed to admire Quine; in recent years Kohlberg has been stimulated by hermeneutics; modern cognitive scientists, in so far as they deal with internal mental events, have had to dissociate themselves from rampant behaviorism; and the structure of knowledge theorists were dealing with issues close to those discussed by many philosophers of science.

Introduction to the criticisms

To set the scene for the extended and interrelated discussions that follow, consider the example of a research physicist. It is rarely, if ever, questioned that this worthy individual comes to his or her work equipped with a conceptual apparatus. For it is evident that the physicist can use concepts such as force, energy, mass, and acceleration; he or she is familiar with relevant theories and empirical laws, such as Newton's laws of motion, the theory of gravitation, Kepler's laws, and Einstein's theories; and possesses a modicum of logical and mathematical skill. Furthermore, it is obvious that the scientist has some sense—although it is hard to describe—of when it is appropriate to apply particular concepts, or perform certain calculations, and so on. Finally, it also seems clear that this mass of information does not form a disorderly array—there is some organization, for the physicist can go about business in an efficient way, can readily retrieve formulae from memory, and can bring appropriate laws and theories to bear as the subject under investigation happens to warrant.

In light of these considerations, it does not seem unreasonable to suggest that the physicist's memory can be conceived of as a vast cognitive structure (or series of structures), and to assert also that a variety of cognitive processes are at work. And insofar as the physicist resembles ordinary mortals, the same can be postulated about them as well. This way of putting matters was, of course, pervasive in Piaget's work, and it is one of the bulwarks of contemporary cognitive psychology (both neo-Piagetian and non-Piagetian). Unfortunately, just what a cognitive structure consists of, and how it differs from (or relates to) cognitive processes and the organized bodies of knowledge that the scientist or ordinary individual has been exposed to, has not always been made clear.

It is evident, furthermore, that the physicist was not born knowing Kepler's laws, Einstein's theories, and the rest. These things were learned, and the cognitive structure must have been painstakingly constructed by the learner. Clearly, then, there is a developmental side to the story, even though the Piagetians, Chomskyans, Vygotskyans, and others, have been in some disagreement about details of the plot.

For some decades many researchers in education and psychology have been contributing to the development of this captivating general model. The learning process has been conceptualized in terms of a dynamic interrelationship between two types of entities—the "structure of the discipline" that is being learned (in our example, of course, this is physics), and the "cognitive structure" that is built up inside the learner as he or she gradually masters that particular subject. Nowadays this has become the standard orientation:

> Teaching is a complex, decision-making and implementing process. It requires a thorough knowledge of the structure of the subject matter. . . . It also requires a thorough knowledge of how students process information and solve problems. By combining subject matter knowledge with an information processing model of the student, instruction can be reasonably planned and revised.[1]

Or, as the science educator Joseph Novak put it in 1977, in his book *A Theory of Education* (which was indebted to the psychological work of David Ausubel),

> Meaningful learning is a process in which new information is related to an existing relevant aspect of an individual's knowledge structure. . . . During meaningful learning, then, new information is assimilated into existing relevant subsumers in cognitive structure.[2]

Finally, way back at the Woods Hole Conference in 1959 (held in the aftermath of the launching of Sputnik, and attended by leading scientists, psychologists, and educators), and in the subsequent report, the then Harvard psychologist Jerome Bruner extolled the virtues of a learner mastering the structure of the discipline to which he or she was exposed.[3] Bruner's notion was incorporated into much of the extensive curriculum development work that took place on several continents during the following decade.

The problem is that all of this is a conceptual quagmire, with pitfalls aplenty; there is potential for the Popperian critic to be of help. The remarks made by Ned Block in his introduction to a collection of papers in cognitive science and philosophy are particularly appropriate:

> A host of crucial issues do not "belong" to either philosophy or psychology, but rather fall equally well in both disciplines. . . . The problems will yield only to philosophically sophisticated psychologists or to psychologically sophisticated philosophers.[4]

The chapters that remain will take up these issues in the following order: First, the "structure of knowledge" pole of the contemporary model will be examined; it will be argued that, although the authors here—Schwab, Hirst and Peters in particular—raise important issues, in some ways their discussions of the topic are curiously out of step with the contemporaneous developments in philosophy of science and epistemology that have been discussed in the earlier parts of the present book. The second chapter will turn to the other pole of the contemporary model, and the research that has been done on cognitive structures of learners will be critiqued. It will be suggested that the empirical techniques that are being used are not always capable of delivering what they promise, and in particular they cannot help but confound cognitive structures with disciplinary structure. In both these chapters some distinctions drawn by Popper will be found to be helpful. The final two chapters take up developmental issues. First, Piaget's theories are examined, and there will be an attempt to uncover the very strong influence upon them of his philosophical presumptions—presumptions that are hostile towards empiricist philosophy. Ideas drawn from the new philosophy of science will be used throughout this critique. Finally, Kohlberg's work on the development of moral reasoning will be up for scrutiny; this research program has undergone many changes since 1958, and it is an ideal venue for the use of the methodological ideas of Imre Lakatos.

Notes and References

1. R. J. Shavelson, "Teaching Mathematics: Contributions of Cognitive Research", *Educational Psychologist*, 1981, **16**, p. 41.
2. J. Novak, *A Theory of Education*. NY: Cornell University Press, 1977, pp. 74–5.
3. J. Bruner, *The Process of Education*. NY: Vintage Books, 1963.
4. N. Block, ed., *Readings in Philosophy of Psychology*. Cambridge, Mass: Harvard University Press, 1980, vol. **1**, p. v.

11

Perspectives on Structure of Knowledge

A Popperian formulation of the issues

It is not particularly insightful to point out that as a person grows to maturity, he or she normally acquires a great deal of knowledge concerning the surrounding social and physical world. Who would dispute that language is acquired, and so is numeracy; that social norms and customs are mastered; that a stock of physical concepts and generalizations is accumulated; and that bodies of organized knowledge—history, biology, calculus, economics, and so on—are learned? The deep issues arise when theories are formulated to explain these phenomena, and when empirical research is embarked upon.

As mentioned in the Introduction, in recent years it has been popular to conceptualize matters in terms of the interaction between two different realms; the cognitive apparatus of the developing person is regarded as interacting with the bodies of knowledge that are regarded, in that particular society, as best representing the surrounding world. As the learner meets with success, the mental or cognitive structures that are built up in his or her memory come to parallel (or to be isomorphic with) the structure of the bodies of knowledge that are being learned. Thus the concepts and relationships in the person's mind are "mirrors of nature", or rather, are mirrors of the disciplines by means of which humans deal with nature. The role of the teacher and parent in all of this is akin to that of a midwife.

Any account of the bodies of research and theory that have been built up in this general area must focus, then, on at least two things—on what has been said about the structures of bodies of knowledge, and what has been said about cognitive structures inside the heads of learners. And in this latter domain, there are concerns that can be called structural (the relationships between the various cognitive elements and processes), and there are developmental concerns (how the cognitive structures and processes change and become "more adequate" over time).

It is clear that all of these are difficult matters to talk about sensibly, let alone to carry out empirical research upon, and unless workers take extreme pains any data they accumulate are likely to have uncertain bearing on the issues in dispute—data collected to throw light on badly-formulated questions contribute to smog, not to enlightenment. Under these uncertain conditions, too, it is easy for schools of thought to arise in which the members are critical of outsiders, and huddle together for mutual internal support; close critical examination of their own presumptions is unlikely to occur. (Insofar as this was Kuhn's message about the dynamics of science, it seems sound.) Under these conditions errors accumulate, rather than being exposed and eliminated. Popper's words are apposite, and could be profitably adopted as a motto by those who labor under such conditions: "But if you are interested in the problem which I tried to solve by my tentative assertion, you may help me by criticizing it as severely as you can. . . ."[1]

There is a different aspect of Popper's work that also is pertinent in the present context: he introduced terminology that is helpful in clarifying the issues in the two domains alluded to above. (However, it should be noted that the metaphysical views that underly this terminology are controversial.) Popper argued that it is possible to distinguish between "three worlds": world 1, consisting of physical or material objects; world 2, a "subjective" world, a world of minds and their contents; and world 3, an "objective" world of knowledge and problems. World 3 "entities" may be the product of minds, but they can exist independently—they have, as it were, a life of their own. (Minds, of course, are housed in world 1 objects, namely bodies; and world 3 entities—theories and arguments and ideas—may also be stored in world 1 objects, for example books.) Thus, according to Popper, "is there a highest number?" is a problem that exists once any number system exists, and the problem is there whether or not any mind currently is aware of the issue. Popper has indicated that one of the many considerations that led him to distinguish these three worlds was his recognition of the distinction between a person's *thought processes* and the *content* of those thoughts; "thoughts in the sense of contents or statements in themselves and thoughts in the sense of thought processes belong to two entirely different 'worlds' ".[2] Popper added:

> it is clear that everybody interested in science must be interested in world 3 objects. A physical scientist, to start with, may be interested mainly in world 1 objects—say, crystals and X-rays. But very soon he must realize how much depends on our interpretation of the facts, that is, on our theories, and so on world 3 objects. Similarly a historian of science, or a philosopher interested in science, must be largely a student of world 3 objects.[3]

Whatever is made of the metaphysics embodied here—and Popper has realized that he is close to Plato's theory of forms (which are timeless, but are accessible only via the light of reason)—his terminology has great heuristic value for the present and the following chapters. In this Popperian language, issues concerning the structure of the disciplines are third world matters, while human cognitive or memory structures exist in the second world. Furthermore, our theories about cognitive structure and its development are third world objects. These labels, though they may appear fanciful, are helpful in preventing conflation of the disparate entities. A major theme in the next few chapters is simply that this conflation has taken place; researchers have been led to ask (and try to answer) strange questions, and confusion results, all because (as the philosopher Norman Malcolm put it) "we don't know what we are talking about."[4]

The remainder of the present chapter will focus upon the literature that developed around the (world 3) notion of structure of knowledge in the 1970s, and which was a major influence upon the post-Sputnik curriculum development projects in the USA and the UK. This is by way of background to the more empirically-oriented discussions that follow. In the subsequent chapter the discussion will turn to the world 2 pole of the contemporary model, the cognitive structures of learners, and the relevant world 3 theories and findings about what happens in the mind of the learner. The remaining chapters will take up the developmental issues. In all these chapters bar the present one, the methodological ideas of Popper and Lakatos will feature prominently.

The rise of "structure of knowledge"

This book is only one of many thousands published in English during the same year, on subjects ranging from accountancy to zoology. Even if one particular subject field—such as education or psychology—is considered, the number is still impressive. But as well as these books, there are mountains of journal articles. It all adds up to a mammoth problem for curriculum planners at all levels who are faced with a dilemma: On one hand there is only a limited time available for an individual to receive his or her primary, secondary and tertiary education; but on the other hand knowledge is accumulating so rapidly, that, even given a whole lifetime, it would not be possible to master more than a small and specialized field. It has long been recognized that the days of the universal genius are over; if present trends continue the world has seen its last Newton or Leibnitz who can master several large fields like physical science, mathematics and philosophy. (Several twentieth-century figures put up creditable performances, but the breed is dying.)

In the course of his or her education, then, the individual is only going to encounter a small sample of the knowledge that is potentially available. What should this sample contain? Should it be a random sample, or should it be biased in a direction that reflects the value judgments of parents, teachers, religious leaders, or the government? Do some branches of knowledge have more worth than others, or alternatively, is some knowledge essential in the sense that it forms a foundation upon which all the rest is necessarily built?

In the past these questions have been tackled by philosophers, and philosophers of education—such men as Plato, Kant, Rousseau, Spencer, Dewey, and Russell. Indeed, much of the educational work of philosophers of the past can be interpreted as being directed at establishing criteria for selection of curriculum content. As a result of these quests, Plato came to have a higher regard for mathematics and philosophy than for poetry and drama; Locke stressed the importance of first-hand experience, and he gave much practical advice (such as the importance of acquiring skills connected with the management of a country estate); Rousseau denigrated bookish education that consisted only of "words"; Spencer held that scientific training was superior to the study of the classics; Dewey concluded that educative experience must be centered around the social nature of life in and out of the school and in the contemporary world. All of these men believed that they had discovered objective grounds for the selection of curriculum content (although that might not always have been precisely how they would have phrased it); the problem has been that others have not agreed with them!

In the last few decades, about the time that Hanson and Kuhn and Popper were publishing their major works, in both Britain and the United States a number of philosophers and educationists were "homing-in" on another approach. They focussed on the nature of knowledge itself; and they decided that bodies of knowledge have certain important structural features, and that furthermore there are only a small number of different *types* of knowledge. If this line of argument is sound, it has obvious educational and curricular implications (some of which are being grasped by computer scientists and researchers in artificial intelligence, who wish to create computers that can "think" and behave very much as humans do).

As might have been expected, this notion of structure of knowledge is one which many contemporary philosophers have found appealing. For the structure of a branch of knowledge is conferred upon it by its concepts and their interrelationships, and these things—concepts, relations and the characteristics of knowledge—are perennial centers of philosophical interest. (As was seen earlier, much of the work that led to the new philosophy of science focussed on such matters.) However, it cannot be claimed that it was *solely* the writings of philosophers on these topics that led to the rise of contemporary interest in the structure of knowledge.

By the late 1950s in the United States, science education in particular was facing a crisis. It was not only the presence of Sputnik in American skies; the rapid accumulation of knowledge, touched on earlier, was felt most in the natural sciences (where knowledge was reputed to have been doubling about every five years). Obviously, it was not possible to continue cramming more and more topics into the curriculum, and so a new solution had to be found—a curriculum based on new assumptions had to be devised to cope with a situation that had no foreseeable end. The National Academy of Science became concerned, and a conference was held at Woods Hole in 1959. It was here that a solution to the crisis was conceived partly in terms of the structure of knowledge.

The consensus at the conference seemed to be that there was little merit in a curriculum that led a student to master a large number of particular facts. The curriculum should achieve something more basic—it should prepare the student in such a way that he or she could deal effectively with whatever facts turned up in the future. And the way to achieve this, to make the student "at home" in the discipline being studied, was for the curriculum to concentrate on structure. As the chairman of the conference, Harvard psychologist Jerome S. Bruner, put it in his report, a student who was familiar with the structure of the discipline was

> well on his way toward being able to handle a good deal of seemingly new, but in fact, highly related information. . . . Grasping the structure of a subject is understanding it in a way that permits many other things to be related to it meaningfully.[5]

Unfortunately, the conference was rather vague about the precise nature of the panacea that it was recommending, and it was not until the early 1960s that the work of Joseph Schwab, Paul Hirst and others threw some light on what was involved in the structure of a discipline.

Schwab's view of structure

According to Joseph J. Schwab

> three different sets of problems constitute the general problem of the structure of the disciplines. First there is the problem of the organization of the disciplines: how many there are; what they are; and how they relate to one another. Second, there is the problem of the substantive conceptual structures used by each discipline. Third, there is the problem of the syntax of each discipline: what its canons of evidence and proof are, and how well they can be applied.[6]

The first of these problems was one that Schwab himself did not pursue at great length, and it is here that the work of Hirst and Peters is particularly relevant. However, the number of disciplines that are identified obviously depends upon the criteria used to distinguish one discipline from another, and Hirst and Peters used the criterion of difference in structure (and by implication Schwab agreed with them). So the acceptability of their solution to the first problem is dependent upon their success in making sense of the notion of structure.

Now, as indicated in the last half of the passage quoted from Schwab, two main aspects of structure have been identified: the substantive and the syntactical. The substantive structure of a discipline is its "conceptual structure", which Schwab explained as follows:

> enquiry has its origin in a conceptual structure, often mathematical, but not necessarily so. It is this conceptual structure through which we are able to formulate a telling question. It is through the telling question that we know what data to seek and what experiments to perform to get those data. Once the data are in hand, the same conceptual structure tells us

how to interpret them, what to make of them by way of knowledge. Finally, the knowledge itself is formulated in the terms provided by the same conception.[7]

What Schwab was arguing, in short, was the non-controversial point that the concepts of a discipline have a directing influence on enquiry, together with the truism that the facts and theories of a discipline—the interrelationships whose existence gives credence to Schwab's usage of the term "structure"—are expressed in terms of these same concepts. It is clear, too, that conceptual structures for Schwab played much the same role as Kuhnian paradigms.

There are several points here about which Schwab was not clear. In the first place, it is far from certain that all disciplines do have a structure in the sense of possessing a body of concepts which are not isolated but are interrelated by laws and theories. (Kuhn recognized this; he claimed that many disciplines are pre-paradigmatic, for no clearcut frameworks have yet emerged.) Many of what have traditionally been called the humanities are not comparable with the physical and biological sciences in this respect—their concepts are often vague and the relations between them are largely unknown. (John Wilson has offered a similar criticism; structure of knowledge theories "become implausible in such cases as 'moral knowledge', 'religious knowledge' and 'aesthetic knowledge'."[8]) Indeed, it is noticeable that Schwab drew all his detailed examples from scientific fields where his ideas seem to have been initially formed. Furthermore, in a number of areas ranging from economics to ethics there are rival sets or networks of concepts and interrelationships; in other words there is no one conceptual structure that all students of the discipline would accept—in Kuhnian terms, there are rival (and perhaps incommensurable) paradigms. And yet, such a field might still be regarded as a discipline, and the rival conceptual networks (an example would be Freudian and behavioristic psychologies) might both be identified as belonging to the same discipline. Considerations such as these at least raise the possibility that whether or not an area of human endeavour is identified as a discipline has little to do with its possession of a Schwabian substantive structure. (It is not being questioned that *some* disciplines might have the feature that Schwab has described.)

A second major issue that requires clarification in this part of Schwab's work is his basis for deciding that different disciplines have different conceptual strucutres. (Two things—say two languages—could be different, but their structures might be similar.) The setting up of criteria to judge differences between various networks of concepts and relationships is a process that is fraught with difficulties. It is worth discussing these in some detail.

On occasion, the argument that different disciplines have different conceptual structures was only a thinly disguised way of making the truistic claim that different disciplines have different concepts. Thus Schwab described "the tremendous role" of the concept of gravitation in the science of mechanics, he referred to the fact that our knowledge of the workings of the human body has "embedded" in it "one or another concept of the nature of an organism", and he pointed out that "back of our knowledge of heredity" there lies a "conception of particles behaving as do the terms in the expansion of a binomial". After citing more examples of similar ilk, he drew the conclusion that, "In general then, enquiry has its origin in a conceptual structure."[9] But Schwab's disguised truism rests on another, for it is also a truism that each concept is different from every other, and so it seems fruitless to attempt to distinguish between disciplines on the grounds of differences in concepts. Even branches of what would be regarded as a typical example of a discipline have different concepts and so would themselves become fully-fledged disciplines if it were concepts that were the defining factor. Thus electricity, physical optics, hydrostatics, mechanics, quantum mechanics, and thermodynamics are six branches of the discipline of physics, and the concepts of each of these branches are different. If disciplines have different structures, and if differences in structure are simply differences in concepts, then these six branches of physics must be considered as disciplines in their own right. And of course, rival Kuhnian paradigms within a discipline (assuming for the sake of argument that these do exist) seem to have different structures (witness Freudian and behaviorist psychologies), and so these must be regarded as different disciplines—which leads to the nice paradox that if a discipline contains rival paradigms, then it doesn't, because they are not in the same discipline but are disciplines in their own right!

It is apparent from Schwab's writings that he did not mean to imply any of this. He meant, presumably, that the concepts of all of physics—or more likely of all the natural sciences—have something in common that warrants the claim that there is an underlying conceptual structure. Either the concepts are alike in some way, or else the relations between them have some common characteristic; but Schwab did not say what this common element was. Obviously, it would not do for Schwab simply to classify concepts as being scientific, historical, philosophical, religious, and so on, because then his whole argument would become trivial: science has a structure in that its concepts are all of the same type—they are the same because they have been defined as being scientific. Why were they defined in this way? So that it could be argued that science is a distinct discipline with concepts that differ from those of other disciplines!

Unfortunately no other more promising basis for classification of concepts or of the relations that link them was established by Schwab. The disciplines often cited as paradigms have a great variety of concepts. Some concepts in each discipline are directly related to what Dewey called the experiental continuum—the realm of observables and of human experience; but other concepts in the disciplines are of great theoretical complexity, having only tenuous links with Dewey's realm of experience. The one concept may appear in more than one discipline, and two concepts from the one discipline, say "force" and "dielectric constant" in physics, may seem intuitively to be less alike than two concepts from different disciplines, for example "force" in physics and "power" in history. Schwab left all these issues undiscussed, with the result that the claim that each discipline has a distinctive substantive or conceptual structure is barely intelligible.

The second aspect of structure identified by Schwab was syntactical structure (which comes close to what is often meant by "methodology"):

> if different sciences pursue knowledge of their respective subject matters by means of different conceptual frames, it is very likely that there will be major differences between one discipline and another in the way and in the extent to which it can verify its knowledge. There is, then, the problem of determining for each discipline what it does by way of discovery and proof, what criteria it uses for measuring the quality of its data, how strictly it can apply canons of evidence.[10]

Schwab appeared to be setting out a program for further investigation: Do different disciplines have different methodologies, different ways "of discovery and proof"? He suspected that they do, but apparently he left the matter open—it was only likely, but not certain, that because of their difference in "conceptual frames" different disciplines would have different "syntaxes". Obviously it would not have been satisfactory just to assume that they do; and it would have been pointless to define what was meant by "disciplines" in terms of differences in methodology, and then to set out to investigate whether or not disciplines actually do differ in this way. Schwab did not make his position perfectly clear, but it is at least possible that for him it was not a question of definition—it was a contingent matter whether or not disciplines had distinct methodologies or syntactical structures. If this was his view, if it was a contingent matter, then investigation cannot proceed until criteria are established to determine which methodological differences are relevant ones. For it could be argued that physicists use different methods or syntaxes in different branches of their discipline, that is, they differ with respect to some or perhaps even all of the things that Schwab suggests that they have in common—ways of discovery and proof, the criteria used to judge the quality of data, the strictness with which canons of evidence are applied, and the route or pathway leading from the data through interpretation to conclusion. Presumably, in Schwab's view, these differences within physical science are not significant. But by what criteria is such a judgment made? On what grounds can it be concluded that the syntactical differences between researchers in quantum mechanics and physical optics are less significant than those between the quantum theorist and the historian? Unfortunately, Schwab lapses into silence.

There is another serious complexity to be noted: The basic assumption in the last passage quoted from Schwab, to the effect that different disciplines are "likely" to have different ways of verification, can be vigorously disputed. The point is that the "new philosophy of science" would suggest that at a fundamental level all disciplines have pretty much the same methodology—science is less certain a field than was traditionally believed, and it is on a par with other more tentative domains. And it will be recalled from the discussion of hermeneutics, that many regard the hypothetico-deductive method as being central to *all* domains that aspire to knowledge.

There is yet another deficiency. Schwab's work harbors the assumption that it is possible to draw a significant distinction between methodological or syntactical issues and conceptual or substantive ones. After all, there would be little point in his maintaining that there are these two aspects to the structure of a discipline if he also believed that the distinction was an untenable one because the substantive could also be categorized as syntactical and vice versa. Unfortunately for Schwab, this is precisely the situation.

The state of methodology of a discipline—its "ways of discovery and proof", its "canons of evidence" and so on—is so closely related to the theories and concepts current in the discipline that the two aspects cannot be distinguished in any non-arbitrary manner. Consider as an example one of the major foundations of contemporary astronomy, the so-called "red shift". This is a form of the Doppler effect in which the wavelength of an emission from a moving source is distorted (the familiar example is the changing note of the whistle of a speeding train); the light received from the distant galaxies seems to be shifted toward the red end of the spectrum, and this is interpreted as being due to the recession of the source, the velocity of which can be calculated. Data of this type have led to the theory of the expanding universe. Now, was the measurement of this red shift a syntactical or a substantive achievement? On one hand, on Schwab's criteria it certainly was a syntactical advance, for it led to new ways of discovery and proof, to new criteria for judging the quality of data, and it opened a new pathway leading from data through interpretation to conclusion. But on the other hand it obviously was a theoretical advance. Concepts and theories not previously thought relevant to astronomical phenomena (the classical work on the Doppler effect) became part of the substantive structure, and new problems emerged concerning theories of the nature of the universe. Furthermore, a great deal of theory had to be assumed in order to make the measurements and calculations involved in determining the extent of the red shift.

A similar situation exists in other natural sciences and in the social sciences. Even one of Schwab's own examples can be turned against him. At one stage he was contrasting the syntax of everyday discourse with that of science:

> the syntax that leads us to assert that the electron is a particle with a small mass and a negative electrical charge is far more complex. The statement most certainly does not rest on the fact that I have looked at an electron and that my colleague has also looked and nodded agreement. It cannot arise from such a syntax because the electron is not visible.[11]

This passage is surprising. It is not as a result of syntax that physicists assert that an electron has a small mass and a negative charge; this concept of the particle follows from the present state of atomic theory. The degree to which the background of theory has been overlooked by Schwab is indicated by his bald assertion that "the electron is not visible". It is theory that shows that an electron is not visible; many laymen and highschool pupils expect the scientist or the teacher to show them such things as electrons, and it is only when the relevant concepts, models, laws and theories, as well as the "syntax", have been mastered that such an expectation can be seen to be misguided. And, after all, it is only theory that explains what is going to count as an electron. Schwab goes some of the way towards recognizing this, for in places he seems to acknowledge that what he calls syntax is related to the conceptual framework. But he ends by establishing an artificial dualism between conceptual and methodological matters, and the almost satirical words of the arch-enemy of dualisms, John Dewey, are pertinent:

> When a man is eating, he is eating food. He does not divide his act into eating *and* food. But if he makes a scientific investigation of the act, such a discrimination is the first thing he would effect. . . . When we give names to this distinction we have subject matter and method as our terms. . . . This distinction is so natural and important for certain purposes, that we are only too apt to regard it as a separation in existence and not as a distinction in thought.[12]

But as Dewey emphasized, the distinctions made by thought do not always accurately reflect actual experience. And yet to leave matters here is not quite fair to Schwab, for from an educational point of view—if not from a philosophical one—he was attempting to communicate an important insight by means of these distinctions "in thought", namely, that there is more to mastering a discipline than learning the mass of facts that it has accumulated.

Peters and Hirst on Structure

R. S. Peters and P. H. Hirst—central figures in the "London School" of philosophy of education—have written on similar themes to Schwab, and it might be expected that, as professional philosophers, their work would avoid these errors. Whether this is so remains to be seen.

At the outset, Hirst states that his views on the structure of knowledge and the curriculum are "based fairly and squarely on the nature of knowledge itself".[13] This is to claim a great deal. It is tantamount to saying that his position follows as some sort of corollary—a necessary consequence—of what we mean by "knowledge". It is not to make the contingent claim that knowledge has been found by empirical investigation to have certain features, and that these features lend support to Hirst's views on the curriculum. Hirst cannot be claiming this for the reason that the features possessed by knowledge, the "nature of knowledge itself", cannot be determined by empirical enquiry but result from conceptual analysis.

Such a strong claim needs to be justified with an analysis of the concept of knowledge, to make explicit the precise way in which its "nature" is related to a particular view concerning the curriculum. Hirst's influential piece of writing on this general topic, his essay "Liberal Education and the Nature of Knowledge" (1965), failed to give such a justification, and so did his later book of essays (1974).[14] The book which Hirst and Peters produced in collaboration, *The Logic of Education* (1970), recognized but again failed to deal satisfactorily with the central issue:

> What we really want to know at this general level is whether the domain of objective experience and knowledge is, for example, one complex body of interrelated concepts, a unity of some sort, a number of similar forms of experience and knowledge with parallel relations between the concepts in each area, or whether it has some other implicit organization. To answer this question necessitates an examination of the conceptual relations embedded in the many forms of public expression we have and of the serious claims to objective tests that are associated with these. An examination of this scope cannot be undertaken here; for this we must refer the reader elsewhere. Much of the work in this area is controversial.[15]

However, the books to which they referred their readers also failed to offer the requisite analysis of the concept of knowledge, essentially being works on the general issues arising in the philosophy of logic, mathematics, science, and history. Nowhere did Hirst and Peters justify the claim that Hirst first made in 1965 and which they put forward jointly in 1970:

> Detailed studies suggest that some seven areas (of knowledge) can be distinguished, each of which necessarily involves the use of concepts of a particular kind and a distinctive type of test for its objective claims.[16]

This position closely paralleled the one held by Schwab, and at first sight would appear to be subject to the same criticisms. The task, then, is to examine Hirst's celebrated essay of 1965 to see if he was able to avoid these various pitfalls.

Hirst's discussion went somewhat deeper and in effect he further divided Schwab's two aspects of structure. The substantive category was broken into concepts and relationships, and the syntactical into tests against experience and techniques, giving four aspects to the structure of knowledge:[17]

1. Each form of knowledge has "certain central concepts that are peculiar in character to the form".
2. "In a given form of knowledge these and other concepts . . . form a network of possible relationships in which experience can be understood. As a result the form has a distinctive logical structure."
3. A form of knowledge, "by virtue of its particular terms and logic, has expressions or statements . . . that in some way or other . . . are testable against experience."
4. "The forms have developed particular techniques and skills for exploring experience and testing their distinctive expressions."

Hirst claimed that only seven "forms of knowledge" have these four distinguishing aspects of structure: mathematics, physical sciences, human sciences, history, religion, literature and the fine arts, and philosophy. Later, in response to criticism he tinkered slightly with these divisions, without introducing major changes.[18] He also admitted that the forms have evolved, not realizing the "can of worms" that was opened by this frankness—if forms evolve, different societies and different epochs may have their own favored forms, and so the question arises as to which *version* of the forms *ought* to be accepted, i.e., the question of justification arises, as John Wilson pointed out.[19] Hirst did not deal with the related question of the status of rival paradigms that might exist within a given form—each with their different bodies of concepts, relationships, and tests against experience.

Hirst's important conclusions about the numbers of forms of knowledge, and their four defining characteristics, was reached on the basis of an argument as sketchily developed as that put forward by Schwab. At the very least it would be expected that Hirst identify for his readers the four structural aspects of each of the seven forms of knowledge; but he did not do this, and it is to be suspected that he could not have done so in a way that would not have been open to serious objection along the lines that Schwab's work was criticized.

One of the objections to Schwab was that he provided no criteria to distinguish between different types of concept, and therefore he was unable to show what the wide range of scientific concepts all had that the concepts of other disciplines lacked. Hirst made no further contribution here, but merely asserted that the "central concepts" of each form of knowledge were "peculiar in character to the form". If anything, this was an obfuscation, because it was not all concepts that were peculiar but only the central ones. How was this latter type to be distinguished within each form? It is to be hoped that it was not by finding which concepts were peculiar according to some arbitrary but as yet unspecified criterion and then defining these as "central".

Another objection to Schwab focussed on his failure to produce criteria for the identification of relevant differences between the methodologies or syntaxes of the disciplines. Here, too, Hirst added nothing; discussing Hirst's work as early as 1969, John Wilson wrote "I am not at all clear what these criteria are."[20] (In 1979 Wilson added that when he looked at some of Hirst's so-called forms of knowledge he felt "a certain malaise."[21]) Hirst's distinction between "tests against experience" and "techniques and skills" heightens rather than lessens the problems. For within any one discipline, e.g. physics or even the whole of physical science, there are remarkable differences in the ways statements are tested against experience (compare quantum mechanics with physical optics), as well as considerable variations in techniques and skills; and, of course, there could be enormous differences across rival paradigms within the one discipline. (On the other hand, if Feyerabend is right in saying that anything goes, then there are no binding methodological practices at all!) Hirst needed to establish several sets of criteria in order to justify his claim that the tests, skills and techniques used in all branches and paradigms of the one form of knowledge differ in a non-significant way compared with the differences between the seven forms.

Furthermore, Hirst would have had to argue convincingly, and at length, against the view that several of the forms have similar tests, techniques and skills. For example, there is a *prima facie* case that mathematical techniques play an important and even central role in the physical sciences and also the human sciences; observation, collection of data, use of control groups, and other techniques used in the empirical testing of hypotheses are important methodological features of both the human and the physical sciences, and some at least are used in historical research; and some branches of philosophy and religion (such as metaphysics and theology) seem to use identical tests and techniques. All this points to the need for the criteria that Hirst failed to provide.

Schwab was also charged with setting up an artificial dualism between conceptual and methodological aspects of a discipline, and Hirst, too, must face this indictment. In his essay he did not point out that the tests against experience and the techniques appropriate to a discipline were determined by the first two aspects of structure, the concepts and their interrelationships.

In 1970, however, in the book he wrote with Peters, Hirst took steps to strengthen his case. In the first place, the argument that each form of knowledge had its own type of central concept was developed in an important way reminiscent of the philosophy of Immanuel Kant:

> all our concepts seem to belong to one of a number of distinct, if related, categories which philosophical analysis is concerned to clarify. These categories are marked out in each case by certain fundamental, ultimate or categoreal concepts that provide the form of experience in the different modes. Our understanding of the physical world, for instance, involves such categoreal concepts as those of "space", "time", and "cause". Concepts such as those of "acid", "electron", and "velocity", all presuppose these categoreal notions.[22]

At first sight this is persuasive: Each of the seven forms of knowledge have a group of irreducible categoreal concepts that their remaining concepts presuppose. But what is the force of "presuppose" in this line of argument? In what sense do the other concepts of physical science—"electron", "velocity", and so on—presuppose such concepts as "space", "time" and "cause"? The answer, presumably, is that when subject to conceptual analysis, the secondary or derivative concepts will be found to be definable in terms of the categoreal concepts.[23] "Velocity", for instance is "rate of change of spatial position"; and "rate" and "spatial position" are close relatives of the concepts of "time" and "space" respectively.

If discussion is broken off at this point, the case seems to rest with Peters and Hirst. But a further, revealing question can be posed: What, in fact, determines the defining characteristics of the concept of velocity? The answer, of course, is not philosophical analysis but contemporary theory in physical science. The present state of the science of physics determines what concepts of physics are categoreal and what ones are not; as the work of T. S. Kuhn and others discussed earlier has shown, several well-known incidents from the history of the science illustrate the fact that major revolutions have in effect been changes in the categoreal concepts and the defining characteristics of concepts, changes that have necessarily been reflected at other levels within the discipline. Hirst and Peters made a mistake here—they asserted it was the task of philosophical analysis to clarify categories of concepts, such as concepts involved in "our understanding of the physical world". However, the introduction of concepts and theories in an attempt to understand the physical world is not the task of philosophy but of science. It has taken the work of Einsteins and Newtons, not of Hirsts and Peters, to establish that the concepts of time, space, and others, are basic to our understanding of the physical world.

This is an important point that can be generalized. The categoreal concepts of human science, physical science, history, religion, and so on, are categoreal not because philosophical analysis says that they are but because of the present state of theory in human science, physical science, history, religion and so on. (After all, if a discipline is a Quinean network—a view discussed in Chapter 2 with respect to science—no knot can be established as absolutely more central and important than any other; but those who *use* the net may decide to treat some knots, or some areas, as being more important.) But if this is the case, then the procedure adopted by Hirst and Peters comes down to this: They have chosen seven areas of theory, taken the basic or categoreal concepts of each (using the theory in each area to determine which concepts were categoreal), and then defined the seven areas in terms of the possession of certain categoreal concepts. But in doing this, in using the theories from seven forms of knowledge in order to establish that there are seven forms of knowledge, they come suspiciously close to arguing in a circle.

In reply to this it could be acknowledged that the specific concepts identified as categoreal in science, in history, and so on, are determined by present theory in these fields. Nevertheless, it could be maintained, humans being the kind of creatures they are, experience must be of certain kinds—spatio-temporal, moral, and so on—which are marked by the possession of categoreal concepts although these latter have undeniably changed during the long period of the development of human knowledge.[24] It is not circular to take the readily observed divisions of knowledge and then to look for what it is that is central to each individual discipline.

Two criticisms can be leveled at this line of argument. In the first place, even if it is a fact that human experience must be of certain kinds, it is not necessary that these kinds be treated or conceptualized in particular ways. Given a basic range of human experience, it is still a contingent matter how people at different times and places will come to conceptualize it, and on this analysis the existence of the present forms of knowledge will be the result of this contingent pattern of past events in our intellectual history. Secondly, the procedure that has been outlined for identifying disciplines is too good—it can be used to show that even small branches of a subject are in fact discrete disciplines, or that the most trivial pursuits are worthy of this honorific. For the procedure of taking readily observed divisions of knowledge, and then looking for concepts that are central in each division, is a procedure that can always be followed no matter what subjects are taken as a starting point. The point is that any subject, or any branch of a subject, or any paradigm within a subject —whether it be physics, or thermodynamics, or physical optics, or the study of bingo or chess, or cookery—necessarily has concepts, and some of these will be more central than others in the light of present knowledge. So it has more than the appearance of futility to ask "what are the forms of knowledge?" and then to answer by taking some of the subjects that are seen to exist at present (why these rather than others?), then determining the central concepts of these favoured subjects (which can always be done), and then using possession of these concepts as a characteristic which determines that these subjects are in fact "forms of knowledge".

Hirst and Peters made even less headway in remedying the other weaknesses in Hirst's essay of 1965. They completely failed to touch on the question of criteria for the determination of relevant differences in methodology; and they did not see that the distinction between conceptual and methodological matters, which was embodied in their various aspects of structure, was artificial. This latter is surprising, for Hirst and Peters were at pains to argue a similar point in a slightly different context a little earlier in their book; they criticized the *Taxonomy of Educational Objectives* of Bloom and his co-workers on the grounds that it tried to distinguish between "different types of intellectual abilities and skills":

> But valuable though this attempt may be in certain respects, it shows no awareness of the fundamental, necessary relationships between the various kinds of objectives that can be distinguished. A knowledge of the meaning of terms can certainly be thought of as in a different category from a knowledge of empirical facts or an acceptance of a rule of behaviour. But clearly, in any given case, an achievement in any one of these categories might be interrelated, even necessarily, with achievements in the others.[25]

Concluding dilemma

It would appear, then, that the case for the structure of knowledge is not merely "not proven", it is based on faulty assumptions. The concepts, laws and theories of a discipline on one hand, and its methodological features on the other, form what Dewey would have regarded as a continuum rather than distinct categories; and it has not yet been shown that typologies of concepts and methods can be established on a basis that does not already assume the existence of different disciplines, an assumption that structure of knowledge theorists cannot make without circularity. A reasonable case can be put that the growth of present-day forms of knowledge has not reflected a so-called "logic of knowledge", as Schwab, Hirst and Peters seem to maintain; if Kuhn or Lakatos are right, progress is more stumbling than that. If more radical writers are correct (for instance, the sociologist Michael Young),[26] the process reflects not logic but the social, cultural and ideological factors revealed by studies in the history of ideas, sociology of knowledge, and social and cultural history.

The long and short of the preceding discussion has been to create a dilemma: The notion of the structure of knowledge is loaded with pitfalls, and is of dubious help; yet on the other hand a person who has mastered a discipline seems to have knowledge that transcends merely factual recall of the domain—the expert seems "at home" in the discipline, and seems to have an ordered understanding of it. Perhaps the root of the problem is that the structure of knowledge theorists have given too clean a picture; it is only a slight parody to state that on their account each discipline has *a* pristine structure. Furthermore, they overlook many of the points emerging from recent epistemological work, especially that done on the nature of science—work that debunks numerous myths, and makes the attainment of knowledge, and the logical features of knowledge itself, less clearcut and absolute.

If the points that were made throughout the present chapter are considered in relation to what was covered earlier, the picture that emerges is of each discipline being like a network—there are multiple linkages and criss-crossing of relations, but the overall form the net takes depends on how it is being grasped by whomsoever is fishing with it. This is not to say that anything will do, or that there are no constraints; after all, a net is not infinitely malleable. And the net itself is a *public* entity—although it is in the third world; it can be the subject of discussion among both experts and learners. The relation between various concepts in physics can be talked about, the pros and cons can be laid out. The fact that a Newton and an Einstein will want to relate the concepts differently is a complexity, but it is not a crippling one. As Popper would remind us, there are better and worse answers although there may be no *absolute* answers.

Although, then, a discipline itself is a somewhat murky entity, the picture becomes even more cloudy when an individual's *understanding* of a discipline is being dealt with. What is in the person's mind is not public—it is in the "subjective" world 2—and the cognitive structure of a learner may depart quite dramatically from the best public consensus about the discipline. The cognitive psychologist Donald Norman puts it as follows:

> Conceptual models (evidently Norman's expression for what in this chapter has been called the discipline's "structure") are devised as tools for the understanding or teaching of physical systems. Mental models are what people really have in their heads and what guides their use of things. Ideally, there ought to be a direct and simple relationship between the conceptual and mental model. All too often, however, this is not the case.[27]

It is to what is in a person's head as he or she masters the structure of a discipline that the discussion now must turn.

Notes and References

1. K. Popper, *Conjectures and Refutations*, op. cit., p. 27.
2. K. Popper, *Unended Quest*, op. cit., p. 181.
3. Ibid., p. 183.
4. N. Malcolm, *Memory and Mind*. Ithaca: Cornell University Press, 1977, p. 249.
5. J. S. Bruner, *The Process of Education*. NY: Vintage Press, 1963, p. 7.
6. J. J. Schwab, "Structure of the Discplines: Meanings and Significances", in G. W. Ford and L. Pugno, (eds.) *The Structure of Knowledge and the Curriculum*. Chicago: Rand McNally, 1965, p. 14.
7. Schwab, op. cit., p. 12.
8. John Wilson, "The Curriculum: Justification and Taxonomy", *British Journal of Educational Studies*, XVII, February 1969, p. 38.
9. Schwab, op. cit., pp. 11–12.
10. Ibid, p. 14.
11. Ibid, p. 22.
12. J. Dewey, *Democracy and Education*. New York: Macmillan, 1955 reprint, pp. 195–6.
13. P. H. Hirst, "Liberal Education and the Nature of Knowledge", in R. D. Archambault, ed., *Philosophical Analysis and Education*. London: Routledge, 1965, p. 125.
14. Paul H. Hirst, *Knowledge and the Curriculum*. London: Routledge, 1974, esp. ch. 6.
15. R. Peters and P. Hirst, *The Logic of Education*. London: Routledge, 1970, p. 62.
16. Ibid.
17. Hirst, op. cit., pp. 128–9. These points are discussed more fully in D. C. Phillips, "The Distinguishing Features of Forms of Knowledge", *Educational Philosophy and Theory*. 3, 1971, pp. 27–35.
18. P. Hirst, *Knowledge and the Curriculum*, op. cit.
19. John Wilson, *Preface to Philosophy of Education*. London: Routledge, 1979, ch. 4.
20. J. Wilson, "The Curriculum: Justification and Taxonomy", op. cit., p. 39.
21. J. Wilson, *Preface to Philosophy of Education*, op. cit., p. 113.
22. Peters and Hirst, op. cit., p. 64.
23. "In conceptual analysis we usually settle for making explicit defining characteristics in the weak sense." Peters and Hirst, op. cit., p. 5.
24. Wilson also offers arguments along these lines. See *Preface to Philosophy of Education*, op. cit., esp. p. 116.
25. Peters and Hirst, op. cit., p. 61.
26. M. F. D. Young, *Knowledge and Control*. London: Collier-Macmillan, 1971.
27. D. Norman, "Some Observations on Mental Models", in D. Gentner and A. Stevens, eds., *Mental Models*. Hillsdale, NJ: Lawrence Erlbaum, 1983, p. 12.

12

On Describing a Student's Cognitive Structure

When cognitive researchers study the changes that occur as a learner gradually masters a discipline, they face a particularly insidious problem. Paul Hirst touched upon it in his famous (and, as was seen in the previous chapter, otherwise justly-criticized) essay "Liberal Education and the Nature of Knowledge", but the significance of the passage has been noted by only a few commentators:

> From what is said of "effective thinking", it is perfectly plain that the phrase is being used as a label for mental activity which results in an achievement of some sort, an achievement that is, at least in principle, both publicly describable and publicly testable—the solving of a mathematical problem, responsibly deciding who to vote for, satisfactorily analyzing a work of art. Indeed, there can be effective thinking only when the outcome of mental activity can be recognized and judged by those who have the appropriate skills and knowledge . . . public terms and criteria are logically necessary to specifying what the abilities are.[1]

Ludwig Wittgenstein[2] made essentially the same point much more pithily: "An *inner process* stands in need of outward criteria." (It is important, in order to forestall misunderstandings which might arise later, to stress that the point of quoting these passages is not to introduce surreptitiously the claim that there are no inner processes.)

To put the issue that is being introduced here in concrete form, consider research on a native speaker of English who is learning to speak Russian. The instructor (or researcher) poses a question: to be understandable it must be well formed in terms of the structure of the foreign language. The student cogitates and then answers in Russian, as was expected. If the student is good, the answer will be well-formed. After all, this is what it *means* to learn Russian: sensible questions asked in or about Russian can be answered in kind. And of course the point can be generalized to the learning of physics, or mathematics, or geography, or. . . .

It would be illegitimate, not to mention naive, for a researcher to note that the answer to a question in Russian was given in Russian, and to consider this as evidence that the student's cognitive processing had taken place in Russian and that it had the structural features of that language. An answer, if it is to count as an answer at all, *must by conceptual necessity* reflect the structure of the language or discipline presupposed by the question—there is no other alternative. This is the nub of Hirst's statement. The analysis of such an answer by itself will throw little if any light on the mental processes by which it was derived. Thus, to revert to the example, it is not uncommon to meet people who can speak a foreign language but who internally work in their native tongue (they translate the Russian question into English, solve it, and then turn the answer back into Russian). Or to take another and more extreme example, from the fact that a hand-held calculator will give an arithmetical answer to an arithmetical problem, one cannot deduce much about its internal structure; it may be programmed to work internally in either an "algebraic" or "reverse Polish" mode, but publicly it must perform according to the rules of the discipline of arithmetic. If it fails by these standards (if it answers "2 + 3 = " with "7") one suspects that the wiring is defective or that the battery is nearly flat.

This leads directly to another point. If correct performance is no guide to the student's internal structure, neither is faulty performance. Yet it is sometimes suggested that an analysis of error can pinpoint where a student's structure is badly constructed. Certainly "the square root of 9 is 4.5" suggests the student might believe that square roots are obtained by dividing by two (but there are other possible sources for the error), and the mistake indicates that the requisite part of the public discipline of arithmetic has not been mastered. However, even if the student's precise error is identified, this information by itself does not serve to indicate where the faulty information is stored within the student's cognitive structure. The error, in other words, gives information about the student's mastery of the "public" discipline, not about the internal goings on (except the obvious information that the student divided by 2).

To turn again to the hand-held calculator, if it misbehaves like this during a calculation and turns up 4.5 instead of 3, the source of the error could lie in various places. No doubt an electronics engineer could discover where the fault was located, but the point is that this could not be done merely by analyzing the nature of the error. (The only way to finesse these problems is to trivialize the notion of cognitive structure, and to *define* it as being isomorphic—when complete—with the structure of the discipline being learned. The notion that a successful learner has internalized the structure of the discipline being learned makes this attractive, of course, but it does have the effect of making the concept of cognitive structure redundant. In general there seem to be no grounds for believing that the problems of psychology can be defined away in this manner, although, as will be seen, some researchers have taken this unpromising path.)

All this seems elementary, and unlikely to trip any researcher. Nevertheless, the confounding of the two things—disciplinary structure and cognitive structure—frequently takes place. Piaget even manages to conflate and confuse three things at times: (a) the structure of a part of the external world,

(b) the structure of our theories dealing with the structure of this part of the world, and (c) the structure of the psychological entities with which we master such theories or deal with such parts of the world.[3] There is no prima facie reason for believing that these three things (if they exist) are identical, or even that they are tightly connected, and they certainly are not merely three different names for the same thing.

As was seen in the previous chapter, Popper has provided terminology that can be used to sharpen the issues here. Thus, the structure of disciplines is a third world matter, while human cognitive structures exist in the second world (while our theories about them exist in the third), and human nervous systems exist in the first. What would count as isomorphism or similarity between such disparate ontological realms is, at best, an unresolved mystery.[4] Piaget was guilty of conflating or collapsing these three realms (and as will be seen, he was not alone).

It is fitting to allow Popper the last word in this section. He has asserted a number of theses that are relevant to the preceding discussion:

> (1) That every subjective act of understanding is largely anchored in the third world.
> (2) That almost all important remarks which can be made about such an act consist in pointing out its relations to third world objects.
> This, I suggest, can be generalized, and holds for every subjective act of "knowledge": all the important things we can say about an act of knowledge consist of pointing out the third world objects of the act—a theory or proposition—and its relation to other third-world objects, such as the arguments bearing on the problem.[5]

And, a little later Popper adds that any "psychological process" that leads to understanding

> must be analyzed in terms of the third-world objects in which it is anchored. In fact, it can be analyzed *only* in these terms.[6]

Research on the cognitive structure of a learner

Confusion similar to that found in Piaget, that is, confusion and confounding of the Popperian three worlds, can be found in the work of contemporary cognitive psychologists in the information-processing tradition. (To point to difficulties is not to denigrate these researchers or to belittle their work; they are struggling with issues of great complexity. It is no favor, however, to allow one's admiration to mask one's critical faculties—on the contrary, all will profit from strong and direct criticism. As Popper once remarked, "We have to try to adopt a highly critical attitude towards those theories which we admire most."[7])

To focus initially on one influential stream of work within this tradition, consider the claim made by Richard J. Shavelson in a well-known paper:

> A structure of a subject matter, ultimately, rests in the minds of the "great scientists". . . . content structure may be viewed as the reverse side of the cognitive structure coin: for example, a textbook provides data from which to infer the author's cognitive structure.[8]

However, the manner in which an individual scientist's cognitive structure is organized (in world 2) is one thing; the way he expresses his ideas in textbooks or papers is quite another. The former may well reflect personal psychological idiosyncracy; it cannot be ruled out *a priori* that there were significant structural differences between the way Newton and Einstein *internally* organized their knowledge, nor can it be ruled out that there are marked differences between the cognitive structures of a contemporary experimental physicist and a theoretical one. How these individuals structure or organize their *public* or world 3 pronouncements is altogether a different kettle of fish—it is determined by contemporary literary tastes, by the rules and standards of their peers in the scientific community, by the canons deemed appropriate in terms of other contents of world 3, and by the level of understanding they regard their intended audience as possessing. (No doubt "structure of knowledge" theorists like Paul Hirst would want to argue that first, these physicists would only be judged as experts because the "objective" standards of the discipline exist; and second, that despite the different forms their papers and textbooks might take, the same logical or conceptual, or substantive and syntactical—as opposed to psychological and cognitive— structure would be present).

There is another consideration: Training students to be scientists is not to train them to reproduce the idiosyncratic structure of some competent or prestigious individual, rather it is to train them in the world 3 canons of the discipline. Thus Shavelson is surely wrong to suppose that the public structure of science—the knowledge structure—resides in, and is identical with, the private cognitive structures of individual scientists. To suppose this is to confuse world 2 and world 3, that is, the realm of the logical—the realm of concepts and their interrelationships—with the domain of the psychologi- cal—the domain of cognitive processes. The one is not necessarily a guide to the other, any more than knowledge of the official structure of Russian is a guide to the way a student linguist has cognitively organized the language (or, it might be added, any more than knowledge of the structure of Russian is a guide to the way Tolstoy or Stalin or Nureyev has internally organized it). Again, the central point is that whatever the manner in which the material is internally organized (and no doubt it is organized in some way), the student has to *perform* by the public norms of the language or of the discipline.

Possibly what has led Shavelson and others astray is the fact that if the cognitive structures of scientists did not exist we never would have come to possess the structure of branches of science, for we would have no science. In a later paper Shavelson wrote that "the objective world of knowledge was arrived at mentally—i.e., by the hard, rigorous, creative thinking of scholars, a subset of whom we now call scientists."[9] Certainly this is true; as Popper pointed out, third world entities may well be created by second world ones, but this does not mean that they are identical. And Shavelson's point can be turned on its head, for arguably the reverse is no less true—without the disciplines of science, there would be no one who could be called a scientist whose cognitive structure could become an object for psychological study. (This also is part of what Hirst was suggesting: without the "public" discipline, there could be no scientists—for there could be no way to recognize them as such!)

It is worth lingering over Shavelson's work, for he explicitly discussed key tools used by members of the research community and in so-doing exposes the slippery nature of the problems. In several related papers in different journals he discusses two ways of measuring "cognitive structure" and a way of measuring "content structure". (It is worth stressing that he did not invent these; he was discussing tools well known to many researchers.)

Cognitive structures of learners can be measured either by word association or by graph construction (Shavelson mentions, but does not discuss, several other methods including achievement testing). In the word association method the student is given a list of words drawn from the discipline that has been learned (or which is about to be learned). In physics, the list might include "conductor", "electron", "circuit", and so forth. One of the tests Shavelson uses in his own research has instructions that read, in part, as follows:

> You will be given a key word which represents a concept in "physics", and you are to write down as many other words which the key word brings to mind as you can. Write as many words as you can which the key word brings to mind.[10]

Responses are tabulated, and sometimes numbers are generated, but the net result is that the researchers can see what other terms the student associates with the stimulus words.

There is, of course, no reason to think that the student's cognitive structure is being measured in this kind of experiment—the student's "public" understanding of the "structure" of physics is what is being grappled with. From the fact that certain words are elicited in response to a key word, it does not follow that they stand in any given structural relation to it in memory. Consider an analogy: It is easy to imagine a number of computers, all with different memory banks and different programs, that were so arranged that they would generate the same list of words from their respective memories when given the same stimulus. A user of any one of these computers would have no firm grounds for inferring anything about the structure of the memory of the particular computer he or she was using on the basis of the way it responded to any questions. All that could be inferred would be the relations between the words actually listed—and this is an inference about the public domain of words and concepts, not an inference about the computer's private, inner domain.

So, to repeat, if the notion of cognitive structure is to mean anything at all, it must have something to do with how information is organized or structured internally. (That is, it would seem to be embodied in world 2.) It is reasonable to suppose (unless one is a radical behaviorist) that this structure is what allows an individual to retrieve and then to act upon relevant information; but it does not follow that this structure can be inferred from data that are only about the individual's actions. This is not to prejudge what resourceful researchers may be able to accomplish in the future, but they will need an argument to show that they have been able to manipulate behavior so as to allow valid inferences to the internal structures that helped to produce that behavior. There is not much point in them dressing up their behavioral findings in "mentalese" and offering these as "findings" about inner mechanisms or structures.

To return to Shavelson and his word association test: After reporting various ways to produce a score or to generate numbers from the results, he remarks that the

> Studies cited above provide some evidence supporting the hypothesis that the word association techniques measures some aspect of a student's cognitive structure.[11]

And he goes on to let the conceptual cat out of the bag; in his own study on instruction in physics,

> word association data were collected before, during, and after instruction. If these data measure some important aspect of cognitive structure, then the cognitive structure of the students receiving instruction should resemble the subject-matter structure more closely with each day of instruction.[12]

It is no surprise that his prediction was confirmed! In a similar way, one could "predict" that word association data collected on a student of the Russian language would come closer to the "disciplinary structure" of Russian as instruction progressed—but this would not be evidence about how the student's cognitive structure was organized, rather it would show the student's increasing ability to reproduce the "objective" structure of the foreign language in terms of which all of his or her performances have to be given. (One would hope that this indeed would be the result obtained after instruction.) There is then, in this work, systematic confusion of the two types of structure.

Turning to the second technique, the graph-construction method for measuring cognitive structure:

> The subject is given an alphabetical list of key words and asked to build a linear tree graph by connecting pairs of words . . . with a line representing the "similarity" between the words.[13]

This technique is misrepresented in the same way as before. Shavelson writes

> With this method, the order in which words are connected by lines on the graph and the resultant proximity among words take on particular importance in examining cognitive structure.[14]

There is no need to repeat the criticism at length. Judging the relatedness of key concepts of a discipline is a task within the structure of that discipline—it is a world 3 task—and is no more of a guide to cognitive structure than the answering of Russian questions is a guide to the cognitive structure of the language student. Any number of cognitive organizations might lead to the performance, but the performance (as Hirst insisted) is always going to be a performance in the public domain, judged by the public criteria of the appropriate discipline. It is worth stressing again that this is not to deny that there is a cognitive domain in each student; the point simply is, as the psychologist David Kieras puts it, "internal representations can not be uniquely identified from behavioral data".[15]

Matters only marginally improve when Shavelson's discussion turns to measurement of the structure of a body of knowledge such as physics. This, Shavelson reports, is done by first selecting a standard textbook; then counting the frequency of use of terms and selecting a small number of those most frequently used ("inertia", "mass", "force", "time"....); then every sentence or formula in the text that contains two or more of these key terms is diagrammed using a standard sentence-diagramming technique; the results are then converted into digraphs; and finally the individual graphs are combined to build up the final structural picture.[16]

At best the technique outlined here measures grammatical structure, but it does not begin to come to grips with the problems of logical and conceptual relationships that are central to the understanding of the structure of disciplines. As Wittgenstein and others reminded philosophers long ago, grammatical form is not a reliable guide to logical form. Furthermore, the problem of markedly different, alternative formulations of bodies of knowledge is ignored. Indeed, the whole body of analytical literature on structure of knowledge—some of which was discussed in the previous chapter—has been by-passed.

There is one last hope. Perhaps Shavelson and other cognitive psychologists are using the expressions "structure of knowledge" and "cognitive structures" differently from the way philosophers would use them. So it is appropriate to close this avenue of escape:

> A subject-matter structure in instructional materials is referred to as *content structure*: the web of concepts (words, symbols) and their interrelations in a body of instructional material.[17]

And,

> The structure in a student's memory is referred to as *cognitive structure*: a hypothetical construct referring to the organization (relationships) of concepts in memory.[18]

The second of these definitions nicely encapsulates the issue. The argument being put forward in this chapter does not deny that a knowledgeable learner has a memory, and has a stock of concepts and rules; rather, the focus is on how much can be learned about the *organization* or *structuring* of these concepts or of this knowledge without confounding the two disparate structures. In replying to this line of criticism (made in a precursor of this chapter that appeared as a paper in a journal with which he was associated), Shavelson once again unknowingly added fuel to the fire; he wrote

> I defined cognitive structure, broadly, as a hypothetical construct referring to concepts and their interrelations in memory. . . . Cognitive structure, then, was defined as the student's *public understanding* of (say) physics.[19]

The running together of these two disparate definitions as if they were synonymous is to run afoul of all the difficulties that have already been alluded to; world 2 and world 3 are being conflated.

Some objections

There are several objections that are likely to be raised against the points made thus far.

The psychologist who believes that "cognitive structure" is a useful notion might be tenacious, and not want to abandon the view that when a student answers a question correctly, whether it be in physics or arithmetic or Russian, then at that moment his or her cognitive structure must closely resemble (or match, or be isomorphic with) the structure of the relevant discipline. After all, when a student correctly answers a physics question with "$E = MC^2$", at that instant the relevant ingredients have obviously "come together" in his or her mind. Furthermore, and even more significantly, it could be argued that it is likely that a student who gets the problem wrong has a cognitive structure that differs in some significant way from that of the relevant discipline (this is likely, perhaps, but not certain because the error could be due to some other factor such as faulty reading of the problem).

It is not clear that this line of objection leads anywhere fruitful. To repeat the point made by Kieras, as well as numerous philosophers, there are many ways that a given performance—or belief, for that matter—could be generated. To cite some mathematical examples, there are often many different algorithms that can lead to the successful solution of an algebraic problem; or again, two hand-held calculators working in completely different modes can successfully solve the same arithmetic problem. Or, to take an example from a different field, it has long been recognized by philosophers of science that theories in science are "underdetermined" by the facts that have been established; in other words, an infinite set of theories can be generated to account for the same set of facts (for instance, by a process sometimes known as de-Occamization).

It follows from all this that any number of theoretical mechanisms can be inferred to account for the facts concerning the student's performance—no particular configuration of the student's cognitive structure is made necessary by the details of his or her performance. Certainly, some configurations may be ruled out, but this still leaves an infinite set of possibilities. And to make the central point even more strongly, there is absolutely no reason to believe that an entity (whether a person, an animal, or a machine) which can undertake successfully a complex task "T", must thereby be internally structured in a way that copies, parallels, or is isomorphic with, "T".[20]

But there are two new points that are worth making in response to this first line of objection. First, those who push the objection are perhaps being misled by a truism, namely, that the student's successful world 3 performance (he or she identifies "E" as being equal to "MC^2") and also the unsuccessful performance (a bungled attempt to solve a problem involving knowledge of Snell's law in optics) are *describable* in world 3 terms, that is, in terms of the structure of the relevant discipline. As argued earlier, the discipline must by conceptual necessity provide the public framework in terms of which the relevant performances are both described and assessed as successes or failures. However, from the fact that the student's performance is describable in this way, it does not follow that the "internal mechanisms" which generated the performance have the same structure as the public discipline.

Second, it is apparent that the objection relies heavily upon the murky notion of "close resemblance" or "isomorphism" between a cognitive (or memory) structure and the structure of a discipline. Some thorny metaphysical issues are raised here, not least of which is the precise relation between world 2 and world 3. Disciplines exist, and so do human memories, but the senses in which they exist appear to differ, as Popper's discussion of his "three worlds" makes clear. The discipline of physics (as opposed to the textbooks in which it is described) is not a physical thing; the relations between its concepts are logical ones—the concepts are linked by definitions, or by logical implication, or by chains of inference. Cognitive (or memory) structures exist in the same sense that any of the abstract entities postulated in the natural or human sciences can be supposed to exist; the relationship between concepts internal to memory structures may be, in a sense, physical but they certainly are not logical—perhaps the concepts are stored physically (possibly encoded in the form of electrical or chemical traces), and they are linked by physically existing pathways (or at the very least by psychologically existing pathways, if this notion has any sense) such that, within the memory system, access to one concept may lead to access to another. To put it another way, the concepts "nucleus" and "electron" may be linked associationalistically in a person's memory, but this is not how they are linked in the discipline!

Another objection that could be raised to the earlier discussion is that many of the points made about cognitive psychology could be made about physics, and yet physics is obviously a successful science. A number of the entities studied in physics are unobservable—the interior of stars and black holes, and the fundamental ingredients of matter (quarks and the rest)—and physicists explore these by making inferences from that they *can* observe (such as readings on laboratory instruments). Logically, there are innumerable hypothetical mechanisms that could be invoked to account for this data, and yet this has not prevented physicists from making headway and from reaching a reasonable degree of agreement. What is sauce for the goose is sauce for the gander—why should the same procedure be objected to in psychology? (Chomsky sometimes argues along these lines.)[21]

In brief, the answer to this is that inferences about unobservables, although risky, must indeed be made and then put to the test. But scientists have to be sensitive to the conceptual pitfalls that lie in the inferential path. Without unduly romanticizing them, theoretical physicists are relatively clear about what they mean by a "quark" or a "black hole": they do not confuse these entities with the instruments by which they have carried out their investigations; they try not to multiply theoretical entities beyond demonstrated necessity; they are sensitive to the existence of rival hypotheses; and they do pay some attention to philosophical or "meta" issues. (Many of the greatest physicists of the late nineteenth and twentieth centuries were also reasonable philosophers.) What is sauce for the goose is sauce for the gander here as well! Why should psychology be looser? The difference between physics and psychology was put, somewhat uncharitably, by Wittgenstein:

> The confusion and barrenness of psychology is not to be explained by calling it a "young science"; its state is not comparable with that of physics, for instance, in its beginnings. . . . For in psychology, there are experimental methods and conceptual confusion.[22]

Problem solving and computer models

It may be thought that the criticisms leveled against Shavelson's approach to cognitive research are not applicable to researchers who use quite different methods. So it is appropriate to turn to psychological work that is closer to the artificial intelligence (AI) tradition.

For well over a decade James G. Greeno has been studying the psychological processes that operate when children solve simple problems in such fields as elementary physics, arithmetic, and geometry. In the latter field, for example, he interviewed a small number of geometry students on a weekly basis throughout the school year, and at each interview he had them work through—aloud—a few problems pertinent to their current work. Knowing what the students had been taught, and knowing what their chains of reasoning had been while solving problems, he was able (he thought) to infer what cognitive processes were involved. He was then successful in programming a computer ("PERDIX") to replicate the students' performances. In a sense the computer program became a test of Greeno's conjectures. As he put it, PERDIX is a "representation" of the "processes that students use". And, he continued,

> The procedures represented in PERDIX are hypothetically the same as those that students typically use in solving the same kinds of problems. Therefore, PERDIX is a candidate for a model of the knowledge that students acquire in order to solve problems in geometry.[23]

The expressions "hypothetically" and "is a candidate" in this passage are significant; but in life many candidates can run for office, and there is a long road to travel between nomination and election as victor. The nomination of a candidate is only the beginning, not the end, of the struggle.

Several issues here require further discussion:

1. In the first place, a skeptic can ask what reason there is to suppose that Greeno has even come close to pinning-down the cognitive structures of the students he studied. They were asked to perform tasks in the discipline of geometry, and to make progressive reports during their work; that is, they were set a world 3 task. *A priori*, then, it might be expected that their reports would consist of good or bad geometry, rather than being sketches of their current psychological (world 2) states.

Consider one of the problems that was assigned. It involved two sets of crossing parallel lines; the measure of one of the angles between the intersecting lines was 40 degrees, and students had to calculate the measure of another angle in a different part of the diagram. Mathematically, the problem was such that the answer could be reached validly only by constructing a chain of reasoning, but there were several ways in which this could be done. Furthermore, several geometrical principles had to be used (theorems about vertical and supplementary angles).

Now, what did the student protocols reveal? As might have been predicted from the foregoing mathematical analysis, successful students constructed various valid chains of inference, using the necessary geometrical principles.[24] What else, the skeptic might ask, was it possible for them to have done? They took, as they had to, the mathematical steps (the world 3 steps) necessary for them to reach the solution. Once again, then, the confounding of disciplinary and cognitive structures has taken place; the students obviously had mastered the relevant mathematics and had internalized this in some fashion, but the nature of the internalization cannot be inferred from their public performances.

2. The subsequent construction of the PERDIX computer program does not significantly strengthen Greeno's case (although certainly it is an impressive feat in its own right). I may be able to train my pet parrot to duplicate one of my standard verbal performances, but this does not mean that what is going on inside the bird-brain is going on inside me.[25] And there is the example of Weizenbaum's computer program ("ELIZA") which mimics quite convincingly the performance of a human psychiatrist. The psychiatrist asks his or her questions for complex reasons (which may, for example, derive from Freudian theory), whereas ELIZA was loaded with a series of gimmicky items (along such lines as "Tell me more about your mother") for the purpose of keeping the "conversation" going in a relatively undisjointed fashion. Indeed, Greeno should have taken Weizenbaum's work to heart, for the point of ELIZA was to demonstrate how a computer may erroneously appear to be

quite human.[26] Thus, the moral is that PERDIX may *appear* to act like a human geometry student, but appearances can be deceptive and in this case may be less than skin deep. As a commentator put it at a conference,

> Greeno has made use of a relatively new methodology in cognitive psychology, one that still has some grave shortcomings. . . . A rule-based system is a convenient way of instantiating the theory in the computers of today but it is not necessarily isomorphic with the structures found in the minds of Greeno's subjects.[27]

3. Greeno has drawn conclusions from his empirical data that are not really conclusions at all—they simply were assumptions underlying the research from the beginning, which he made explicit at the end. It appears that Greeno has had a long-standing commitment to the notion of conceptual structure—a commitment that predates much of his empirical work. In the first few years of the 1970s he coauthored several papers with references to structure in the titles. It is revealing to examine the content of one of these; a paper coauthored with Egan, which appeared in 1973.

After an introductory paragraph, the paper describes two experiments (in the aptitude–treatment interaction tradition) in which students learned concepts of probability by means of programmed texts. One group of students was taught relevant rules and formulae and applied these to problems, while the other group worked through the same examples but had to infer or discover the rules for themselves. Ability tests were given to members of both groups, and so was a post-test consisting of probability problems. The results indicated that students of low, medium and high ability performed differently in the "rule" and "discovery" groups—there was, indeed, an aptitude–treatment interaction and students of low relevant ability performed better when instructed by the rule method. Higher ability students taught by the discovery method appeared to do better on problems requiring a high degree of interpretation.

After some ten and a half pages devoted to reporting these matters, the authors' conclusions come like a bolt out of the blue:

> These data indicate that the result of learning by discovery is a well-integrated, cognitive structure.

And

> The result of learning by rule is primarily the addition of new components to cognitive structure rather than the reorganization of existing components.[28]

Conclusions are not "indicated" by data at all; conclusions are *drawn* or *reached* by researchers. And to reach conclusions, chains of reasoning are followed, and such chains contain premises. The empirical data merely constitute one set of premises, but there must be others—there must be premises that provide a link between the data and the conclusions.[29] Furthermore, investigators who accept the same data can reach wildly different conclusions if they use different links in the course of their chains of reasoning. One absolute requirement is that a term which appears in the conclusion (such as "cognitive structure") must appear somewhere in the premises; but in the case of Egan and Greeno it does not—it appears only in the opening paragraph of the paper where the authors summarized the conclusions they eventually were going to reach. In the *body* of their paper the crucial expression is conspicuous by its absence.

What, then, is the chain of reasoning of Greeno and Egan? It is as follows:

Premise (in summary): Data gathered during the research indicate certain differences in performance on probability problems between students of differing ability taught in different ways; etc.

Conclusion: Therefore, cognitive structures of students have changed in certain ways (e.g., discovery learning increases the integration of cognitive structure).

This reasoning is invalid; it is a *non-sequitur*. There is an immense "logical gap". To bridge it, at the very least some premise referring to cognitive structures is required, and so is a premise referring to how these structures become well-integrated. And, of course, these premises cannot merely be asserted—they have to be established. Palpably, the experiments reported by Egan and Greeno do not give them warrant to assert such premises, for their work only directly involved students working through programmed texts and solving problems. (They *thought*, needless to say, that they were depicting cognitive structures, but thinking this does not make it so. Evidence, or argument, is required.)

These missing and vital linking premises constitute, then, the underlying assumptions that the experimenters brought with them to their work. They merely have stated them—misleadingly—as conclusions. (Of course, another way of putting all this is that there are hosts of rival or alternative explanations that could be offered to account for their reported data. It is a simple fact of logic that a reader is not forced, by the data, to accept *any* conclusions about cognitive structures—as was seen in Chapter 2, theories are underdetermined by data.)

A final point needs to be made here. In responding to some of the preceding criticisms of his work Greeno made a point that, in effect, undercuts many of his own arguments together with those of Shavelson. He pointed out that

Ability to use the information of a subject also depends on the way in which that information is structured in memory, and the optimal organization for use may not correspond closely to the organization that is used in presenting and discussing the concepts, propositions, and principles themselves.[30]

From which it would seem to follow that data about how the concepts were presented publicly might not be a reliable guide as to how the information is structured in memory!

Reaction times

The discussion thus far has stressed one point: If a student succeeds (or fails) at some intellectual task, it might be possible to infer that he or she knows (or is ignorant of) some relevant and requisite item of knowledge. However, it is not possible to infer *from this alone* that the student's cognitive apparatus is in any particular configuration. In short, the structure of the student's cognitive structure cannot be determined from this data.

What in addition, then, would researchers need to discover in order to be able, in conjunction with the data about success or failure at the task, to infer something about the structure of the student's internal structures? Some researchers believe the answer lies in reaction time data.

Consider a hypothetical but nonetheless feasible experiment in what is known as the "fast-process" research tradition.[31] A simple question is devised and then phrased in different ways, for example negatively and positively. (Thus, "If John is taller than Bill, is Bill shorter than John?" and "If Bill is not as tall as John, is John not as short as Bill?") The question might also be worded so that the answer to one form of it is "Yes", and to another form "No". Different groups of subjects are then exposed to these alternate forms of the question via a computer console. The time taken for answers to be selected is measured (in microseconds) by how long it takes for the "Yes" or "No" button to be pushed. The results typically are that questions posed negatively take longer to solve, and that correct statements can be recognized more rapidly than incorrect ones. From this sort of data, inferences can be drawn about the complexity of the corresponding mental operations, the processes by which people judge the identity of statements couched in alternative forms, and so forth.

Sternberg has given a clear account of the logic of the "additive" and "subtractive" methods used here. The general idea is that if a complex mental process is made up of parts (say $a+b+c+d$), and if the time taken for the whole process is known, the time taken for various parts can be determined by devising related tasks that have one less or one more part.[32] The ingenuity of some of the experiments in this research tradition cannot be denied, and on the whole the experimenters are sophisticated about the assumptions they are making.

Nevertheless there are problems in trying to pin down the architecture of cognitive structures using such methods. Deciding whether two similar sentences actually are the same is a process that usually takes microseconds; solving a physics problem typically takes thousands of times longer (on the order of minutes). Eventually headway might be made, but it is a long way off. And there is another problem—while it may be the case that all humans process negative and positive statements the same way, and make comparative judgments about sentences in the same way, it does not seem to be the case that they solve physics problems the same way. But even if the *methods* they use happen to be the same (i.e., if the basic psychological processing is the same), it is not clear that the way they have *internally ordered* or interconnected their knowledge of physics must be the same.[33] Some may have internally arranged the subject historically, others by topic; some may have concentrated on memorizing principles and may need to reconstruct, as required, less central information; some tie the concepts of physics closely with those of mathematics or chemistry; and so forth. In all cases there will no doubt be complex idiosyncratic interconnections between what is remembered about physics and what is known in a variety of other areas. Furthermore, it cannot be said that any one organization of physics is best—it all depends upon the purposes, interests, background, and so forth, of the individual. What was best for Einstein would not be best for a Herbert Spencer or a Leonardo or the pilot of a jumbo jetliner.

None of this is to deny that for certain purposes it may be rewarding to study the psychology of experts. Herbert Simon and others have studied expert and novice chess players, and it is pertinent to note that the differences here do not seem to be differences in the basic processes each group has available, but rather are differences in noting and remembering significant features of the layout of the game, or differences in ability to compute the effects of moves. (It is not psychological processes, but knowledge of chess, that breeds experts.) But, again, if similar things were to be discovered about expert physicists, this would still not be revealing about the way "physics" was "structured" within their cognitive apparati.

Which structure should guide the teacher?

The question thus starts to surface: Why is it necessary to pin down how a discipline such as physics is structured within a learner, if defects in the public performance can easily be determined and are sufficient guide as to how the learner might increase his or her knowledge? What is the point of anything more? Determining the basic psychological processes that are at work is one thing, but mapping the idiosyncratic details of an individual's cognitive structure would seem to be—even if it were possible—too much of a Herculean task at this stage of the game.

The point at issue here can be put more strongly. If a young physics student gets a problem wrong because he or she does not know Einstein's formula ($E = MC^2$), then it matters little how his or her cognitive structure is organized. No matter how it is organized, the formula has to be known, and the teacher should bring it to the student's attention. As the philosopher David Hamlyn has argued, a curriculum decision about what ought to be taught in a subject, and in what order it ought to be taught, "is not a matter for psychology. I would emphasize this point."[34] And a little later in the same essay, he added:

That is to say that the best person to say how the teaching of, say, mathematics should proceed is the mathematician who has reflected adequately, and perhaps philosophically, on what is involved in his own subject.[35]

There is a somewhat more troubling case. Suppose that the student does know the formula, in that he or she can state it correctly when asked, "What is Einstein's formula?" But the student does not think to use the formula when tackling certain problems. Is this not a case where the cross-links in the student's cognitive structure are defective? Maybe so, but again the point is that a precise mapping is not required from a cognitive psychologist. The student has not made a connection, perhaps because it was not taught; good teachers are quite accustomed to reteaching a topic, bringing out points that experience has shown them their pupils have not mastered. (It needs to be re-emphasized that it is not being questioned here that there is some cognitive mechanism at work in the pupil, leading him or her to make the mistake. It may be a challenge for the psychologist to describe this mechanism, but this is not required in order for teachers or subject-matter experts to carry out effective teaching.)

Paul Hirst summarizes the pertinent issues well:

Concepts are acquired by learning the complex use of terms in relation to other terms and their application in particular cases. A subject's logical grammar and the order within it must be respected in all teaching methods, but this leaves a vast area in which experimental investigations about the effectiveness of different methods can and must be carried out.[36]

But Hirst stresses that

The logical grammar involved and the various possibilities for the logical sequence to be used, are matters for determination by an analysis of the subject to be taught, not for empirical investigation.[37]

On the misleading aspects of models

Models are important for guiding research, but they have a dark side. It is well known to philosophers of science that models can be misleading; they have features that are not at all analogous to, or isomorphic with, the phenomena being represented. Thus, to take a now out-dated example, billiard balls in revolution may faithfully capture some aspects of the structure of atoms, but they have irrelevant attributes (such as color and wind resistance). Mary Hesse called these aspects of a model the "negative analogy". The point of this for the present discussion is that it is hard not to be misled, when thinking about cognitive structures, by features of the models that are being used. In particular, cognitive scientists must guard against using, in a naive way, the language appropriate to the model ("billiard ball" language) when discussing the primary phenomena themselves.

Consider the way cognitive structures and schemata are given representation as networks or flow diagrams of the sort computer programmers are wont to draw. The literature is full of these impressive charts, and the accompanying texts refer to them in ways like the following: "representations" of cognitive or memory structures, "models", "measures" of cognitive structure, "diagram illustrating interrelations of memory structures and", "the processing of a problem by our system is based on a set of schemata", and so forth.[38]

There are a number of ways in which these diagrams, and even these ways of writing about cognitive structures, can be misleading. (But it should be emphasized that it is not being asserted that all researchers—especially the ones quoted here—are always misled.)

1. In the first place, these diagrams have a reassuring atmosphere of reality and concreteness about them. In this scientific age, even lay people have seen flow diagrams of industrial processes (such as oil refining), and have gazed in wonder at diagrams of the structure of complex molecules (and there can be little doubt that complex molecules exist). Cognitive structures depicted in a similar way as networks seem just the sorts of things that could have "psychological reality", and of course the sense of solidarity and permanence engendered by the term "structures" reinforces this. (The cognitive realm may be real, and it may have structure or organization, but it cannot be solid, physical, or spatial in the same way as the molecular realm.)

The sense of spatial and physical reality of the network begins to fade when it is realized that alternative ways of depicting the very same "structure" exist (not to mention the fact that innumerable rival structures could be hypothesized). Consider a simple analogy. The US taxation form is, in fact, a booklet filled with items requiring a response. These are set out in a slightly disguised tabular form—the taxpayer works through the items and instructions one by one. Many of the items, however, pose choices; and according to which alternative is selected the taxpayer is directed to different items, or different pages, or sometimes a completely different tax booklet. (Thus, "Are you married or single?"; "If filing a joint return, use tax schedule D": "If filing a separate return, use schedule. . . ."). Now, an alternative way of organizing the tax form would be in the style of a flow chart. Nodes on the chart would indicate the questions the taxpayer has to answer, and arrows or lines would lead to the next appropriate question; where choices exist several arrows would lead out from a node.

Similarly, in many cases of models of cognitive structure the material is presented as a diagram; but it could have been presented the way it was originally fed into the computer, that is, like a taxation form—a long series of statements and instructions often of an "If-Then" or "Either-Or" form. (Klahr and Wallace seem to deliberately avoid diagrams in their book and instead offer their readers illustrations of long tables of propositions and instructions that are programmable in a computer.)[39] Long tables or strings of sentences are less picturesque, less striking, less "solid", and less misleading in that they are less likely to engender the feeling of "psychological reality". The central point is that when alternative representations exist, the issue arises as to which—if any—of them is the one that approaches "closest" to reality. The issue is not entirely pre-empted by picturesqueness. Kieras makes, if not the same point, one that is related:

> It should be clear that internal representations can not be uniquely identified from behavioral data. Unfortunately, many in cognitive psychology have not understood or recognized this basic limitation on cognitive theory. Apparently their problem lies in a basic confusion on the logical status of various sources of knowledge used in the process of constructing psychological theories. . . . However, others, such as Anderson (1976, 1978) argue that the effort to determine what kind of representation people really use was misguided to start with.[40]

2. Picturesque models of cognitive structure—which are models in spatial terms—are involved in a three-way confusion. On one hand there are the spatial relations in the model itself: Nodes representing concepts, skills, or whatever, are linked by long or short lines to other nodes representing related concepts or skills. The greater the distance between any two points in the diagram, and the greater the number of intervening lines and nodes, the less closely related are these two particular points. Thus, in many of these diagrams, "concept relatedness—that is, semantic distance—is the central organizational principle", and:

> The length of lines connecting concept nodes indicates the strength of association between concepts. For example OSTRICH and CANARY are both instances of BIRD, but OSTRICH is further from BIRD than CANARY, thus indicating that canaries are semantically closer to the concept BIRD than ostriches are.[41]

On the other hand, there are the conceptual and logical relationships between the concepts of the discipline being studied by the student (such as physics). And, finally, there are the psychological or associationistic bonds or relationships within the cognitive apparatus of the student. The three types of relationship—spatial, conceptual, and psychological—are quite distinct and, as far as is now known, quite irreducible. Indeed, to confuse the picture even more, it must be admitted at this late stage in the argument that the tripartite Popperian distinction that has been used as a framework throughout may be oversimple. In a recent work on "mental models", Donald Norman distinguished between *four* different things:

> the *target system*, the *conceptual model* of the target system, the user's *mental model* of the target system, and the *scientist's conceptualization* of that mental model. . . . A *conceptual model* is invented to provide an appropriate representation of the target system, appropriate in the sense of being accurate, consistent, and complete. Conceptual models are invented by teachers, designers, scientists, and engineers.[42]

To illustrate Norman's point with an example: The behavior of physical matter could be a target system, in which case the discipline of physics would be the conceptual model; a student's conceptual structure or understandings of physics would be the user's mental model, and the cognitive researcher's model of what was happening in the mind of the student would be the scientist's conceptualization. At the risk of adding more straws that will break the camel's back, Norman's typography leaves out two more things: the structure of the biological or neural machinery that makes it possible for a student to form a mental model, and the biological or neural machinery that made it possible for the original scientists to construct the discipline (i.e. the conceptual model).

Whatever classification of domains is settled upon, it is clear that confusion arises when terminology appropriate to these various domains (each of which embodies different types of relationships) is not kept distinct. When a student learns that a proton is part of an atom, he or she has not reduced the distance between the two concepts (this is "model" talk), and he or she has not come to appreciate that there is a strong association between "atom" and "proton" ("psychological mechanism" talk). The student has learned there is a conceptual connection—a proton is part of an atom ("discipline" talk). Or, for another example, re-examine the quotation given above: "OSTRICH is further from BIRD than CANARY, thus indicating that canaries are semantically closer to the concept BIRD than ostriches are." The notion of "semantic closeness" is apt to be misleading, for all that can be meant is, for example, the rather trivial fact that a person is more likely to cite a canary than an ostrich when asked to name a bird. When you know that both canaries and ostriches are birds you have formed a conceptual link, and for most purposes in life (except, perhaps, party guessing games) it matters little which *particular* bird comes to mind when one is asked to name an example.

3. To consider another case in which graphs, flow-charts, and block diagrams exacerbate problems, notice the strangeness of Egan and Greeno discussing the degree of "integration" of a cognitive structure. Is a system that is composed of a geometrical theorem written down at Harvard, and its corollary written at Stanford, lacking in "integration"—and, if so, why? (Are spatial, logical, or psychological relations the key here?) "Degree of integration" is a particularly murky notion. Students know what they know; when they know some topic in physics, then they know it—they know the relevant concepts and their interrelationships. If they only partially know the topic, then they will know only some of the concepts and relations. Now, if their cognitive structure could be "inspected", it would be seen to contain these (few) concepts and relations (or their correlates); the issue of the structure lacking integration would not arise (taken for what it was, it would be integrated). Degree of integration only becomes an issue when what the student knows is compared with what could be known, in other words when the full range of concepts and relations found in the subject matter (e.g. physics) are taken as standards. So, once again Hirst and Popper are vindicated, and Egan and Greeno's talk of well integrated and relatively poorly integrated structures is seen to be a misleading way of referring to how well or how poorly students have mastered the subject they are studying.

Yet again, was Bruner hoping for something sensible when he wanted the growing child to "internalize events into a 'storage system' that corresponds to the environment?"[43] It will be recalled that in an earlier section of this chapter the problem was raised of how to characterize the "correspondence" or "isomorphism" between a world that physically exists in time and space, and a world of concepts that are related conceptually and logically but *not* spatially and temporally. It is worth noting in this context that Norman Malcolm has raised many of the relevant issues, and he has written:

> My aim in asking such questions is, of course, to induce the realization that we have no idea of how to answer them, and that this is because we don't know what we are talking about.[44]

Conclusion

One must not go overboard. The research problems of interest to Egan and Greeno, and the others, probably can be rephrased in less troublesome ways (although it may not always be an easy matter to do so). The point is that often the modes of expression that follow naturally from the models they are using are misleading, and they overlook the logical priority of the subject the learner is studying. To stay with Egan and Greeno for purposes of illustration, it seems that what is of concern to them is that students taught in different ways master different amounts of material and acquire the relevant skills to different degrees. This is a clear statement, but it is in Popperian world 3 terms. It is by judging the students against the discipline they are learning that the researcher detects deficiencies in them. It is not by inspecting their cognitive structures (which are not the sorts of things that are easily inspectable), nor is it by judging the mysterious "degree of integration" of these structures.

Notes and References

1. P. Hirst, "Liberal Education and the Nature of Knowledge", in R. D. Archambault, op. cit., p. 119.
2. L. Wittgenstein, *Philosophical Investigations*. NY: Macmillan, 1968, section 580.
3. J. Piaget, *Six Psychological Studies*, NY: Vintage Books, 1968, pp. 147, 152–3.
4. N. Malcolm, *Memory and Mind*, op. cit., Chapter X.
5. K. Popper, *Objective Knowledge*. Oxford: Oxford University Press, 1972, p. 163.
6. Ibid., p. 164.
7. John Watkins uses this as the frontispiece to his *Science and Skepticism*, op. cit.
8. R. J. Shavelson, "Methods For Examining Representations of a Subject-matter Structure in a Student's Memory." *Journal of Research in Science Teaching*, 1974 (11), p. 232.
9. R. J. Shavelson, "On Quagmires, Philosophical and Otherwise: A reply to Phillips", *Educational Psychologist*, 1983, **18**, p. 84.
10. Shavelson, "Methods For Examining Representations. . .", op. cit., p. 239.
11. Ibid., p. 241.
12. Ibid., p. 341.
13. Ibid., p. 242.
14. Ibid., p. 242.
15. D. E. Kieras, "Knowledge Representation in Cognitive Psychology", in L. Cobb and R. M.

Thrall (eds.), *Mathematical Frontiers of the Social and Policy Sciences.* AAAS Selected Symposia, **54,** 1980, p. 31.

16. R. J. Shavelson, "Some Aspects of the Correspondence Between Content Structure and Cognitive Structure in Physics Instruction", *Journal of Educational Psychology.* 1972, (63), p. 226.

17. R. J. Shavelson, "Some Methods for Examining Content Structure and Cognitive Structure in Instruction". *Educational Psychologist,* 1974 (11), p. 111.

18. Ibid., p. 116.

19. R. J. Shavelson, "On Quagmires, Philosophical and Otherwise: A Reply to Phillips", op. cit., p. 83.

20. There is a relevant discussion of simulation and explanation in psychology in Jerry Fodor, *An Introduction to the Philosophy of Psychology.* NY: Random House, 1968.

21. See N. Chomsky, *Language and Mind.* (Enlarged ed.) NY: Harcourt Brace Jovanovich, 1972, and N. Chomsky, *Rules and Representations.* NY: Columbia University Press, 1980.

22. L. Wittgenstein, op. cit., p. 232.

23. J. G. Greeno, "A Study in Problem Solving", in R. Glaser (ed.) *Advances in Instructional Psychology.* (I), Hillsdale, NJ: Erlbaum, 1978, pp. 13–14.

24. J. Greeno, ibid., p. 23–8.

25. See J. A. Fodor, *An Introduction to the Philosophy of Psychology.* NY: Random House, 1968.

26. D. C. Dennett, *Brainstorms.* Montgomery, VT: Bradford Books, 1978, p. 116.

27. H. M. Halff, "Discussion: Process Analyses of Learning and Problem Solving" in R. E. Snow, P. A. Federico, and W. E. Montague (eds.), *Aptitude, Learning and Instruction,* (2), Hillsdale, NJ: Erlbaum, 1980, pp. 90, 92.

28. D. E. Egan and J. G. Greeno, "Acquiring Cognitive Structure by Discovery and Rule Learning". *Journal of Educational Psychology,* 1973, (64), p. 96.

29. D. C. Phillips, "What Do the Researcher and the Practitioner Have to Offer Each Other?" *Educational Researcher,* 1980, **9,** 11, pp. 17–20.

30. J. Greeno, "Response to Phillips", *Educational Psychologist,* 1983, **18,** p. 76.

31. See R. Lachman, J. Lachman and E. Butterfield, *Cognitive Psychology and Information Processing: An Introduction.* Hillsdale, NJ: Erlbaum, 1979.

32. R. J. Sternberg, *Intelligence, Information Processing, and Analogical Reasoning.* Hillsdale, NJ: Erlbaum, 1977.

33. D. C. Phillips, "Muddying the Conceptual Waters: Research on Cognitive Change", in D. DiNicola (ed.), *Philosophy of Education 1981: Proceedings of the Conference of the Philosophy of Education Society.* Champaign, IL: P.E.S., 1981.

34. D. W. Hamlyn, "The Logical and Psychological Aspects of Learning", in R. S. Peters (ed.), *The Concept of Education.* London: Routledge, 1967, p. 33.

35. Ibid., p. 43.

36. P. H. Hirst, "Liberal Education and the Nature of Knowledge", in R. D. Archambault (ed), op. cit., p. 59.

37. Ibid.

38. Greeno, 1979, op. cit., pp. 29, 68; Greeno, 1980, op. cit., pp. 9, 10–13; Lachman, Lachman, and Butterfield, 1979, op. cit., p. 309; Shavelson, 1974, op. cit., pp. 119–20.

39. D. Klahr and J. G. Wallace, *Cognitive Development.* Hillsdale, NJ: Erlbaum, 1976.

40. D. E. Kieras, "Knowledge Representation in Cognitive Psychology", in L. Cobb and R. M. Thrall (eds.), *Mathematical Frontiers of the Social and Policy Sciences.* AAAS Selected Symposium 54, 1980.

41. R. Lachman, J. Lachman, and E. Butterfield, *Cognitive Psychology and Information Processing: An Introduction.* Hillsdale, NJ: Erlbaum, 1979.

42. Donald Norman, "Some Observations on Mental Models", in D. Gentner and A. Stevens, eds., *Mental Models.* Hillsdale, NJ: Erlbaum, 1983, p. 7.

43. J. S. Bruner, *Toward a Theory of Instruction.* NY: Norton, 1966, p. 5.

44. N. Malcolm, *Memory and Mind,* op. cit., p. 249.

13

Change and Development of Cognitive Structures: Piaget as Theorist

Whatever is inside the head of a student—or for that matter the head of a subject-matter expert—and however what is there is structured, it did not arrive in that state instantaneously. Children are not born being able to read, Einstein was not born knowing physics, and presumably Mozart—although precocious—was not born knowing how to write music. Whatever cognitive structure a person has, was itself constructed over time. There is, then, an inescapable developmental aspect to the story that is unfolding in the present group of chapters.

Thinking in terms of a hierarchy or sequence of developmental stages is a pervasive feature of the modern mind.[1] Erik Erikson formulated a hierarchy of stages in the development of the mature human personality; Havighurst had a sequence of developmental tasks; Gesell collected photographs of typical children of different ages; Dr. Spock wrote of the stages of baby growth in language understandable to the average parent; and Kohlberg investigated the stages of development of moral reasoning. But it was Piaget (together, often, with Inhelder) who brought the notion of developmental stages into the forefront of the modern consciousness.

First appearances

There can be little doubt that Jean Piaget did much to put teeth into the notion that as a child develops it constructs a set of cognitive structures. Several aspects of his stage theory were touched upon in the previous chapter, but much remains to be scrutinized. (It will turn out, during this critique, that there are many parallels with the work of the modern philosophers of science met earlier.)

Piaget approached his work as much as a theorist and philosopher as he did as an empirical researcher—so that the appropriate critical approach is as much to look for theoretical and philosophical flaws as it is to find empirical counterevidence. For, as Popper has pointed out

158

every *rational* theory, no matter whether scientific or philosophical, is rational in so far as it tries to *solve certain problems*. . . . Now if we look upon a theory as a proposed solution to a set of problems, then the theory immediately lends itself to critical discussion. . . . Does it solve the problem? Does it solve it better than other theories? Has it perhaps merely shifted the problem? Is the solution simple? Is it fruitful? Does it perhaps contradict other philosophical theories needed for solving other problems?[2]

It is not easy, however, to answer these Popperian questions about Piaget. In the first place, his writings were voluminous, and his ideas must be traced through books like *Biology and Knowledge, Genetic Epistemology, Structuralism, Psychology and Epistemology, Behavior and Evolution, Psychology of Intelligence,* together with his well-known earlier and more purely psychological volumes. But, perhaps even more seriously, Piaget's work has several internal problems that makes analysis of his ideas no easy matter: (1) the material is convoluted; (2) it is often very badly argued; and, (3) it often obfuscates or evades the central points at issue. Thus, the frustrated Theodore Mischel was led to write in a book review that

since the issues are not just empirical but heavily conceptual, their resolution requires the sort of skill in conceptual analysis that is the stock in trade of much recent Anglo-American philosophy. Piaget, perhaps because of his European background inclines him to think of philosophy as general speculations which can have no resolution, has not concerned himself with work in analytic epistemology that would be directly relevant to the issues that do concern him.[3]

Several examples will illustrate the dimensions of these related problems:

1. *Convolution:* The following passage may well be making an interesting point, but nothing much is apparent because it is so dense. The parallels with passages from Hegel are startling. The quotation is taken from an exposition of the key explanatory concept "equilibration":

In the equilibration of the integration and the differentiation, the necessity for negations is equally clear. On the one hand, to differentiate a totality, T, in subsystems, S, means not only to confirm what each of these possesses but also to exclude, or deny, the characteristics each system does not have. On the other hand, to form (to integrate) a total system, T, means to free positively the characteristics common to all the S, but this also means to distinguish—this time negatively—the common features of special characteristics not belonging to T. In short, the differentiation is based on negations and then, in turn, the integration implies them. The totality T is modified and remains superior in rank to S, but within a new enlarged totality.[4]

In order to assess the holistic aspects of Piaget's thought, and also the explanatory theories he develops, one first has to decipher passages such as this, assuming of course, that there is something here to be deciphered.

2. *Paucity of argument:* This example is taken from a dialogue Piaget had with the psychologist Richard I. Evans in 1973. Piaget answered a question about the difficulties encountered in moving back and forth between the disciplines of psychology and philosophy:

All epistemologists, of whatever school, are implicitly calling on psychology. Even if they maintain that they want to avoid any aspect of psychology, that is already a psychological position. The logical positivists, for example, claim to avoid psychology, in maintaining that logic can be reduced to language—to general syntax and semantics. Despite themselves, they have taken a psychological position. What we must keep in mind, then, is that every implicit psychological assumption could be, and should be, verified. This verification is what is missing from epistemology and philosophy. When you get into the field of verification, you are still concerned with the same problems, but they become more precise. Facts help to clarify them.[5]

Are the problems here rooted in the exposition, or do they result from weakness in the underlying position? In the first place, Piaget seems to be using the term "psychology" rather broadly; only this way can a case be made that the avoidance of psychology (such as the refusal to allow psychological aspects into a theory about the nature of logic) is itself a "psychological position". In normal usage—the usage Evans clearly intended in asking his question—the avoidance of psychology is certainly a position, but it is a higher order or "meta" or even philosophical position. The problem is compounded when Piaget goes on to say that assumptions should be verified. It is not at all clear if he means that this should hold true also in epistemology and philosophy. It is not clear what even *counts* as verification in these fields and many epistemologists would oppose the suggestion—one that Piaget does make in various places, as will emerge later—that facts (including the facts that Piaget gathers in his interviews with children) help to clarify the problems of epistemology and philosophy. Of course, this is the very issue Evans was puzzled about and which he was discussing with Piaget. The latter's answer was merely begging the question.

3. *Obfuscation:* The final example to illustrate the difficulties in dealing with Piaget's prose, and the philosophical thought which may (or may not) lie beneath it, is a footnote attached to a discussion of cognitive structures in *Genetic Epistemology*; the issue is pertinent, given the investigation of the status of such structures in the previous chapter:

The reader may ask here whether "structures" have real, objective existence or are only tools used by us to analyze reality. This problem is only a special case of a more general question: do relations have objective independent existence? Our answer will be that it is nearly impossible to understand and justify the validity of our knowledge without presupposing the existence of relations. But this answer implies that the word existence has to be taken to have a multiplicity of meanings.[6]

Here Piaget was attempting to have his cake and eat it too; after about eighty words the reader is no closer to understanding whether or not he thought structures have "objective reality". The last sentence is a particularly delightful evasion that brings the reader back full circle. One wonders why Piaget bothered to put pen to paper at all.

Being charitable is a civilized virtue, and no doubt one could find reason to exercise it in Piaget's case. But charity also begins at home, and what is required is a sufficient reason—in the name of philosophy—to extend it to Geneva.

A characterization of Piaget as philosopher and theorist

If there is any philosophical or theoretical merit in Piaget's writings, it cannot lie entirely in the sophistication or ingenuity of many of his specific arguments and formulations, which too often were defective in the ways that have been illustrated. Rather, much of the interest must arise from the direction in which he was attempting to move (that is, it must come from the problems with which he was grappling, together with the general manner in which he was attempting to solve them). In giving a characterization of this, it is convenient to use the terminology coined by William James.

It will be recalled from Chapter 8 that in his *Pragmatism*, James argued that on the basis of temperament one could divide philosophers into two broad categories—the "tender-minded" and the "tough-minded"; he added that most "have a hankering for the good things on both sides of the line." Tender-minded philosophers tend to be rationalistic, intellectualistic, idealistic, optimistic, religious, freewillist, monistic, and dogmatic;[7] tough-minded philosophers, on the other hand, are likely to be empiricist (they go by "facts"), sensationalistic, materialistic, pessimistic, irreligious, fatalistic, pluralistic, and skeptical.[8]

Piaget has to be classed among the tender-minded, even though, significantly, he had a slight hankering for toughness. Raised in the Continental rationalistic tradition, he saw serious "gaps" in empiricism. And he had what Brian Rotman calls a "Kant connection",[9] although he modified the doctrines of the master in significant ways; it is here that his attempt at toughness, at "going by the facts", is of great interest. Furthermore, he was a holist (not to mention a structuralist) in the neo-Hegelian sense of this term (discussed in Chapter 7); it is relevant in this context to note that William James wrote that "rationalism means the habit of explaining parts by wholes".[10]

What is the chief way in which Piaget attempted to modify or toughen the tender-minded syndrome? To put it briefly and somewhat crudely, like those in the Kantian tradition he held that all human experience is mediated by categories (or, in his terms, structures). However, these are not innate but are developed or constructed by the individual as a result of interaction with the environment. Experimental psychology and biological theory are able to cast as much light on the nature and operation of these structures as can philosophical investigation. Hence the joining, in some of his book titles, of epistemology with psychology, biology, and genesis. Brian Rotman's words are worth quoting to help set the stage for the later discussion, although the picture is slightly oversimplified:

> . . . it is worth recalling in general terms how thoroughly Kantian Piaget's theory of mind is. Apart from his earliest studies, all of Piaget's work on children's cognitive structure is dominated by the Kantian picture of a cognizing mind constructing the world according to the intellectual categories and the forms of spatio-temporal intuition. Naturally Piaget

presents his model of mind in terms not available to Kant, namely the structuralist language of algebraic groups of operations; but the organizing framework is precisely the same. It is true that within this framework Kant and Piaget diverge on method. Piaget's approach is concerned with the empirical question of how children and hence adults come to possess these faculties.[11]

In the following discussion, the focus will be upon the way in which Piaget took this modified Kantian philosophy, and with it tried to solve a cluster of theoretical problems in developmental psychology, problems that cluster around a central puzzle: Why does the individual develop at all? At first sight, to call this a puzzle may itself seem puzzling, but the issue can be driven home by using an analogy drawn from the new philosophy of science discussed in earlier chapters. (It is an analogy that has been noted by a number of writers.) As it develops, the child undergoes massive changes in world-view, and accompanying massive changes in cognitive structure, and this seems to be analogous to what has happened during the history of science, when (in Kuhn's terms) there have been major paradigmatic shifts. But the earlier discussion showed that it is always possible for a scientist to stick to his or her guns in the face of new and recalcitrant experience—it is always possible to make changes in a world-view in such a way as to minimize the impact of the new data. (The data can be ignored, or *ad hoc* hypotheses added, or the hard core can be protected by blaming an auxiliary hypothesis for the anomalous data, and so on.) In short, theories—whether those of a scientist or of a child—are underdetermined by nature. Thus the scientist is not *forced* to undergo revolutionary change, so why should the developing child?

The construction of structures

Initially, then, it seems relevant to focus upon Piaget's account of the development of cognitive structures in the individual child, a topic that was touched upon in the previous chapter. To simplify the exposition, and also to highlight some features that will be crucial later, it will be a useful device from time to time to pursue the comparison between the Piagetian child and a mature scientist.

Consider a scientist who is researching the behavior of plastic materials under certain conditions of temperature and pressure. He* will bring with him to his work what has been variously described as a paradigm, a disciplinary matrix, a conceptual scheme or a *Weltanschauung*. In the following discussion the expression "scientific world-view" will be used as a label for this important, if abstract, entity. As the earlier chapters have shown, the structure, and development, of scientific world-views has been the focus of interest in a great deal of recent work in philosophy, philosophy of science,

---

*To avoid confusion, the scientist will be "he", and the Piagetian child "she".

and philosophy of education, not to mention educational and cognitive psychology.

Armed with his intricate intellectual apparatus, the scientist will work with his plastic materials. And if the research should prosper, his knowledge will grow. The oddities that he turns up—the appearance of unexpected properties or phenomena, the apparent breakdown of laws, or the failure of a theory to predict changes in the experimental material—will have to be accommodated.

Now, as indicated earlier, there are some striking similarities between this prototypical scientist, and the child as depicted by Piaget. For the Piagetian child, at whatever stage of development, brings with her to the activities of her daily life (such as playing with a ball of clay) a world-view with rather similar components to that of the scientist. The child's conceptual scheme will be far less sophisticated, and will perhaps be changing at a different rate to that of the scientist, but it will still be made up of concepts, rudimentary laws, theories and principles, and some elementary mathematics and logic.

Piaget, however, distinguishes between the parts of this world-view which involve "knowledge of environmental data, which will eventually enable the subject to comprehend the exterior world objectively", and the parts which are logico-mathematical.[12] Concepts belonging to the first part are not merely "copies" of reality, Piaget insists; concept formation is dependent upon the subject engaging in physical activity, and the process also involves "co-ordination". Sometimes Piaget refers to the resulting groups of concepts as "causal structures".[13] The logico-mathematical structures, on the other hand, arise from the process of "reflection" upon these co-ordinated actions rather than from the actions themselves. And, as Piaget points out, these latter structures, "in the human child, are even to be observed in elementary form before there is any systematized physical knowledge".[14] The following passage is a good summary:

> I should like now to make a distinction between two types of actions. On the one hand, there are individual actions such as throwing, pushing, touching, rubbing. It is these individual actions that give rise most of the time to abstractions from objects. . . . Reflective abstraction, however, is based not on individual actions but on co-ordinated actions. Actions can be co-ordinated in a number of different ways. They can be joined together, for instance; we can call this an additive co-ordination. Or they can succeed each other in a temporal order . . . Now all these forms of co-ordinations have parallels in logical structures, and it is such co-ordination at the level of action that seems to me to be the basis of logical structures as they develop later in thought.[15]

Armed, then, with a variety of structures, the child plays with some clay, and in the course of ongoing experience she will turn up oddities that will need to be accommodated. (At this stage it would be possible to digress to discuss the highly "inferential" nature of Piaget's conclusions; the evidence that a scientist possesses or lacks certain concepts and skills is quite direct compared with the evidence that a child possesses or lacks such things.)[16]

The structure of cognitive structures

It is important to note at this stage that the scientist under scrutiny does not possess a disorderly array of concepts, laws, and logico-mathematical structures. There seems to be some *organization*, but the details of this are controversial, as was argued in the previous chapter. But, as will be recalled from that earlier discussion, and also the discussion in Chapter 2, the pervasive image is of a network. The more abstract theories and concepts of the world-view are located deep inside the mesh, while concepts and empirical laws closely related to the observable realm (for example, concepts such as temperature and volume which can easily be defined in terms of operations) are near to the edge of the network. Even if a small area within a particular science is taken for examination, the network analogy is appropriate. The words of Carl G. Hempel are worth re-quoting from Chapter 2:

> A scientific theory might therefore be likened to a complex spatial network: its terms are represented by the knots while the threads connecting the latter correspond, in part, to the definitions and, in part, to the fundamental and derivative hypotheses included in the theory. The whole system floats, as it were, above the plane of observation and is anchored to it by rules of interpretation. These might be viewed as strings which are not part of the network but link certain points of the latter with specific places in the plane of observation.[17]

It will be recalled that a similar interpretation, but applied to the whole of a scientific world-view and not just to specific theories within the field of science, is held by W. V. O. Quine. In his influential paper "Two Dogmas of Empiricism", Quine chose the image, not of a network but of a forcefield:

> The totality of our so-called knowledge or beliefs, from the most casual matters of geography and history to the profoundest law of atomic physics or even of pure mathematics and logic, is a man-made fabric which impinges upon experience only along the edges. Or, to change the figure, total science is like a field of force whose boundary conditions are experience.[18]

In Quine's view, the logico-mathematical portions of this "field of force" are located well away from the boundaries; they are relatively stable but even these portions *could* be changed in order to preserve from change some other more favored part of the net.

In contrast to the scientist, a greater portion of the intellectual equipment of the Piagetian child is in a state of flux. Although her passage from infancy to adulthood forms a developmental continuum, for descriptive purposes it can be divided up into the well-known periods and sub-periods (it is this descriptive part of Piaget's work, of course, that has become so famous with lay people and educators). As the child progresses, it seems as if her mental structures—according to Piaget's account—become more comprehensive and better integrated or *equilibrated*:

> According to this point of view, intellectual operations, whose highest form is found in logic and mathematics, constitute genuine actions, being at the same time something produced by the subject and a possible experiment on reality. The problem is therefore to understand how operations arise out of material action, and what laws of equilibrium govern their evolution; operations are thus conceived as grouping themselves of necessity into complex systems,

comparable to the "configurations" of the Gestalt theory, but these, far from being static and given from the start, are mobile and reversible, and round themselves off only when the limit of the individual and social genetic process that characterizes them is reached.[19]

Piaget did not specifically refer to the overall intellectual structure of the child as being in some sense "layered", or as being a network with the relatively unchallengeable portions near the center. As commented upon earlier, he did claim that there are two types of structures present in the mental equipment of the child—the logico-mathematical ones and the ones that embody concepts pertaining to the nature of the physical world. Even in one of his earlier books, *The Child's Conception of Physical Causality* (first published in English in 1930), he distinguished between these, which he called the logical structures or formal category, and the real structures or category, and he pointed out that they had parallel and interacting courses of development.

A reader is hampered from forming a clear picture of the overall organization of these structures by severe terminological difficulties. A typical case is the following paragraph from *Six Psychological Studies*:

> Logic in the child (as in the adult) is evidenced in the form of operational structures; i.e. the logical act consists essentially of *operating*, hence of acting on things and toward people. An operation is, in effect, an internalized action which has become *reversible* and co-ordinated with other operations in a grouping, governed by the laws of the system as a whole. To say that *an operation is reversible* is to say that every operation corresponds to an inverse operation, as is true, for example, for logical or arithmetic addition and subtraction. An operation never exists in isolation. It is dependent on an operational structure such as the "groups" in mathematics . . . or lattices or the structures that are more elementary than groups and networks, which we call "groupings". Each of these structures involves law of totalities which define the operational system as such and a particular form of reversibility (inversion in the group, reciprocity in the lattice, etc.).[20]

The picture that can be built from all this shows the intellectual equipment of the Piagetian child (or for that matter, of the adult) as being made up of a *number* of structures. Each of these structures is a system in the holistic sense that its parts are dynamically interrelated so that the "whole is more than the sum of the parts". Furthermore, in the child these structures are in a state of flux. They are changing or developing, moving always towards a more stable equilibrium. A slight alteration (or accommodating change) to any part of one structure will alter the whole structure; this follows as a corollary of Piaget's holism. Finally, the various individual structures are not entirely independent, but are themselves dynamically interrelated. And to highlight the similarity and differences between Piaget's view and that of the philosophers and methodologists discussed previously, the logico-mathematical structure has, for Piaget, a somewhat privileged position. It is, to be sure, not safely enmeshed and protected the way it is depicted by Quine and others; on the contrary, it is much closer to the "firing line" of contact with the physical surroundings. The privileged position of this structure lies in its primacy. The other structure, composed of concepts and relations directly pertinent to contact with the physical environment, would not be what it is were it not for the mediating influence of this logico-mathematical structure. As Piaget put it:

> Physical knowledge or experimental knowledge in general (including the geometry of the actual world) proceeds on the other hand by abstraction based on characteristics of the objects as such. We must therefore expect the role of perceptive fact to be greater in this second field. *But—and this is essential—in this field also, perception never acts alone. Only by adding something to perception do we discover the characteristic of an object.* And what we add is precisely nothing but a group of logico-mathematical limits which alone make perceptive reading possible . . . there is no experimental knowledge which can be qualified as "pure", detached from all logico-mathematical limits consisting of classifications, functions, and so forth.[21]

The words which have had emphasis added here have an unmistakable Kantian ring.

It appears that there are good grounds for the argument that there is only a trivial difference between Piaget and the views so far cited of many contemporary philosophers. This difference consists, basically, of a dispute over the best sort of pictorial representation for a cognitive structure. The philosophers opt for something like a network, with the logico-mathematical elements lying near the center, while Piaget opts for several networks, one of these being logico-mathematical in nature. In both images there exists the possibility that the concepts, laws and theories which are constructed to deal directly with the physical environment will reflect the influence of logico-mathematical portions of the world-view.

Accommodatory mechanisms and the problem of change

For Piaget more than for Quine or Hempel, and certainly more than for Kant, questions of genesis and of change are primary. (In a sense, Piaget was more of a kindred spirit to Kuhn and Lakatos.) How do cognitive structures develop? What changes take place as the child has new experiences with the toys in her crib? Furthermore, if each individual constructs her own structures, then how is it that the process has the same results for everyone? To put it bluntly, Piaget faces a particularly severe form of the problem that has plagued all biologically and functionally-oriented positions in the social sciences—the problem of accounting for change.

A skeptical note can be introduced here in order to highlight the problem facing Piaget. It seems reasonable to suppose that not all adults accommodate to anomalous experience in the same way. Some of us, when challenged, rethink our presuppositions, but we rethink them differently from the way our friends rethink theirs; others adopt simple *ad hoc* hypotheses, or merely deny that the new evidence is relevant. Some become victims of groupthink, as Irving Janis calls it; some will sublimate; and for others the diverse processes known to resolve cognitive dissonance will bring relief. In such cases, our individual cognitive structures will change along different lines. If Piaget is right, however, there seems to be no such diversity among children. It is, perhaps, comforting but rather romantic to suppose that children are innately wiser, in that all of them unerringly select the "most adequate" strategy by which to adjust, when those who begot them are so obviously floundering. We are entitled to ask Piaget about the "homeostatic" mechanism that is at work in children, and to explain why it apparently stops functioning in adults.

Some light can be shed by again considering the scientist, who on the basis of his present world-view (embodied in his cognitive structure) is making a prediction about the elasticity his plastic material will display when it is cooled a few degrees nearer absolute zero than he has ever chilled it before. He performs the experiment, and the results shatter his prediction. Which part of his scientific world-view requires adjustment? Contemporary literature in the philosophy of science contains an abundance of advice on this matter, but—as will be recalled from Chapter 2—the overall thrust is that experience alone cannot dictate that a change be made to a specific portion of a scientific world-view. To revert to the earlier metaphor, because the world-view is structured like a network, experience that seems to threaten a specific part of the net can—but need not—be dealt with by changing this part which is most closely "aligned" with the experience. But it is equally possible to alter some other portion of the net to compensate, perhaps by adding *ad hoc* hypotheses, or by altering some law or theory, or perhaps by going deep into the net and changing the geometry (e.g., from a Euclidean to a non-Euclidian form) or even the logic. It all depends on which portions the scientist, or the scientific community, decides ought to be kept intact. Thus, if our scientist finds his prediction does not come true when his plastic is chilled near to absolute zero, he could abandon his hypothesis and be forced to change the part of his conceptual network containing his concept of the plastic material; but alternatively, he could accommodate by altering the portion of his network pertaining to elasticity ("the law of change of elasticity with temperature does not hold within x degrees of absolute zero"), or he could hold that his measuring procedures fail at such extreme temperatures, and so on. These changes all preserve the stock of information already established in science, and they successfully accommodate the new experimental result—they successfully restore "equilibrium". They will, however, differ with respect to implications for future research, but this may not become apparent for some time.

This, as we have seen, is the message often found in the writings of the recent philosophers of science—Imre Lakatos, Paul Feyerabend, and W. V. O. Quine. Feyerabend even stresses that it has sometimes been fruitful (in cases from the history of science) to ignore evidence that challenges portion of the present world-view, in the hope that something will eventually turn up to account for it. Quine's words are a good summary of this general orientation:

Any statement can be held true come what may, if we make drastic enough adjustments elsewhere in the system. Even a statement very close to the periphery can be held true in the face of recalcitrant experience by pleading hallucination or by amending certain statements of the kind called logical laws. Conversely, by the same token, no statement is immune to revision. Revision even of the logical law of the excluded middle has been proposed as a means of simplifying quantum mechanics . . . A recalcitrant experience can, I have urged, be accommodated by any of various alternative re-evaluations in various alternative quarters of the total system.[22]

In the light of these contemporary trains of thought, Piaget's discussion of the process determining the direction of change of the individual child's cognitive structures seems remarkably deficient. Consider the following passage from *Genetic Epistemology*:

To my way of thinking, knowing an object does not mean copying it—it means acting upon it. It means constructing systems of transformations that can be carried out on or with this object. Knowing reality means constructing systems of transformations that correspond, more or less adequately, to reality. They are more or less isomorphic to transformations of reality. The transformational structures of which knowledge consists are not copies of the transformations in reality; they are simply possible isomorphic models among which experience can enable us to choose. Knowledge, then, is a system of transformations that become progressively adequate.[23]

At first sight, Piaget's acknowledgement that there are several "possible isomorphic models" is reminiscent of the philosophers' argument that there are several ways a world-view can be constructed (or reconstructed) to cope with experience. But even without going further afield in Piaget's writings some problems emerge. In the first place, he stresses several times that these alternative models, or structures, which can be developed are isomorphic— isomorphic with reality, and hence, presumably, with each other. It is far from clear what is meant here, but the most straightforward interpretation would be that the models have the same "logical structure", that is, the same arrangement of "elements", otherwise, how could they possibly be isomorphic? In this case, the alternative models would be essentially the same, for it would be only a translation problem to move from one to another. The following two sentences are isomorphic in this straightforward sense; to arrive at the second from the first is a simple translation exercise:

(1) The cat is on the table.
(2) Rfc ayr gq ml rfc ryzjc.

Now, according to the positon advanced by the contemporary philosophers of science, there can be no question of isomorphism between the alternative world-views that can conceivably result when a scientific world-view is adjusted as a consequence of facing anomalous experience. For one scientist might advocate the adoption of an exotic geometry in order to accommodate, while another may argue for the addition to the corpus of science of a specific *ad hoc* hypothesis, and a third may suggest that some fundamental physical principle (like the conservation of parity) requires revision. The elements in these three world-views would not be the same; there would be no isomorphism. And yet all three world-views would presumably account for previously established scientific knowledge and explain the new and challenging experience.

Changing structures: "biological Kantianism"

A related problem emerges from Piaget's claim that "knowledge . . . is a system of transformations that become progressively adequate". In various of this writings[24] he acknowledged, like a good Kantian, the impossibility of obtaining an absolute gauge of external reality by means of which we could appraise the adequacy of our cognitive structures. So the test of adequacy became a functional—and in the final analysis, a biological—one.[25] It was central to much of Piaget's writing (as it was to Dewey's) that humans are part of physical (or external) reality, and have evolved within it. Piaget, like Dewey, believed that probably the most important of the adaptive mechanisms which have helped the human species to flourish is the capacity to exercise intelligence. In much of his voluminous work on this general issue, Piaget did not talk of the resulting knowledge (or the resulting intellectual structures) as being adequate mirrors of reality, but he preferred, not surprisingly, to use biological phraseology:

> It is in this sense that intelligence, whose logical operations constitute a mobile and at the same time permanent equilibrium between the universe and thought, is an extension and a perfection of all adaptive processes. Organic adaptation, in fact, only ensures an immediate and consequently limited equilibrium between the individual and the present environment. Elementary cognitive functions, such as perception, habit and memory, extend it in the direction of present space (perceptual contact with distant objects) and of short-range reconstructions and anticipations. Only intelligence, capable of all its detours and reversals by action and by thought, tends towards an all-embracing equilibrium by aiming at the assimilation of the whole of reality and the accommodation to it of action, which it thereby frees from its dependence on the initial *hic* and *nunc.* [26]

During these biologically oriented discussions Piaget seems never to have considered seriously the possibility that, at any instant in time, there are a *number* of non-isomorphic, equally functional or "adequate" ways in which the external world could be conceptualized. There may be several configurations of the child's network or world-view that allow the same answer to be given to questions put to the child by a researcher. Or, to put it slightly differently, there seem to be no good grounds to support Piaget's assumption that there is only one particular configuration of a cognitive structure that will set it in equilibrium. If an individual is in a state of equilibrium when he or she has theories and beliefs (and so on) that facilitate "satisfactory" dealings with the environment, and if rival sets of theories can function this way (as the principle that theories are underdetermined by nature indicates), then it follows that the process of equilibration alone is not sufficient to assure that individuals will come to construct identical (or even highly similar, on whatever criterion) cognitive structures.

There are passages—that again are hard to interpret—that indicate Piaget may have had further considerations in mind to account for the supposed fact that we all come to share the one set of physical theories and interrelated logico-mathematical structures that he regarded as truly adequate. He seemed to postulate a biological link or chain between the cognitive structures of the adult and the realities in the external world, an aspect of his thought that was closely related to his alliance with contemporary structuralism.

The nature of this link is explicated in great detail in *Biology and Knowledge*, and it is conveniently summarized in the concluding paragraph of *The Child and Reality*. The conscious mechanisms of humans—what John Dewey somewhat vaguely called the capacity to think or carry out inquiries—are extensions of (and for Piaget they were isomorphic with) biological or organic mechanisms that occur throughout the animal kingdom, but these in turn are determined by physico-chemical causes in the external world:

> This isomorphism of conscious implication and of organic causality can be conceived as a special case of correspondences between deduction and material reality which characterize the whole circle of sciences. Let us suppose the logico-mathematical structures placed in sufficient isomorphism with organic structures, then the latter explained causally in an efficient manner by a "generalized" physico-chemistry ... until the biological fact is encompassed. This physico-chemistry itself could not help becoming mathematical and deductive, thus based, as a point of departure, on its point of arrival ... It is in the perspective of such a circle, or if we prefer, of such a constantly increasing spiral that it is probably fitting to situate the problems of relation between life and thought.[27]

One thing, at least, is very clear here: the argument involves an important confusion. By some sleight-of-hand, or slip of the argument, the mathematical description of the cognitive structures in the mind of the individual has become transformed into the mathematical structure of the physical (and biological) world. And this is not an isolated manoeuvre of Piaget's. As indicated in Chapter 12, there are places where he confused (or confounded or conflated) all three of Popper's worlds—he ran together such things as the structure of a part of the world, the structure of our theories dealing with the structure of this part of the world, and the structure of the psychological structures by which we master such theories or deal with such parts of the world.[28] If Piaget had convincing reasons for flying in the face of commonsense (or rather, of commonsense metaphysics), that is, if he was not merely confused, then he owed his readers a more forthright account.

Carol Feldman and Stephen Toulmin point to essentially the same confusion in a related aspect of Piaget's work:

> Nowhere, it seems, are the differences between the problem involved in *formally representing* a theory and the problems involved in *empirically testing* it so difficult to keep separate as in the area of cognition. Just because the theoretical system in question can plausibly be presented as corresponding to some mental system in the mind of the actual child, we may be led to conclude that the formalism of the theoretical system must be directly represented by an isomorphic formalism in the mind of the child. In their account of the development of spatial knowledge, for example, Piaget and Inhelder (1956) deliberately blur the distinction between topology and Euclidean geometry as formal systems for describing (a) the spatial relations which constitute the phenomena the child copes with, and (b) the forms in the child's

mind. In this way, ontological reality is assigned to the hypothetical mental structures of the theory simply on the basis of the formal expressions by which they are represented in the theory.[29]

There seems no escaping the conclusion, then, that notions like isomorphism and equilibration (and the related assimilation, accommodation and homeostasis) cannot do the work Piaget required of them. There is a growing body of critical literature on these, which it is not necessary to summarize here.[30] One passage from Brian Rotman's lengthy discussion should suffice;[31] it is taken from a context where Rotman had been attacking Piaget's "biological Kantianism" for failing to recognize that any evolutionary-oriented account of the development of knowledge in the individual (Piaget, it turns out, believed ontogeny recapitulates phylogeny) conflicts with the description of such development as a linear progression through a fixed series of stages.[32] On the notions of equilibrium and equilibration Rotman stated:

> But, as we have seen, there is no reason to suppose that increasingly stable equilibrium —whatever this is finally to mean—pursues a single path. Certainly the evolution of species, whether thought of in terms of equilibrium, or in any other way, cannot be described as a linear progression. There is, therefore, the question of which of the many paths forward from protozoa to their more complex descendants is the line of true progress, since presumably they have all evolved according to the identical laws of equilibrium.[33]

There are several routes for escape from this dilemma. It could be acknowledged that individuals have different conceptual structures (and thus notions like equilibration could be kept as central); or one could stress more than Piaget did the importance of social pressures in determining the direction of cognitive development (this is the line taken by, among others, the Soviet psychologists Vygotsky and Luria, and David Hamlyn[34] thinks it is the key to a significant conceptual weakness in Piaget); or one could fall back to a modernized version of Kantianism by stressing the existence of innate structures (which are, perhaps, produced by the genetic inheritance of our species). This last position is the one adopted by Noam Chomsky; he regards Piaget's viewpoint as "obscure in crucial respects" and he argues:

> Piaget develops a certain "constructive interactionism": new knowledge is constructed through interaction with the environment. But the fundamental question is evaded: *how* is this knowledge constructed, and why *just this kind* of knowledge and not some other? Piaget does not give any intelligible answer, as far as I can make out. The only answer that I can imagine is to suppose an innate genetic structure which determines the process of maturation. Insofar as he considers it wrong to give such an answer, he falls back into something like the empiricism that he wants to reject. What he postulates is nowhere near sufficient, it seems to me, to account for the specific course of cognitive development.[35]

The attack on empiricism

This passage by Chomsky raises the issue of Piaget's attitude towards empiricism: why, indeed, did he reject it? In many of his books there are passing references to the matter, but perhaps the most detailed discussion is in a paper written with Barbel Inhelder, "The Gaps in Empiricism".

It rapidly becomes apparent that Piaget—and presumably his coauthor —had little understanding of the empiricist philosophical tradition as it had developed in the English-speaking world in the late nineteenth and twentieth centuries. There is no mention of Russell or Ayer or any of the dozens of others who might have been expected to be candidates for discussion. They did mention Herbert Spencer—it is to be hoped that they were not serious in considering him to have been the deepest representative of the tradition they were attacking; they referred to "classical associationist empiricism" and to behaviorism; they mentioned Chomsky's successful attack on Skinner's theory of verbal behavior; and they made passing reference to Quine.

This latter, rather than being a sign of profundity, turns out to be their Achilles' heel:

> ... the great logician Quine was able to show the impossibility of defending a radical dualism of analytic and synthetic judgments (this "dogma" of logical empiricism, as Quine amusingly termed it). Moreover, a collective study by our Centre for Genetic Epistemology has been able to verify Quine's objections experimentally by finding numerous intermediaries between the analytic and synthetic poles.[36]

The point, of course, is that Quine was not putting forward a psychological or experimental hypothesis; he was making a conceptual point, and experimentally "verifying" it is as much out of place as it would be if the proposition under consideration was that "all black objects are black". Anthony Quinton has a forthright statement of the general point that Piaget and Inhelder seem to have not grasped:

> As distinct from such earlier empiricists as Locke, Hume and Mill, the members of this tradition, which has been the standard or classical form of epistemology, in Britain at any rate, in this century, have been quite definite that their purpose is to give logical analysis of knowledge as it actually exists and not a genetic or historical or psychological account of its growth. In Reichenbach's useful phrase, they are offering a rational reconstruction of our knowledge which sets out the reasons that logically justify our beliefs and not a narrative of the causes that in fact led us to adopt them.[37]

Piagetians consistently overlook this issue of justification of knowledge-claims. In Chapter 4 of his book *Psychology and Epistemology*, for instance, Piaget discussed empiricism under the heading "The Myth of the Sensorial Origin of Scientific Knowledge", and it was only the psychological issue of origin, rather than the modern epistemological issues of logical analysis and justification, that was identified as relevant.

So, in "The Gaps in Empiricism", Piaget and Inhelder systematically misrepresented modern empiricism by psychologizing it;[38] the bulk of their discussion focussed on associationism and behaviorism, and there was some exposition of experimental studies. They started on this track in the first paragraph of their paper, where they introduced empiricism in these terms:

> ... we find a central idea: the function of cognitive mechanisms is to submit to reality,

copying its features as closely as possible, so that they may produce a reproduction which differs as little as possible from external reality. This idea of empiricism implies that reality can be reduced to its observable features and that knowledge must limit itself to transcribing these features.[39]

This was no mere slip; the move of introducing the functioning of cognitive mechanisms was important, for it allowed Piaget and Inhelder to link up the three main points they wished to make—the three "gaps" they see in empiricism. If they had opened with a more philosophically-oriented account of empiricism (even the *Dictionary of Philosophy*[40] would have given them nine alternatives to choose between), then at least two of their points (and possibly all) would have been discarded as irrelevant.

The first gap in empiricism, according to Piaget and Inhelder, was that "biologists have shown that the relationship between an organism and its environment . . . is one of constant interaction".[41] Here they were simply mistaken; as discussed in Chapter 2, this is no "gap" at all, for empiricism relates not to the details of the processes by which knowledge is acquired, but rather it concerns the logical justification of knowledge-claims. There is no reason why an empiricist, *qua* empiricist, cannot accept the fact of organism–environment interaction.

The second "gap" Piaget and Inhelder saw in empiricism concerns mathematics, a field which they pointed out "clearly escapes from the constraints of outer reality".[42] In their discussion, Piaget and Inhelder covered material they had often presented before—the use of geometry by the Egyptians, Cantor's updating of mathematical procedures known to children and primitive societies, and the like. But again, the discussion was curiously uninformed about twentieth-century disputes in the philosophy of mathematics, or the views on mathematics held by writers in the empiricist tradition—Bertrand Russell's name is conspicuously absent. The issue of rival geometries (Euclidean and non-Euclidean), and which of them is applicable to the universe, was never mentioned. Brian Rotman, himself a mathematician, concludes that "Piaget's characterization of mathematics and of its creation is limited by certain misconceptions".[43]

The remaining "gap" in empiricism was introduced in the following way:

Thirdly, as man acts upon and modifies reality, he obtains, by transforming his world, a deeper understanding than reproductions or copies of reality could ever provide. Furthermore, cognitive activity can be shown to have structural properties.[44]

This, of course, was a reaffirmation of the Piagetian viewpoint rather than an argument against empiricism. But, once again, the crucial point is that empiricists need not deny that humans may act upon (and even modify) "reality"; and many have regarded empiricist philosophy as quite compatible with the development of "deeper understanding" of the physical world. The issue is not the methods of inquiry that are adopted, but the logical justification or status of the knowledge that is obtained. To drive this home, it is worth quoting from Bertrand Russell's account of the nature of the physical world (although the overlap with Quinton's message earlier will be apparent):

> ... we do not, in fact, experience many things that we think we experience. This makes it necessary to ask ... in what sense physics can be based upon experience, and *what must be the nature of its inferences if it is to make good its claim to be empirically grounded.*[45]

In so far, then, as in his theorizing he stressed interaction with the environment, and eschewed *a priori* or innate structures or categories, Piaget—as Chomsky pointed out—approached close to the empiricism he thought he had effectively criticized. Piagetian cognitive structures are modified (or undergo accommodatory changes) as a result of their facing recalcitrant experience, and equilibrium will only be attained (if ever) when there are no more surprises coming from further experience. The effectiveness of a structure is judged, in other words, in experiental terms. All this reeks of empiricism. It seems that, in trying to psychologize or biologize Kant, Piaget innocently wandered across the border into tough-minded territory.

The relevance of psychology for epistemology

In his attacks on empiricism, Piaget misrepresented certain issues by psychologizing them. Does the same criticism apply more generally—did he err in coupling epistemology with genesis, psychology, and biology (a coupling he flaunted in his book titles)?

At first glance it may seem that Piaget was advancing an exciting thesis. In the opening pages of his *Psychology and Epistemology*, he appears to hold a conception of epistemology that would be endorsed, not only by Quinton and Russell, but also by Popper, Reichenbach and many others:

> Epistemology is the theory of valid knowledge, and even if this knowledge is never in a state and always forms a process, this process is essentially the passage of a lesser to a greater validity.[46]

He then went on to make the bold assertion that psychology can make a contribution to epistemology thus conceived.

Several contemporary philosophers, who are well aware of the distinction between the genesis and the justification of beliefs and knowledge-claims, seem to have been favorably impressed by this Piagetian epistemological program. As early as 1953 Wolfe Mays read an enthusiastic paper on precisely these issues to the Aristotelian Society;[47] and more recently Susan Haack has attempted to evaluate the arguments, pro and con, concerning the relevance of psychology to epistemology, and she comes down in support of Piaget's stance (as opposed to Popper's, which she takes as representative of the view that there is a well-nigh unbridgeable gulf between the two disciplines):

> But Piaget, unlike Popper, seems willing to include the historical, sociological and psychological questions which arise in the study of the growth of knowledge, as part of epistemology. The use of such locutions as "developmental epistemology" and "scientific

epistemology" signals a generous view of the scope of epistemology . . . Piaget is committed to a thesis which Popper strenuously denies, viz., that psychological data can be relevant to questions of the validity of theories.[48]

Unfortunately, a closer reading of Piaget's writings raises serious problems about his position. The last passage quoted from Piaget, which Haack also cites, is one of the few where he used the term "validity". The examples he gave to flesh out this general statement—and certainly many of his other general discussions—indicate that he actually had something quite different in mind. In brief, he was concerned with the "logical structure" of bodies of knowledge—with the architecture of cognitive structures—rather than with what Quinton, Popper, Reichenbach and others would call the validity or justification or warranting of the items of knowledge *qua* knowledge. This is clearly demonstrated in a passage, which occurs within two pages of the last quotation from Piaget, where he spelled out what he took to be involved in establishing the validity of "norms" (by which, in this discussion, he meant rules or principles such as conservation and transitivity):

> Next is the problem of the validity of these norms. The logician must now formalize structures suitable to these successive stages, pre-operatory structures (without reversibility, transivity, or conservations but with qualitative identities and oriented functions, likewise qualitative with corresponding but quite elementary, trivial MacLane type of "categories") or operative structures (with "group" or "grouped" characteristics).[49]

For an alternative account of Piaget's position, consider the opening pages of *Genetic Epistemology*, where Piaget proceeded without using the term "validity" at all. He started by saying that genetic epistemology attempts to "explain knowledge" on "the basis of its history" and especially by the "psychological origins of the notions and operations upon which it is based".[50] Now, in this way one certainly can "explain knowledge", in the sense of showing from whence it has come; but there is nothing so far in this account to show that the items under consideration are indeed knowledge—or, to put it in Dewey's terms, that the items have "warranted assertibility".

Piaget continued by pointing out that genetic epistemology, conceived in this way, "runs into a major problem, namely, the traditional philosophical view of epistemology". This looks promising, but it quickly becomes apparent that Piaget again was skirting around the issue of the validity or justifiability of the knowledge-claims:

> For many philosophers and epistemologists, *epistemology is the study of knowledge as it exists at the present moment; it is the analysis of knowledge for its own sake and within its own framework* without regard for its development.[51]

The words that are emphasized here are amenable to interpretation in terms of analysis of validity of knowledge-claims, but Piaget did not clearly state that this is what he understood traditional epistemology to be concerned with. His words also can be interpreted as saying epistemology is concerned with analysis of the structural relations between the items of (so-called) knowledge.

This second interpretation of Piaget's understanding of epistemological validity is made plausible by the preceding discussion in the present chapter, which has highlighted Piaget's interest in the "architecture" and dynamics of conceptual structures. Piaget's further discussion in *Genetic Epistemology*, and his examples here and also in *Psychology and Epistemology*, heavily tip the scales in this latter direction.

Piaget's answer to this "major problem" his genetic epistemology faces at the hands of traditional philosophers is a triumph of obfuscation. He merely reasserted his original position, dressed up in different language so that it appeared to be a rebuttal of the objection:

> Scientific knowledge is in perpetual evolution: it finds itself changed from one day to the next. As a result, we cannot say that on the one hand there is the history of knowledge, and on the other its current state today, as if its current state were somehow definitive or even stable. . . . Scientific thought is . . . a process of continual construction and reorganization.[52]

Thus, the structure of Piaget's argument early in *Genetic Epistemology* may be summarized as follows:

Piaget 1:   Genetic epistemology considers genesis is relevant to understanding present knowledge.
Traditional objection: This is confused. Genesis is irrelevant to validity.
Piaget 2:   It is not confused, because genesis is relevant to understanding how present knowledge evolved.

The examples Piaget uses to illustrate the genetic epistemological method do nothing to save the day. He again mentioned Cantor's work in mathematics, Einsteinian and Newtonian physics, the structures developed by the Bourbaki group of mathematicians, time and speed in physics, the doctrine of object-permanence in the light of contemporary microphysics, and the notion of change.[53] In discussing these examples, he never showed how understanding genesis or psychological origin establishes the truth, validity, justifiability or warranted assertibility of these various knowledge-claims. In fact, it is far from clear what the examples do show; sometimes the point seems to have been that the scientist or mathematician has made new use of primitive (or child-like) structures of thought, and sometimes Piaget seemed concerned to explain why a piece of work overcame psychological barriers to its acceptance.

It is interesting to reflect upon what would have to be argued in order to establish that issues concerning genesis were relevant to whether or not knowledge-claims were valid or justifiable. It would need to be shown that there are some psychological or developmental processes, the unadulterated operation of which ensures that a true or valid or warrantedly assertible endpoint would be reached.[54] Piaget was right in believing that the dominant tradition in epistemology denies that this can be shown, and the recent philosophers of science who were discussed earlier have strongly reaffirmed this negative conclusion.[55] As indicated throughout the present chapter,

Piaget was not able to make a breakthrough and he often nimbly sidestepped the central issues.

Conclusion

Piaget's attempt to orient the foundations of epistemology towards biology and psychology—the attempt to toughen the tender-minded syndrome—must be rated as a failure. And it is a little more than ironical to find the following words in his introduction to *Insights and Illusions of Philosophy:*

> ... philosophy, as its name implies, is a "wisdom", which man as a rational being finds essential for co-ordinating his different activities, but is not knowledge properly so-called, possessing safeguards and methods of verification characteristic of what is usually called "knowledge".[56]

If this same insight had infused the rest of Piaget's work, a different conclusion might have been warranted for the present discussion.

Notes and References

1. For the logic of such theories, see D. C. Phillips and Mavis Kelly, "Hierarchical Theories of Development in Education and Psychology", *Harvard Educational Review*, **45**, August 1975.
2. K. Popper, *Conjectures and Refutations*, op. cit., p. 199.
3. T. Mischel, "Can Genetic Epistemology be Divorced from Epistemology?" *Contemporary Psychology*, (21), 1976, p. 164.
4. J. Piaget, *The Development of Thought*. NY: Viking Press, A. Rosin, trans, 1977, p. 11.
5. R. I. Evans, ed., *Jean Piaget: The Man and His Ideas*. NY: Dutton, 1973, p. 34.
6. J. Piaget, *Genetic Epistemology*, op. cit., p. 23.
7. W. James, op. cit., p. 23.
8. Ibid., p. 22.
9. B. Rotman, *Jean Piaget: Psychologist of the Real*. Ithaca, NY: Cornell University Press, 1977, pp. 24–31.
10. W. James, *Essays in Radical Empiricism, and A Plurative Universe*. NY: Dutton, (A Pluralistic Universe, Lecture 1.) 1971.
11. B. Rotman, op. cit., p. 151.
12. J. Piaget, *Biology and Knowledge*. Chicago: University of Chicago Press, 1971, p. 28.
13. J. Piaget, *The Principles of Genetic Epistemology*. W. Mays (trans), London: Routledge, 1972, p. 24.
14. J. Piaget, *Biology and Knowledge*, op. cit., p. 28.
15. J. Piaget, *Genetic Epistemology*. NY: W. W. Norton, E. Duckworth (trans), 1971, p. 18.
16. D. C. Phillips. "The Piagetian Child and the Scientist: Problems of Assimilation and Accommodation", *Educational Theory* (28), Winter 1978.
17. C. G. Hempel, *Fundamentals of Concept Formation in Empirical Science*. Chicago: University of Chicago Press, 1952, p. 36. See also A. Pap, *An Introduction to the Philosophy of Science*. London: Eyre & Spottiswoode, 1963, p. 52.
18. W. V. O. Quine, "Two Dogmas of Empiricism", in his *From a Logical Point of View*. NY: Harper and Row, 1961, p. 42.
19. J. Piaget, *Psychology of Intelligence*. NJ: Littlefield, Adams, 1969, pp. 16–17.
20. J. Piaget, *Six Psychological Studies*. NY: Vintage Books, A. Tenzer (trans.), 1968, p. 121, Piaget's emphases.
21. J. Piaget, *Psychology and Epistemology*. NY: Viking Press, A. Rosin (trans.), 1972, pp. 72–3.
22. W. V. O. Quine, "Two Dogmas . . ." op. cit., pp. 43–4.
23. J. Piaget, *Genetic Epistemology*, op. cit., p. 15.
24. For example, see *Biology and Knowledge*, Section 23.

25. This is a theme in *Biology and Knowledge*, Section 23. See also T. Mischel, "Piaget: Cognitive Conflict and the Motivation of Thought", in T. Mischel (ed.), *Cognitive Development and Epistemology*, op. cit.

26. J. Piaget, *Psychology of Intelligence*, op. cit., p. 9.

27. J. Piaget, *The Child and Reality*. NY: Viking Press, A. Rosin (trans), p. 172.

28. For two examples located close together, see *Six Psychological Studies*, op. cit., pp. 147, 152–3.

29. C. Feldman and S. Toulmin, "Logic and the Theory of Mind". *Nebraska Symposium on Motivation 1975: Conceptual Foundations of Psychology*. Lincoln: University of Nebraska Press, 1976, pp. 416–17.

30. See as introduction to this literature: Mischel, 1971, op. cit.; Phillips, 1978, op. cit.; also Sophie Haroutunian, *Equilibrium in the Balance*. NY: Springer-Verlag, 1983.

31. Rotman, op. cit., p. 118.

32. Ibid., p. 106.

33. Ibid., p. 116.

34. D. Hamlyn, *Experience and the Growth of Understanding*. London: Routledge, 1978, pp. 58–9.

35. N. Chomsky, *Language and Responsibility*. NY: Pantheon Books, 1979, pp. 84–5.

36. J. Piaget and B. Inhelder, "The Gaps in Empiricism", in A. Koestler and J. R. Smythies (eds), *Beyond Reductionism: The Alpbach Symposium*. London: Hutchinson, 1972, p. 544.

37. A. Quinton, *The Foundations of Knowledge*. Reprinted in R. Chisholm and R. Swartz, eds, *Empirical Knowledge*. NJ: Prentice-Hall, 1973, p. 544.

38. For a recent discussion of psychologism, and Popper's attitude towards it, see M. A. Notturno, *Objectivity, Rationality, and the Third Realm*. Dordrecht, Netherlands: Nijhoff, 1985.

39. Piaget and Inhelder, "The Gaps in Empiricism", op. cit., p. 118.

40. *Dictionary of Philosophy*. D. Runes (ed), NJ: Littlefield Adams, 1967, pp. 89–90.

41. Piaget and Inhelder, "The Gaps in Empiricism", op. cit., p. 119.

42. Ibid., pp. 118, 122–7.

43. B. Rotman, op. cit., p. 131.

44. Piaget and Inhelder, "The Gaps in Empiricism", op. cit., pp. 118–19.

45. B. Russell, op. cit., p. 128. (My emphasis.)

46. J. Piaget, *Psychology and Epistemology*, op. cit., pp. 7–8.

47. W. Mays, "The Epistemology of Professor Piaget", *Proceedings of the Aristotelian Society*, 1953, **54**, pp. 49–76.

48. S. Haack, "The Relevance of Psychology to Epistemology", *Metaphilosophy*, **6**, 1975, p. 175.

49. J. Piaget, *Psychology and Epistemology*, op. cit., pp. 9–10.

50. J. Piaget, *Genetic Epistemology*, op. cit., p. 1.

51. Ibid., pp. 1–2. (My emphasis.)

52. Ibid., p. 2.

53. Ibid., pp. 3–8 and *Psychology and Epistemology*, pp. 7–21.

54. Perhaps Piaget can be seen as an early representative of the "reliabilist" trend in epistemology. See the symposium in *The Monist*, 1985, **68**, nos. 1 & 2.

55. For example, the work of Lakatos and Feyerabend suggests that no methods can be ruled out, or counted upon, in the search for scientific truth.

56. J. Piaget, *Insights and Illusions of Philosophy*. W. Mays (trans), NY: Meridian, 1971, p. xiii. For a more generous interpretation of Piaget as philosopher, see James Marshall and Michael Peters, "New Perspectives on Piaget's Philosophy", *Educational Theory*, Spring 1986, 36, pp. 125–136.

14

Kohlberg's Stages of Moral Development: A Lakatosian Critique*

Just under a decade ago the *New York Times* ran a series of articles on the current state of various academic disciplines. Eventually it was psychology's turn to face the scrutiny of the press. The story could not have been an easy one to write, but the author jumped skillfully from Skinner to I.Q. to evaluation methodology without saying much and without missing footing by slipping into the morass of Freudianism, Chomskyanism, information processing models, and the like. Nevertheless, there was one interesting passage:

> Drawing on Piagetian evidence that cognitive development involves a series of stages that emerge as the child interacts with its environment, Dr. Lawrence Kohlberg of Harvard has demonstrated that similar stages of moral development emerge as the individual gains experience in making moral judgments. His theory is now being put to work in several schools and in a Connecticut prison.[1]

This authoritative statement nicely exemplified the then—and still—current myth that the stage theory of moral development has, in fact, been "demonstrated" and all that remains is to put it to work.

To the skeptic, however, the article better illustrates the old principle that one ought not to believe all that is written in a newspaper. During the past few decades there has been considerable controversy, amongst methodologists and philosophers of science, over what constitues a satisfactory "demonstration" of a theory; as should be apparent from the preceding chapters, many would reject this whole approach to understanding the growth of scientific theories (holding instead that theories are replaced, or overthrown, but that none are ever proven to be true). Thus, it is not clear that Kohlberg, or any one else, *could* have "demonstrated" anything. Although there are many researchers at work using Kohlberg's theoretical framework, truth in science is not established on the basis of a head-count. There are important critics and there are many unresolved technical issues that need to be considered. Whether the specifics of Kohlberg's work are focussed upon, or whether a somewhat

*Much of this chapter is based on earlier material coauthored by Jennie Nicolayev.

179

broader view is taken and more general issues about the nature of scientific research are examined, the situation is not nearly as simple as those reading the *New York Times* over Sunday brunch may have concluded.

The discussion that follows is intended to illustrate the usefulness of the set of ideas developed by Imre Lakatos; these ideas will not be defended here, but rather, they will be applied. For Kohlberg's work raises important general issues, as well as issues particularly of interest to developmental psychologists and educators. Over several decades Kohlberg, together with his students, former students, and colleagues, has been pursuing a vigorous research program; this work is a "moving target", for it is (and must be) in constant flux as the researchers uncover new data and develop more refined techniques. In a paper published in 1982, Kohlberg himself sketched the various changes his theory had undergone during a quarter of a century.[2] The general issue, then, is how such work in progress can be assessed. (Although it involves the making of delicate judgments, only work in the Kohlbergian "mainstream" will be discussed in any detail; work which originated within the tradition but which eventually diverged—such as that of Carol Gilligan—will only be mentioned in passing. Gilligan's work, for all its major differences, also retains important elements in common with that of Kohlberg.[3])

A preliminary statement: Lakatosian research programs revisited

The question of how to assess individual theories in order to determine if they are scientific has, in the past, been given a great deal of attention. In recent times, however, this focus has been changed by the work of Lakatos and others,[4] which grew out of the Popperian tradition and which was, in part, in opposition to the theses put forward by Thomas Kuhn (a story recounted more fully in earlier pages). As Paul Feyerabend has summarized this new train of thought:

> The methodology of research programmes develops standards for the evaluation of (scientific, or, more generally, conceptual) change. The standards apply to research programmes, not to individual theories; they judge the evolution of a programme over a period of time, not its shape at a particular time; and they judge this evolution in comparison with the evolution of rivals, not by itself.[5]

The point of this new orientation is that scientific thought is in constant flux: new experimental results are being obtained, new phenomena are being encountered, novel perspectives are arising from the work of theorists, and old facts and anomalies are being reinterpreted or explained away. According to Lakatos, it is difficult, if not impossible, to find criteria for "instant rationality",[6] that is, criteria by which the worth of current events in science can be judged. Today's "crucial experiments" may be shown by later events not to be crucial at all and anomalous experimental results that now might be regarded as only a small "cloud in the clear sky" may, in the light of subsequent events, turn out to be revolutionary.[7]

Faced with these realities, the methodologist is in a difficult position with respect to giving advice about what practices are illegitimate in science. Not all *ad hoc* hypotheses are to be eschewed; the writing off, as anomalous, of results that are difficult to explain has not always been a fruitless stratagem; and so on.

In brief, as will be recalled from the earlier discussion, the position reached by Lakatos was that successive changes in a branch of science—or what he calls a research program—should be progressive. Changes or "improvements" to theories, the stratagems adopted to accommodate difficult experimental findings, and so forth, should always be content-increasing:

> Mature science consists of research programmes in which not only novel facts but, in an important sense, also novel auxiliary theories, are anticipated; mature science—unlike pedestrian trial-and-error—has "heuristic power".[8]

In Lakatos' view, a scientific research program is rather like a new game with evolving rules. Central to the activity are certain ingredients that the gamesters do not want to change under any circumstances. In his colorful terminology, these form the "hard core". To preserve this core, there must be other ingredients that are expendable or subject to change in the light of experience. These form the "protective belt". And finally, changes in the program are directed by the "positive heuristic".

> The negative heuristic specifies the "hard core" of the programme which is "irrefutable" by the methodological decision of the protagonists; the positive heuristic consists of a partially articulated set of suggestions or hints on how to change, develop the "refutable variants" of the research programme, how to modify, sophisticate the "refutable" protective belt.[9]

It was suggested earlier that a clear case can be made that the theory of moral development advanced by Lawrence Kohlberg and his associates forms a research program in the Lakatosian sense. (On occasion this has been challenged, but the challenge is easily answered.[10]) Although there were some classic psychological studies of moral behavior by Hartshorne and May in the 1920s, and although Piaget had written on the subject, the date usually associated with the birth of this domain is 1958, when Kohlberg completed his doctoral dissertation. Since that time, there has been a flurry of experimental work, theoretical revision, and reconstruction of experimental techniques. The question is, have these activities been content-increasing? Is the program a progressive one or has it stagnated and, in Popper's words, begun "to lose its empirical character"?[11]

Some aspects of Kohlberg's hard core

(a) Stages of development

A researcher interested in moral behavior, or in how people think about moral issues (these two matters, of course, need not be the same), is not necessarily committed to a developmental orientation, much less to the view that there are clearcut stages of development. It is a hard fact of life that there are many conceptions of the nature of morality and about how humans should act in particular moral situations. It is at least debatable that these rival positions are on a par, each with their own strengths and weaknesses, rather than being located in a hierarchy of increasing adequacy. Instead of conceiving of individuals as moving up a hierarchy, then, one could view them as perhaps randomly distributed between a number of relatively viable alternative positions, among which they move as they find reason to abandon one and adopt another. And it may even be the case that most individuals have come to adopt a stance endorsed by some "significant other"—a parent or other significant relative, or an influential teacher or minister of religion, or a key peer. Another alternative conception, based upon a paper by Henry D. Aiken with which the young Kohlberg was well acquainted,[12] is that there are several levels of abstraction in moral thinking, and everyone uses all of these levels, adopting in a particular case the level of thought that seems most appropriate given the specific circumstances.

Kohlberg and his associates, however, have apparently chosen to disregard such alternative accounts. It has always been part of their irrefutable hard core that an individual's moral reasoning progressively passes through a series of stages. In a paper by James Rest, at that time one of Kohlberg's collaborators, the following forthright account of the stage theory was given:

> Kohlberg (1958, 1959) has characterized the development of moral judgment in terms of a typology of six stages. Each stage is defined as a distinctive orientation to moral problems, and it is claimed that the six stages represent an invariant, universal developmental sequence. . . . The usual method of stage assessment is to present to a subject a hypothetical moral dilemma, ask the subject to tell what he would do in the situation, and ask for reasons for his choice of action. A scorer then classifies the reasoning according to established scoring guides (Kohlberg, 1958). Evidence that Kohlberg's stages depict a natural sequence of development comes from observations that older subjects manifest higher stage characteristics (c.f. Kohlberg and Kramer, 1969), and that when change is induced it tends to be to the next highest stage (c.f. Turiel, 1969).[13]

In addition to clearly explicating the Kohlbergian stage claims, this passage nicely illustrates the Lakatosian point that judging whether a theory is progressive at a particular point in time is impossible. Scientists involved in a program may *claim* that all parts of their theory have to stand up to the evidence, but whether in fact they *allow* all of their theory to face this test can only be revealed by studying the interplay between theory and evidence over an extended time period.

Rest's repeated references to the evidence pertaining to Kohlberg's hard core would lead one to believe that if refuting evidence were found, the Kohlbergians would be prepared to abandon the hard core. Clearly, however, in the almost three decades that the program has existed, the assumption that moral development occurs in fixed stages has not been given up. Indeed, it could not be given up, for then nothing of the program would remain. What would remain of tennis if it were no longer played on a flat, rectangular, specially marked court? Most of the old rules would not be applicable to the new game; old skills would not be useful; and the traditions associated with the game would become antiquated. Similarly, the price for Kohlbergians abandoning the stage hypothesis would be enormous. The words of three of Kohlberg's coworkers give a glimpse of what would be at stake:

> ... how does the researcher collect appropriate data and proceed to identify, validly and reliably, moral development stages? The question is of course crucial, for if the stage constructs cannot be reliably and validly scored, then the empirical significance is problematical.
> The bridge we use to span the gap between theory and data—that is, our research instrument—has three parts: a standard moral interview format, "structural" interviewing techniques, and a standard-form scoring manual.[14]

The point here is that whither goes the stage hypothesis, so goes the research instrument, taking the rest of the hard core with it.

(b) Invariance

When a park ranger at Yosemite expounds on the stages of development of an Alpine meadow, it is well understood that he or she is presenting what could be called a trend theory. There is a tendency for certain stages to occur but it would not be surprising to find a meadow where the stages had occurred somewhat differently. Similarly, certain events might occur in a fairly definite order when an underdeveloped society undergoes rapid modernization; however, sociologists would not be shocked to discover a case where the general trend had not been reflected.

Trend theories are, in fact, the best that can be hoped for in most areas of behavioral research. Any generalizations that are discovered are probabilistic in nature, and rarely (if ever) hold true for all members of a relevant sample or population.

Against this background, the Kohlbergian hard core appears extremely bold: not only are there stages of moral development, but the order in which individuals pass through the stages is invariant. Kohlberg makes it clear that there is not merely a trend for the stages to occur in a fixed order:

> The progression, or set of stages ... implies something more than age trends. In the first place, stages imply invariant sequence. Each individual child must go step by step through each of the kinds of moral judgment outlined. It is, of course, possible for a child to move at varying speeds and to stop (become "fixated") at any level of development, but if he continues to move upward, he must move in accord with these steps.[15]

Or as he put it in an earlier paper,

> the concept of stage implies an invariance of sequence in development, a regularity of stepwise progression regardless of cultural teaching or circumstance. Cultural teaching and experience can speed up or slow down development but it cannot change its order or sequence.[16]

Now the significance of an invariance claim is that it applies to *all* cases; as defined by Webster, "invariant" means "not varying" or "incapable of varying". "B invariantly follows A" means, therefore, that "there can never be an example of a B which does not follow an A". On the face of it, this claim is eminently scientific in the strict Popperian sense; it is a clear, bold claim full of empirical content and hence is easily testable. It would take only one case of variation—one case in which B did not follow A—to refute such a claim.

It is obvious, then, that the insistence on invariance could put the hard core at risk and if the latter is to survive, it must be protected against what would appear, *prima facie*, to be refuting evidence. The easiest path, of course, would be to soften the claim: "there is a tendency for B to follow A" is a generalization that would not be thrown into a jeopardy by cases of B which did not follow A. For their own reasons, however, the Kohlbergians do not choose to take the easy path.

(c) Logical necessity

There may well be developmental sequences in nature that are invariant. Suppose that it is always the case that insects pass through the sequence of egg, larva, pupa, and finally imago (sexually mature adult). It could not be other than what it is; it is necessarily the case that the pupal stage comes after, and not before, the larval stage.

It is clear that, at best, this is a case of empirical or nomic necessity. The laws of nature being what they are, it is biologically impossible for the larval stage to follow the pupal stage. Furthermore, this sequence had to be discovered; it could not be deduced from the initial meanings of the terms "pupa" and "larva" that one necessarily follows the other. ("Initial" is important here, for after some time the word "pupa" might undergo a change of definition, and might come to mean "stage of insect development that follows the larval stage".) In the same way, it could not be deduced from the meanings of the words that lightning precedes thunder. On the other hand, it can be deduced that a black object must be black.

In light of this discussion it is interesting to note that the Kohlbergians introduce "necessity" into their hard core, but it is not merely nomic or empirical necessity (which, in fact, they specifically reject). A much more startling claim is made:

> the step-by-step sequence of stages is invariant. The sequence represents a universal inner logical order of moral concepts, not a universal order found in the educational practices of all cultures or an order wired into the nervous system. Since each new basic differentiation at each stage logically depends upon the differentiation before it, the order of differentiations could not logically be other than it is.[17]

This is truly dramatic. If the claim stands, the hard core is brilliantly protected against any possible counterevidence. For of course, matters of logical necessity are immune from empirical refutation. The generalization that "all black objects are black" is logically true and no evidence could possibly shake it. Indeed, what would even count as counterevidence?

Challenges to the hard core

It is evident that the three aspects of the Kohlbergian research program that have been discussed are closely interrelated: moral development occurs in stages, the order of which is invariant and also logically necessary. The first two claims of this tripartite hard core are pseudo-empirical—it is *apparently* the case that evidence could be found that bears upon them. The third claim, however, is non-empirical, and this must be dealt with first. The focus in the present section will be upon the challenges to the hard core; the ways in which the Kohlbergians have defended their central assumptions will be examined later.

(a) Logical necessity

Kohlberg's startling claim that the stage sequence "represents a universal inner logical order of moral concepts" has attracted some attention in the literature, but on the whole the discussion has been much too gentle.[18] The claim still stands as part of the hard core. Just what the claim amounts to, however, is not perfectly clear.

On a charitable interpretation, there are three things that could be intended when it is claimed that the stages of moral development are logically necessary. On two of these interpretations the claim is clearly incorrect, and on the other, at best only several of the six stages of moral development are logically necessary.

(i) On the first interpretation, the expression "logically necessary" could, perhaps, be used in the sense of "logically possible". However, it is most unlikely that Kohlberg had this in mind. Logical possibility is a most charitable category; a great many things that are physically impossible are logically possible. Thus, everything in the universe, plus a great deal that is not, is logically possible. It is logically possible for pigs to fly, for ants to be a mile long, and for developmental psychologists to be mistaken.

(ii) On a second—and more likely—interpretation, "logically necessary" could be used in the sense of "true by definition". In this sense, it is certainly logically necessary that all bachelors are unmarried and that all black objects are black. Such statements are often identified in the technical literature as being trivially true.

(iii) According to a third interpretation, "logically necessary" could be used in the sense of "is presupposed"; thus "A is logically necessary for B" could mean "A is presupposed by (or is a presupposition of) B". According to this reading, when a person argues for the utilitarian view that moral principles are those which are conducive to the happiness of the greatest number of individuals, it is clear that this view presupposes that the notions of "happiness" and "moral principles" are meaningful. Furthermore, to know the meaning of "moral principles" presupposes that one knows what a principle is. So, to put it another way, the notion of a principle is a presupposition of—and in this third sense is logically necessary for—the utilitarian moral view.

Now in which of these three senses is it the case that Kohlberg's third developmental stage—to take one stage arbitrarily as an example—must, by logical necessity, come after Stages 1 and 2 and not before them? Empirically, of course, it may be the case that the third stage must follow the first two, but that is not the issue. Consider Kohlberg's description of stages one and three:

> Stage 1—*Punishment and obedience orientation.* The physical consequences of action determine its goodness or badness regardless of the human meaning or value of these consequences. Avoidance of punishment and unquestioning deference to power are valued in their own right . . .
> Stage 3—*Interpersonal concordance or "good boy—nice girl" orientation.* Good behavior is that which pleases or helps others and is approved by them. There is much conformity to stereotypical images of what is majority or "natural" behavior . . .[19]

It should be obvious that in neither of the three senses of the expression is it "logically necessary" for Stage 3 to occur after Stage 1. (i) It is not logically impossible for Stage 3 to occur before Stage 1. It is not a logical contradiction, however empirically implausible it may be, to claim that first an individual believes good behavior pleases or helps others, and later the individual moves to the view that the physical consequences of an action determine its goodness or badness. (ii) Neither is it true by definition that Stage 3 must follow Stage 1. "The physical consequences of an action determine its goodness or badness" is not part of the meaning of "good behavior pleases or helps others"; whereas "is unmarried" is part of the meaning of "bachelor", in which case "a bachelor is unmarried" is true by definition. (iii) While it is certainly the case that the moral views endorsed by individuals at both Stages 1 and 3 have presuppositions, it is not the case that the third stage actually presupposes (i.e. logically entails) the first stage.

In general, then, the Kohlbergian claim for logical necessity has not been substantiated. Furthermore, it is not clear why the claim was added to the hard core in the first place. Scientific theories are not strengthened by being made true by definition—certainly the theories of Newton, Einstein and Darwin are not true in this sense. As we have seen, there seem to be good grounds for claiming that the very point of science is that theories are *not* true by definition. Popper puts the point strongly:

> In short, we prefer an interesting and a highly informative theory to a trivial one. All these properties which we desire in a theory can be shown to amount to one and the same thing: to a higher *degree of empirical content, or of testability* . . . with increasing content, probability decreases; or, in other words . . . content increases with increasing improbability. . . . Thus, if

our aim is the advancement, the growth of knowledge, then a high probability cannot possibly be our aim also; for these two aims would be incompatible.[20]

Kohlberg and his coworkers seem not to have thought through these issues carefully enough. Consider these lines from one paragraph in a paper by James Rest:

> One of the main implications of a stage hierarchy is that a higher stage is more complex than a lower stage and that a higher stage logically presupposes the simpler lower stage. . . . Empirical demonstration is important because it would support the theory for why the stages are naturally ordered as they are. . . .[21]

The point on which Rest is seriously mistaken is one that was met in earlier chapters—it is in thinking that matters of logical truth require empirical demonstration. Such matters have a probability of *one*, and in a Popperian sense they have no empirical content for they are true by virtue of the meanings of the terms involved. Thus, there is absolutely no point in empirically demonstrating that all bachelors are unmarried, or that all black objects are black. The fact that Kohlbergians state empirical demonstration *is* important, and that they seek it, is a tacit admission that the claim of logical necessity is a spurious one. (The Kohlbergian response to these points will be discussed later.)

(b) Stage sequence and invariance

As was indicated earlier, the remaining two aspects of Kohlberg's hard core—stage sequence and invariance of order—can be construed as claims to which evidence is pertinent. They therefore face the possibility of refutation. Under these conditions of risk, it becomes important to have a strong protective belt—a belt that will dissipate the force of any counterevidence before it can challenge the core.

There are several types of evidence that would be damaging if brought to bear against the Kohlbergian hard core. First, the assertion that moral development occurs in stages would be shaken if it were shown that in fact there are no clearcut stages, or alternatively if it were shown that many individuals are not neatly classifiable into a stage and instead straddle two or three stages. Second, although the claim for invariance would be shaken by the above-mentioned possibilities, it would also flounder if it were discovered that regression does occur in moral development, that is, if even one case was found where an individual moved "backwards".

(1) The first thing presupposed by a stage theory is that the relevant class of individuals or things can be unambiguously assigned to stages. After all, what sense can be made of a stage theory if few members of the relevant class neatly fit into the stages? The process of assigning individuals or things to stages is not a simple one, however, and always involves the use of theories and the making of inferential judgments (matters Kohlberg seems newly sensitive to,

due to his developing interest in hermeneutics). In assigning an insect to one of the four stages of development—egg, larva, pupa, or imago—the theory used is relatively commonplace and a child can easily be trained to make reliable categorizations. The same is decidedly not true of Kohlberg's theory of moral development; people do not go about wearing their moral stage on their sleeve.

The procedure by which individuals are assigned to Kohlbergian stages is extremely complex; and to make discussion of it even more difficult it has changed substantially from year-to-year. The present analysis will start with a version of the scoring manual from perhaps the heyday of the Kohlbergian program, the late 1970s. (As of late 1985 the "definitive" edition—or, for that matter, any edition—had not yet appeared in published form.) First, the individuals being studied are presented with a number of hypothetical stories, or moral dilemmas, which center on a protagonist who presumably must choose to do either A or B. Corresponding to each story are a series of questions or probes designed to elicit the stage of moral reasoning used by the individual. The point of the interview is not to ascertain which action is recommended by an individual, but rather to locate the reasons given in support of the decision. These reasons are then checked against a voluminous scoring manual, and if a proper fit is found, the response is judged scorable and assigned to the appropriate stage. The entire interview is scored in this fashion and a final tally is then made using various arithmetical techniques. As a result of this process the subject is assigned an overall "stage of moral reasoning". Something of the complexities involved are hinted at in the directions included in the scoring manual itself:[22]

> ... the only unit to be actually stage scored by comparison with the manual is the norm/element moral judgment. This scoring is done by comparing the interview reasoning with the criterion judgments in the manual, by considering the structural descriptions given in the criterion judgment explications, and by using the distinctions between parallel ideas at different stages to help avoid mis-matches. Such interview–manual comparisons can yield a number of possible conclusions: (a) The interview moral judgment does not match any of the criterion judgments listed and so is not stage scorable. . . . (b) The interview . . . clearly matches . . . a stage . . . a score for that stage is given. (c) The interview clearly matches a criterion judgment which is labeled as transitional . . . a transitional score is given. (d) The interview ambiguously matches . . . an ambiguous score is entered. . . . (e) The interview . . . matches (equally well) criterion judgments at two adjacent stages but does not *clearly* match any criterion judgment. An ambiguous transitional score is given. . . . We have instituted a "guess category" for scoring issues which might otherwise seem unscorable by the Standard Form Manual.[23]

The objection to this procedure, however, is not its complexity. Many branches of science involve the use of complex, abstract procedures and a case could be made that such procedures are especially difficult to avoid in the behavioral sciences. Human behavior is affected by many variables and scientific headway in these matters is bound to be no easy task. The trouble with Kohlberg's work is that the complexity of his model does not result in clearcut results, in clearcut assignment of subjects to stages. Even sophisticated researchers find it difficult to unambiguously assign many experimental subjects. It would seem that, at best, the stage device is a rough, heuristic, one which does not approximate the realities of human development. In this respect, the scoring categories of "ambiguous", "transitional", "ambiguously transitional", and "guess", seem especially revealing.

That this is no abstract problem is shown by the work of Haan *et al.*; however, the significant points may not be obvious to any of their readers who pay less than careful attention to the numbers used in reporting the data. Their original sample consisted of 957 individuals, all of whom were given the Kohlberg Moral Judgment Interview; of these, only 54 percent, or 510 subjects, were included in the final analysis because only this percentage could be assigned to a "pure" moral type.[24] Lest "pure" be misinterpreted as meaning that these individuals consistently used only one stage of moral reasoning in their interviews, it is important to note that "pure" means simply that one stage accounted for twice the summed weight of any other. Hence, it is possible that even of this 54 percent, most subjects used more than one stage of moral reasoning. The important point, however, is that almost an equal number of subjects, 46 percent or 447, could *not* be assigned a "pure" type at all, indicating that their "dominant stage" accounted for less than 67 percent of their reasoning (and that other stages therefore accounted for more than 33 percent of their reasoning).

Now certainly it would be pointless to insist that in order for "stage" to be a meaningful concept, all individuals must neatly fall into one particular category. Admittedly, people move in and out of stages, and it would not be at all unusual to find some people moving into Stage 3 but still using remnants of Stage 2 reasoning, thus giving the appearance of straddling two stages. The question obviously is one of degree. When roughly one half of the sample is definitely straddling at least two stages and the other half is more than likely doing so, talk of stages seems somewhat strained. What sense could be made of insect development if at any random point in time 50 percent of the observed population was halfway between two stages, or perhaps even straddling three. There is further evidence to indicate that the problem of straddling stages does not end here. Looking again at the data reported by Haan *et al.*, one finds the following figures listed: ". . . Stage 2 men have the following mean scores *across the six stages:* 0.8, 18.5, 3.9, 2.9, 6.1, 1.5."[25] Clearly, these figures raise serious difficulties for Kohlberg's theory of stages for it would be akin to finding a concrete operational Piagetian child who demonstrated sensory motor, pre-operational, concrete operational, and formal operational reasoning all on one task. The absurdity of this hardly needs to be pointed out.

In his study of the hierarchical nature of moral judgments, James Rest inadvertently reports similar data. In attempting to ascertain whether subjects preferred the highest stage of moral reasoning which they could comprehend,

Rest administered the standard Moral Judgment Interview and noted both the "predominant stage" and "highest stage" used by his subjects. Out of 47 subjects, slightly more than 10 percent (that is, five subjects) were shown as straddling three stages. For example, predominant reasoning used was reported as Stage 2, while highest reasoning used was Stage 4.[26] Had Rest reported lowest stage used as well, one would expect the percentage of subjects straddling three stages to be even higher. The significance of stages is difficult to understand when half of the total developmental possibilities are occupied by a significant number of individuals.

If the notion of developmental stages is abandoned in the field of moral cognition, it follows that invariance becomes a spurious issue. But suppose for the sake of argument that the stage hypothesis is saved; one case of variance in the developmental sequence would then be sufficient to refute the claim of invariance. The available evidence suggests that far more than one case has been encountered.

In a follow-up study of Kohlberg's doctoral dissertation, Kramer examined the longitudinal progress of the original subjects as they moved from adolescence to early adulthood.[27] Between late high school and their second or third years of college, 20 percent of the sample had shown regression in their moral reasoning. That is, where they had pretested at Stages 4 and 5, they were posttesting at Stage 2. In the same paper, Kolhberg and Kramer report another group of people who showed regression, however this group did not seem to follow the above pattern. Although the authors offered *ad hoc* explanations for both of these phenomena, which will be considered later, the point here has been to establish that the claim of invariance has not gone unchallenged.

It should be noted in passing that the incidences of straddling raise an uncomfortable possibility for the invariance hypothesis as well. For while it may be possible that individuals who straddle two stages are all moving in an upward direction, that is from the lower stage to the higher, it is also possible that they may be moving in a backward direction, that is regressing from the higher stage to the lower one. This issue can only be settled by careful longitudinal study.[28] Unfortunately, Kohlbergians often seem to rest their case not on relevant studies of this type, but on the *belief* that their assumption about invariant upward movement could not possibly be mistaken.

The protective belt

In the light of the preceding discussion, there can be no doubt that the Kohlbergian hard core is at risk. The claim of logical necessity has been shown to be untenable, the assertion of invariance is faced with considerable counterevidence, and even the stage assumption—which is basic to the whole program—has been found unintelligible.

According to the Lakatosian position on the structure of research programs, however, this need not herald the demise of the research program for it is the function of the protective belt to dissipate the attack on the hard core. Only if the protective belt fails to function successfully will the research program itself be endangered.

(a) Reinterpretation of the research

One technique for dealing with criticisms is to offer new interpretations of what the research is trying to accomplish; a related gambit is to draw distinctions—ones not driven by theory but driven merely by the *ad hoc* need to ward off attack—so that it can be responded that, although the critical points are sound in their way, they do not apply to *this* work. In other words, these sorts of techniques allow the criticisms to be "bracketed" off as relevant (at best) to other realms.

Consider the lengthy paper that Kohlberg and two coauthors produced in 1983, "The Current Formulation of the Theory", that presents the most up-to-date "snapshot" of the structure of the research program. Here the authors drop the bombshell that in recent years they have been very much influenced by hermeneutics (to which they were sensitized by Jurgen Habermas).[29] They are now able, they say, to "have our psychometric cake and hermeneutically interpret it too".[30] Accordingly, they have adopted a new interpretation of the stages:

> Thus, our stage interpretations are not value-neutral; they do imply some normative reference. In this sense our stage theory is basically what Habermas calls a "rational reconstruction" of developmental progress. Our theory is a rational reconstruction because it (a) describes the developmental logic inherent in the logic of justice reasoning with the aid of (b) the normative criterion of Stage 6 which is held to be the most adequate (i.e. most reversible) stage of justice reasoning.[31]

Whatever it does, this new view does not appear to let the Kohlbergians off the hook. It does not rectify the faulty arguments and inconsistencies in their accounts of the so-called "developmental logic inherent in the development of justice reasoning". The new hermeneuticism merely muddies the water more; like the octopus, they hope to make use of the murkiness to escape from predators! For when empirical or conceptual difficulties are raised, it can now be replied: "You miss the point—our account is normative and interpretive, and thus has to meet different standards."

(b) Scoring

There are a number of ways in which Kohlberg's scoring procedures insulate the hard core against attack. First, they are extraordinarily complex. As Kurtines and Greif have pointed out, for many years the manual has been difficult to obtain (it had still not been published by late 1985); the directions were not clearly spelled out; and short of attending one of the special scoring workshops conducted at Harvard, the independent researcher had either to rely on his or her own judgment much of the time or abandon the study altogether.[32]

Some of the complexity inherent in the procedure has been illustrated by the passage quoted earlier from a version of the scoring manual dating from the late 1970s. But this is only the tip of the iceberg. At least one version of the scoring manual referred to sub-stages for each of the six primary stages, however, no guidelines were presented for scoring these. In recent years, too, a distinction has been drawn between "hard" and "soft" developmental stages; the hard being Piagetian-type stages, and the soft being "existential". This *ad hoc* distinction was necessary to accommodate a criticism made by Gibbs.[33] Furthermore, there came a time when Stage 6 was entirely eliminated from the manual "partly because it is so rare in most populations and partly because a more standard form would probably be required for clear differentiation of Stages 5 and 6".[34]

This raises some obvious problems for the various cases of past research in which Kohlbergians have persistently discovered—or deliberately included in their samples[35]—numbers of individuals at both Stages 5 and 6. Indeed, Kohlberg even noted that at the age of twenty-five, he personally was clearly at Stage 6.[36] Putting this to one side, however, the impression remains that researchers within the Kohlbergian tradition are busy readjusting their scoring procedures to give the results required by their theoretical assumptions. After all, why else would they make distinctions in the scoring manual for which no clear scoring procedures were yet available? Their theory *must* have been giving them direction.

Over the years, the possibility that an individual's moral reasoning will straddle three or more stages was neatly guarded against by several scoring procedures. First, under the responses considered *unscorable*, are those which ". . . approximate equally well criterion concepts at more than two stages or at two non-adjacent stages".[37] Second, when actually computing the issue scores (which then are summed and weighted for a global score), the manual recommends that:

> If two non-adjacent stages were scored, the one receiving fewer points is not represented in the issue total. If they have received an equal number of points, the higher stage is assigned to the issue total.[38]

The above statement is footnoted in the following not atypical manner:

> This rule has been imposed at least temporarily to prevent gross mistakes by inexperienced scorers. A justification for the rule and fuller treatment of the issues of unit, context, stage homogeneity will be provided in a later draft of the scoring manual.[39]

Where neither of these devices flushes out all but the predominant stage, one hope remains. In computing the total or global score the procedure is as follows: The frequency of stages used across all issues is calculated and each stage is then variously weighted depending on whether the stage is "pure", "major", "minor". Pure stages are assigned three points, major stages two, and minor stages one. The points are then totaled per stage and percentages are computed. When, using this procedure, one stage accounts for at least 75 percent of the total, it is assigned as the global stage. When one stage alone does not contribute 75 percent of the total, stages accounting for more than 25 percent are considered; where the percentage is equal, a dual stage is assigned; where unequal a major/minor stage is assigned.

Clearly, both the weighting procedure and the percentages are designed to eliminate as much variation as possible from the final score. Although a subject may very well use four different stages of reasoning during the interview, it is highly unlikely that this fact will survive the scoring procedure. "Pure" moral types are the most advantageous for Kohlbergian theory. The data cited earlier from Haan *et al.*, reporting mean reasoning across all six stages, would not be considered refuting evidence since the figures report stage usage under the accepted 25 percent limit.

It is interesting to note that Kohlbergians apparently feel free to bend this rule when necessary. In the Rest study previously mentioned, it was found that the "predominant stage" used was not a good predictor of level of comprehension of moral reasoning, but that "highest stage used" was. Admissible as "highest stage used" was any response contributing more than 20 percent of the total.[40] This suggests that the decision as to what will count as substantial usage of a stage of reasoning is an arbitrary one.

Within the last few years Kohlberg has made further changes. Following on from his newly-explicit hermeneutical outlook, he stresses that "interviewing and scoring are acts of 'interpreting a text' around some shared philosophic categories of meaning."[41] And he now tries, he says, to "differentiate" the content and the structure when scoring or assessing the stages. Stages are now seen as "ideal types". In an attempt to clarify these matters he writes:

> To briefly explain, an interview transcript is first classified by the content of the choice; second, it is classified by the content of the justification of the choice; and third, it is classified by the value content appealed to in the justification. Only after classifying content according to these three content categories is an interview then assessed by stage or structure.[42]

Neither the logic, nor Kohlberg's new conception of the stages, are easy to comprehend; and the problem comes to the fore of how a stage theory, interpreted in this new way, could ever be put to the test:

> Since the structures themselves can never be observed, the stages that represent them are constructions of ideal types or illustrative exemplars rather than abstracted forms or expressions of the structures themselves. In this context, an ideal type is the theoretical representation of the stage, which itself contains differing mixtures of content and structure. The glossing over of the distinction between content and structure reduces the plausibility of defining the operations that structures were intended to represent.[43]

(c) Regression and Invariance

There are three major ways in which the Kohlbergians have attempted to defuse the evidence of regression and maintain their hard core assumption that movement through the stages is invariant.

(i) As will be recalled, cases of regression were found by Kramer in a follow-up study of Kohlberg's dissertation sample. At that time, Kohlberg and Kramer explained the phenomenon as being "more like functional regression than it is like a structural regression". They went on to claim that such regression is, in fact, a developmental *advance*, presumably because these subjects had faced "universal" challenges to their prior conventional morality and had, so to speak, met those challenges as could be seen by their eventual return to Stages 4 and 5. "Every single one of our retrogressors had returned to a mixed Stage 4 and 5 morality by age 25, with a little more 5 or social contract principle, a little less 4 or convention than at high school."[44]

Their explanation continued, cast in Ericksonian terms, and it was argued that the regression represented ego development rather than moral development. However, after providing this delightful example of Orwellian "newspeak", they made a sober confession:

> The formulation we have just made is inadequate. We have superimposed developmental task "stages" of ego function in adulthood upon childhood stages of moral structure and claimed structural regression was functional advance. Obviously, such an attempt to have one's cake and eat it too is inadequate. A sequel to the paper attempts to correct this inadequacy by defining ego "stages" in terms of metaethical theories and world views . . .[45]

It is interesting that their new frankness did not extend to considering the possibility that their hard core assumption was faulty (illustrating that Lakatos's insights into this matter were valid).

As best as can be determined, the gauntlet—the challenge to write a *correct* explanation in a "sequel"—was taken up by Elliot Turiel, then a student of Kohlberg's. Focussing specifically on the change from Stage 4 to Stage 5, Turiel rejected the earlier explanations put forward by Kohlberg and Kramer and posited instead that those subjects who posttested at Stage 2 only *appeared* to be at Stage 2. In fact, he claimed, their thinking had a more advanced structure and hence could not have been Stage 2 thinking at all. Turiel argued that these subjects were actually in a transitional state for they were leaving the comforts of Stage 4 "Conventional" thinking and entering the much more advanced Stage 5 "Principled" thinking. The cognitive reorganization required by this move was apparently sufficiently complex to mislead the earlier researchers and cause them to incorrectly classify the moral reasoning of their subjects. The "transitional state" or "Stage 4 1/2", as it was commonly called among members of the research community, was thus born.

On the face of it, Turiel's *ad hoc* hypothesis does not seem unreasonable in the context of Kohlbergian theory;[46] Kohlberg himself conceded, in 1983, that Turiel was basically correct. It is conceivable that the shift from Conventional

(Stages 3 and 4) to Principled (Stages 5 and 6) levels of moral reasoning would be the most difficult, hence entailing a special transitional period. As Kohlberg recently put it, disequilibrium and adoption of "some form of subjectivism or relativism is a necessary but not sufficient condition for movement to Stage 5."[47] The fact that this phenomenon seems only to occur among college sophomores lends further credence to this possibility. Nevertheless, there are certain problems with this auxiliary explanation.

First, Turiel's *ad hoc* hypothesis is not content-increasing; it merely describes in different terms something that was already known. What once was labeled regression can now be called Stage 4 1/2 or transition; the function of the re-labeling was to save the theory. Turiel's introduction of a new vocabulary, however, still does not allow for the prediction of which individuals in Stage 4 will go through this period, or which individuals in the transitional state will move on to Stage 5. Neither does it indicate whether transitional states are to be found anywhere else in the hierarchy. Secondly, given the scoring possibilities (unscorable, scorable, transitional, ambiguous, ambiguously transitional, guess) and the scoring procedures (for example, categorizing as "unscorable" something which can fall in two nonadjacent stages), the introduction of a new stage presents enormous coding problems. It was not shown how answers to moral dilemmas which are typical of Stage 4 1/2 would differ from other "transitional", "ambiguously transitional" and "guess" answers. Thirdly, and perhaps most importantly, this explanation does not account for all regressions, as both Turiel and Kohlberg admit.

(ii) The second major strategy adopted by Kohlbergians in efforts to insulate their hard core against the challenge issued by regression, involves the use of a variety of *ad hominem* arguments. These range in subtlety from Turiel's blanket accusation that many findings of regression can only be due to inadequate empirical techniques or poorly formulated theory,[48] to the more indirect approach of Kohlberg and Kramer. It will be recalled that the latter two did report finding a second group of individuals who showed regression and it is worth noting that the authors considered these to be "cases of genuine structural regression".[49] Consisting of "abnormals"—schizophrenics, persons over the age of 65, and incarcerated criminals—the hasty dismissal of this group by Kohlberg and Kramer underscores their implicit suggestion that "normal" patterns of development should not be expected to hold for "abnormal" individuals.

There are at least two problems here. First, Kohlberg and Kramer admit that the schizophrenics were functioning well on psychometric tests and were about to be released from the hospital. The "elderly" were not only college educated but intellectually "intact" for their age norms, and the criminals had all shown prior moral reasoning at Stages 3 and 4. Why these people would have regressed to Stages 1 and 2 then, remains a real puzzle. Secondly, if invariance actually holds, and even more, if it is logically necessary as is claimed, then it should hold regardless of the age group, mental health, or environmental circumstances of the individuals concerned—logical truths are not rendered inoperative by penal servitude or by chronological age.

(iii) Another Kohlbergian method for defusing regression involves blurring the distinction between universal or "all" claims, and tendency claims. In an early paper on cognitive stages and preschool education, Kohlberg illustrated his understanding of invariance with an example of how children develop the concept of a dream. He wrote, "if there is an invariant order of development . . . all children should fit one of the patterns. . . ." Then, in a striking passage, he went on to report his evidence:

> The fact that *only 18 out of 90* children *do not fit* one of these patterns *is acceptable evidence* for the existence of *invariant sequence* in the development of the dream concept.[50]

In a situation where one case out of ninety would be sufficient for refutation, the ignoring of counterevidence that totals 20 percent of the sample is a feat of bluff that would make seasoned poker players blush with envy!

(d) Presentation of research findings

The Kohlbergian hard core, as is perhaps evident from the last example, has been protected from refutation by the manner in which counterevidence is presented and by the way in which difficulties are glossed over in subsequent discussions of the evidence.

Kohlbergian researchers have rarely presented the relevant figures in an unambiguous fashion. Indeed, as the two exasperated psychologists Kurtines and Greif reported in their detailed review of the Kohlbergian literature, there

> appears to be three methods of reporting results. Combining these methods with the two possible ways for reporting results from the global scoring technique, one arrives at five possible combinations of scoring and reporting scores for the Moral Judgment Scale.[51]

To aid in decipherment of their figures the Kohlbergians helpfully provide a verbal gloss. As is the case in virtually all research in the behavioral sciences, the results are probabilistic in nature—the figures illustrate that trends are present, and results may or may not be statistically significant. The results never show that all experimental subjects react in exactly the same way. A nice example of the technique of glossing is found in a paper by John Gibbs in the *Harvard Educational Review*. In a brief section titled "A Research Review", a section notable for its lack of hard data, Gibbs reported on the available literature in terms such as: "were much more likely" (without saying how much more likely), "markedly amenable" (without saying how markedly or how amenable), "found greater change in the upward direction" (without saying how much greater, or how reliable the findings were), "found significant upward change" (without saying how significant), "found positive correlations" (without saying how positive), "has generally supported the hypothesis" (without saying anything about the support, which by implication, was found for the counterhypothesis as well).[52] It is notable that in the very place where Gibbs should have hedged his bets he drew the following conclusions:

> The research reviewed above suggests that Kohlberg's first four moral judgment orientations define a Piagetian stage sequence. . . . The evidence seems rather impressive that the four candidates define a stage sequence in the Piagetian sense.[53]

In view of the discussions in preceding sections of this chapter, it should not require detailed argument to establish that this is entirely spurious. Piagetian-type sequences are supposedly universal in the sense that they apply to all individuals without exception. The vague and probabilistic results reported by Gibbs actually refute, rather than support, such universal claims, for probabilistic data entail that the trends discovered did *not* hold for all members of the relevant sample.

Kohlberg himself must bear responsibility for this distressing tendency to gloss findings, and to discuss them in a fashion that is, at best, misleading. His published works are replete with remarks such as the following:

> Over a period of almost twenty years of empirical research, my colleages and I have rather firmly established a culturally universal invariant sequence of stages of moral judgment. . . .[54]

And elsewhere:

> Using hypothetical moral situations, we have interviewed children about right and wrong in the United States, Britain, Turkey, Taiwan, and Yucatan. In all cultures we find the same forms of moral thinking. There are six forms of thinking and they constitute an invariant sequence of stages in each culture.[55]

Unfortunately, of course, the evidence that is available does not "rather firmly establish" Kohlberg's theory. As Kurtines and Greif noted, after their independent examination of the research literature,

> Not only is there no clearcut evidence supporting the assumption of invariance of stages and their hierarchical nature, but there is also evidence suggesting that these assumptions may be incorrect.[56]

(e) Confirmation and the avoidance of refutation

There are grounds for thinking that a fundamental methodological failing of the Kohlbergians is their insistence upon seeking evidence that confirms rather than refutes their hard core. By now the point is familiar: Any clever researcher, armed with enough sophisticated techniques and given enough time and resources, could find at least some evidence for any hypothesis, no matter how fanciful it might be. A much more valid approach, but far more threatening to the hard core, would be to work for the refutation of errant hypothesis. Karl Popper put the issues lucidly:

(1) It is easy to obtain confirmations, or verifications, for nearly every theory—if we look for confirmations. (2) Confirmations should count only if they are the result of *risky predictions*. . . . (3) Every "good" scientific theory is a prohibition: it forbids certain things to happen. The more a theory forbids, the better it is. (4) A theory which is not refutable by any conceivable event is non-scientific. Irrefutability is not a virtue of a theory (as people often think) but a vice. (5) Every genuine *test* of a theory is an attempt to falsify it, or to refute it.[57]

Is the research program viable?

In light of the available evidence, there is good reason to believe that the hard core of the Kohlbergian research program is implausible. There are no clear stages of moral development—at best they are arbitrary fictions (or "ideal types" by Kohlberg's new admission) having little or no verisimilitude; even if it is assumed that there is something there, the order in which individuals move through these (fictitious/ideal) stages is far from invariant, and the sequence of the stages (if indeed they exist) is certainly not logically necessary. Interviewing and scoring are now revealed to be interpretive and normative activities. More and more *ad hoc* distinctions are being drawn in the attempt to "bracket out" the criticisms and counterevidence. Furthermore, the protective belt seems unable to restore the credibility of the hard core. Should not, then, the research program be abandoned?

While commonsense would dictate an unambiguous affirmative answer to this question, contemporary methodologists and philosophers of science would be somewhat more cautious. Lakatos, for example, made the point that:

> to give a stern "refutable interpretation" to a fledging version of a programme is dangerous methodological cruelty. The first versions may even "apply" only to non-existing "ideal" cases; it may take decades of theoretical work to arrive at the first novel facts and still more time to arrive at interestingly testable versions of the research programmes . . .[58]

There is a lot to be said for this. One cannot expect research programs to spring forth fully developed. It takes time and great effort to think through the issues and propose testable theoretical solutions. Seen in this light, the almost three decades over which the Kohlbergian program has been developing is not an unreasonably lengthy period of time.

This charitable position, however, runs into an insurmountable problem. There are no signs that the Kohlbergian program is maturing, that it is any nearer than it was several decades ago to making specific, testable predictions, or to opening-up previously unknown realms of phenomena. To refer once again to Lakatos, mature scientific programs must be progressive—they must have heuristic power and lead to growth:

> This requirement of *continuous growth* is my rational reconstruction of the widely acknowledged requirement of "unity" or "beauty" of science. It highlights the weakness of *two*—apparently very different—types of theorizing. First, it shows up the weakness of programmes which, like Marxism or Freudianism, are, no doubt, "unified", . . . but which unfailingly devise their actual auxiliary theories in the wake of facts without, at the same time,

anticipating others. (What *novel* fact has Marxism *predicted* since, say, 1917?) Secondly, it hits patched-up unimaginative series of pedestrian "empirical" adjustment which are so frequent, for instance, in modern social psychology.[59]

Precisely these same points can be made against the Kohlbergian research program. Have not, in fact, the auxiliary theories that "save" the hard core, all been devised "in the wake of the facts"? What *novel* facts has the research program *predicted* in the last decade or more? Has not the program been "patched-up" with a series of "pedestrian empirical adjustments"? (It might be noted here that Carol Gilligan was led to uncover some "novel" facts, but this was because she saw a defect in Kohlberg's work—he had studied only males! Using subjects from the other sex, she reached different conclusions about moral reasoning, conclusions which more "mainstream" Kohlbergians are busy trying to accommodate. It is not clear, however, that Gilligan's work avoids many of the problems that have been discussed with respect to Kohlberg's methodology.)

In the final analysis, then, the philosophers of science must come to endorse the conclusion reached by commonsense—the Kohlbergian program is degenerating and has little recognizable merit. (This is not to deny that when it was first introduced the program represented, in Lakatos's terminology, a progressive problemshift.)

It should be emphasized, too, that moral reasoning is an important area of concern, and it is imperative that it continue to be studied. Kohlberg's program has been the dominant one in the field, and as writers from Thomas Kuhn to Imre Lakatos have insisted, research programs in important areas cannot be abandoned, regardless of their weaknesses, until alternatives are available. Research is directionless unless it is guided by some hypothesis or heuristic device, and possibly anything is better than nothing. If there were a rival research program in the same field, however, one of the chief reasons for continuing to embrace Kohlberg would disappear.

Notes and References

1. R. M. Galvin, "Psychology: There are Other Therapists at Work," *New York Times*, August 14, 1977.

2. L. Kohlberg, "A Reply to Owen Flanagan and Some Comments on the Puka–Goodpaster Exchange", *Ethics*, **92**, April 1982.

3. C. Gilligan, *In a Different Voice*. Cambridge, Mass: Harvard University Press, 1982.

4. Imre Lakatos, "Falsification and the Methodology of Scientific Research Programmes", op. cit. (Quotations here will be taken from the 1976 reprint.) Also see *British Journal for the Philosophy of Science;* papers by Zahar, (24), 1973; Musgrave, (25), 1974; and Urbach, (25), 1974.

5. P. Feyerabend, "Zahar on Einstein", *British Journal for Philosophy of Science*, (25), 1974, p. 25.

6. This expression is used by Lakatos in a subheading to his paper, "Falsification and the Methodology of Scientific Research Programmes", op. cit., p. 154.

7. Lord Kelvin once stated that the famous Michelson-Morley experiment was the only "cloud in the clear sky" of the ether theory; later it turned out to be important for Einstein's theory which opposes the ether theory. Ibid., p. 161.

8. Ibid., p. 175.

9. Ibid., p. 135.

10. See D. Lapsley and R. Serlin, "On the Alleged Degeneration of the Kohlbergian Research Program", and D. C. Phillips and J. Nicolayev, "In Its Final Stages?", *Educational Theory*, **34**, Spring 1984.

11. K. Popper, quoted in Lakatos, op. cit., p. 154.

12. H. D. Aiken, "The Levels of Moral Discourse", *Ethics*, (LXII), 1952. On occasion Kohlberg has given reference to this source.

13. J. R. Rest, "The Hierarchical Nature of Moral Judgment: A Study of Patterns of Comprehension and Preference of Moral Stages", *Journal of Personality*, (41), March 1973, pp. 86–8.

14. D. Candee, A. Colby and J. Gibbs, "Assessment of Moral Judgment Stages", Center for Moral Education, Harvard, p. 1.

15. L. Kohlberg, "Stages of Moral Development as a Basis for Moral Education", in C. M. Beck, B. S. Crittenden, and E. V. Sullivan, (eds), *Moral Education: Interdisciplinary Approaches*. Toronto: Toronto University Press, 1971, p. 36.

16. L. Kohlberg, "Cognitive Stages and Preschool Education", *Human Development*, (9), 1966, p. 6.

17. L. Kohlberg, "Stages of Moral Development . . .", op. cit., p. 48.

18. See T. Mischel, (ed.), *Cognitive Development and Epistemology*. NY: Academic Press, 1971, especially R. S. Peters, "Moral Development: A Plea for Pluralism", and W. P. Alston, "Comments on Kohlberg's *From Is to Ought*".

19. L. Kohlberg, "Stages . . ." Appendix 1, p. 87.

20. K. Popper, "Some Comments on Truth and the Growth of Knowledge", in E. Nagel, P. Suppes, and A. Tarski, (eds), *Logic, Methodology and Philosophy of Science*. Stanford: Stanford University Press, 1962, p. 286.

21. J. Rest, "The Hierarchical Nature of Moral Judgment", op. cit., p. 86.

22. The manual is something of a "moving target". It went through many yearly revisions, presenting a problem for "Popperian testing".

23. D. Candee, A. Colby, and J. Gibbs, op. cit., p. 31.

24. N. Haan, B. Smith, and J. Block, "Moral Reasoning of Young Adults: Political-Social Behavior, Family Background, and Personality Correlates", *Journal of Personality and Social Psychology*, (10), 3, 1968.

25. Ibid., p. 187. (My emphasis.)

26. J. Rest, op. cit., pp. 99–100.

27. L. Kohlberg and R. Kramer, "Continuities and Discontinuities in Childhood and Adult Moral Development", *Human Development*, (12), 1969.

28. The need for longitudinal work was noted by W. Kurtines and E. B. Greif in their critical review, "The Development of Moral Thought: Review and Evaluation of Kohlberg's Approach", *Psychological Bulletin*, (81), 8 August 1974.

29. L. Kohlberg, *The Psychology of Moral Development: Essays on Moral Development. Volume 11* San Francisco: Harper & Row, 1984, ch. 3, p. 217.

30. Ibid., p. 220.

31. Ibid., p. 221.

32. Kurtines and Greif, op. cit., esp. p. 455.

33. Kohlberg, *The Psychology of Moral Development*, op. cit., pp. 236–49.

34. *Moral Judgement Scoring Manual*, Harvard: Center for Moral Education, Part III, Instructions, p. 1.

35. J. Rest, op. cit., p. 91.

36. L. Kohlberg and R. Kramer, op. cit., p. 93.

37. *Moral Judgement Scoring Manual*, p. 9.

38. Ibid., p. 13.

39. Ibid.

40. J. Rest, op. cit., p. 100.

41. Kohlberg, *The Psychology of Moral Development*, op. cit., p. 219.

42. Ibid., p. 245.

43. Ibid., pp. 242–3.

44. L. Kohlberg and R. Kramer, op. cit., p. 111.

45. Ibid., p. 118.
46. It is not accurate to regard Turiel, especially in his later work, as a Kohlbergian. But see E. Turiel, "Conflict and Transition in Adolescent Moral Development", *Child Development*, 45, (1), 1974.
47. Kohlberg, *The Psychology of Moral Development*, op. cit., p. 440.
48. Turiel, op. cit., p. 18.
49. L. Kohlberg and R. Kramer, op. cit., p. 112.
50. L. Kohlberg, "Cognitive Stages . . .", op. cit., p. 11. (My emphasis.)
51. W. Kurtines and E. Greif, "The Development of Moral Thought", op. cit., p. 456.
52. J. C. Gibbs, "Kohlberg's Stages of Moral Judgment: A Constructive Critique", *Harvard Educational Review*, **47,** (1), February 1977, pp. 48–9.
53. Ibid., p. 50.
54. L. Kohlberg, "The Claim to Moral Adequacy of a Highest Stage of Moral Judgment", *Journal of Philosophy*, LXX, October 1973, p. 630.
55. L. Kohlberg, "Education for Justice: A Modern Statement of the Platonic View", in *Moral Education: Five Lectures*, Cambridge, MA: Harvard University Press, 1970, p. 70.
56. W. Kurtines and E. Greif, op. cit., p. 469.
57. K. Popper, *Conjectures and Refutations*. NY: Harper and Row, 1968, p. 36.
58. I. Lakatos, "Falsification and the Methodology of Scientific Research Programmes", op. cit., p. 151.
59. Ibid., pp. 175–6.

Glossary

Complete definitions are not given for all terms; rather, the senses that are pertinent in the context of the discussions in the present book are the ones that are focussed upon. For fuller accounts see some such work as A. R. Lacey, *A Dictionary of Philosophy*. NY: Scribners, 1976.

ACCOMPANYING CHARACTERISTICS: Those characteristics that an object may possess—and may always possess—but which are not taken into account when applying some term to that object. (E.g., possession of a particular color is an accompanying characteristic of a tea-cup, for it is not part of the general definition.) [Contrast with "Defining characteristics".]

AD HOC HYPOTHESES: Hypotheses that are added to save a theory or more general hypothesis from refutation; they are added in the light of refuting evidence, and initially the only reason in support of them is that they account for this evidence. Traditional philosophy eschewed their use, but the new philosophy of science recognizes that scientists often use them.

ANTI-NATURALISM: In the sense in which it is most frequently used in this work, anti-naturalism is the view that the social sciences cannot validly use many of the research methods associated with the natural sciences; anti-naturalists in this sense see the social sciences as more closely allied to the humanities than to the sciences. [See "Naturalistic, 2".]

AUXILIARIES/AUXILIARY ASSUMPTIONS: In order to carry out a test of the implications of some scientific hypothesis, material from other areas of science (which for the time-being are taken as being true) must be made use of (e.g., the theories upon which the instruments being used are based, or formulae used for calculations).

DEFINING CHARACTERISTICS: Those characteristics that it is necessary for an entity to possess in order for a certain term to be applied to it (e.g., possession of both a handle and prongs are probably defining characteristics—they might not be the only ones—of a "fork"). [Contrast with "Accompanying characteristics".]

DEMARCATION, PROBLEM OF: The problem, central to the development of Popper's thought, of the criterion (or criteria) that demarcates science from a non-science (or metaphysics).

DUHEM-QUINE THESIS: The view, put forward by both Pierre Duhem and W. V. O. Quine, that science is a complex network that faces the test of experience as a whole; negative evidence can require that an accommodatory change be made, but this change can be made in any part of the network (so long as any secondary changes that are necessary in other parts are made).

ECLECTICISM: The view that a researcher should adopt whatever theories or methodologies are useful in inquiry, no matter their source, and without undue worry about their consistency.

EMIC: An emic account of a situation or setting or event is one written from an internal perspective, e.g., by a participant in that situation or event. The term may also connote that the concepts used in the account are those that are part of the normal terminology of the participants. [Compare with "Etic".]

EMPIRICISM: The position that all knowledge (usually, but not always, excluding that which is logico-mathematical) is in some way "based upon" experience. Adherents of empiricism differ markedly over what the "based upon" amounts to—"starts from" and "warranted in terms of" are, roughly, at the two ends of the spectrum of opinion.

EPISTEMOLOGY: The branch of philosophy dealing with the theory of knowledge—the nature of knowledge, its scope, and the assessment of the reliability or degree of warrant of knowledge claims.

ETIC: An etic account of a situation or setting or event is one written from an external perspective, e.g, by an outside observer. The term may also connote that the concepts used in the account come from the observer's frame of reference rather than from the frame of those *in* the situation or setting. [Compare with "Emic".]

HARD CORE: Term used by Imre Lakatos in his theory of scientific research programs; the hard core is that portion of the program that scientists who adhere to the program have decided to maintain unchanged at all costs. [See "Protective belt"; "Positive heuristic".]

HERMENEUTICS: The discipline of interpretation of textual or literary material, or of meaningful human action.

INCOMMENSURABILITY: According to those inspired by the work of T. S. Kuhn, if two paradigms (q.v.) are rivals, they are incommensurable— statements from one paradigm are not fully translatable into terms appropriate to the other (for they "carve up" reality differently, so that even if they use the same words, the words have different meanings in the different contexts). [See "Semantic holism".]

INDUCTION, PROBLEM OF: The problem of justifying simple inductive reasoning of the form "the N members of class A that have been observed so far have property p, thus all members of class A have property p." Evidently the "thus" requires justification, for the conclusion goes beyond the data provided in the premise.

INSTRUMENTALISM: The view that ideas and theories (including those of science) have the status of intellectual instruments; that is, they must be regarded as good or bad tools rather than being thought of as true or false.

INTERNAL RELATIONS: As opposed to external relationships, internal relations are those in which the entities are altered (i.e., undergo change in properties) as a result of the relations into which they have entered. Thus, gravitational interaction is an internal relationship, and the weights (as opposed to masses) of bodies interacting gravitationally are determined by the relationship. [See "Organicism/Holism".]

LOGICAL POSITIVISM: Name of a position developed in the 1920s by members of the Vienna Circle; its most notorious tenet was the verifiability principle of meaning, which stated that something is meaningful only if it is verifiable empirically (i.e., directly, or indirectly, via sense experience), or if it is a truth of logic or mathematics. [See "Positivism".]

META-LEVEL: If discourse about observable events is regarded as occurring at level 1, then discourse at a higher level of abstraction (e.g., discourse about theoretical or philosophical matters pertaining to, or arising from, level 1) is at a meta-level.

METAPHYSICS: The branch of philosophy dealing with a host of disparate issues that cannot be settled, in principle, by appeal to human observation or experience. (Literally, "beyond or after physics".)

NAIVE FALSIFICATION: The view (sometimes erroneously attributed to Popper) that, although we cannot prove or absolutely confirm our knowledge claims, we can put them to the test and absolutely refute the ones that are faulty. (Popper realized that tests are only tentative, and a negative test-result is always potentially open to reconsideration. This is "sophisticated falsificationism".)

NATURALISTIC: (1) A study or piece of research is naturalistic insofar as it uses qualitative or case-study methods (as opposed to manipulative or experimental methods). This contrasts markedly with the second usage, below. (2) The social sciences are held by some (including Popper) to be naturalistic in the sense that they have no features that offer insuperable obstacles to the adoption of the methods of the natural sciences. (See "Antinaturalism".)

NON-JUSTIFICATIONIST EPISTEMOLOGY: This is also referred to as non-foundationalist epistemology. It is the view that knowledge is not built upon a certain or indubitable base; instead, although knowledge-claims may be well-warranted, there is no warrant or foundation that is so firm that it cannot be open to question.

OBSERVATION SENTENCES/PROTOCOL SENTENCES: According to the logical positivists (q.v.) these are sentences that are entirely verifiable in terms of sense experience; all "higher order" statements in science must be reducible to these basic elements.

ONTOLOGY: A branch of metaphysics (q.v.) dealing with the nature of existence, the ways in which entities belonging to different categories may be said to exist, and so on.

OPERATIONALISM/OPERATIONISM: The view—closely related to the verifiability principle of meaning (q.v.)—that all scientific entities and their properties are definable in terms of the operations by which they are measured or apprehended. The view was developed by the physicist P. W. Bridgman, but was influential in the social sciences and psychology.

ORGANICISM/HOLISM: The view that in certain systems or organic entities, the whole is more than the sum of its parts. The parts are dynamically or internally interrelated, so that the whole has properties not found in the totality of the isolated parts (Hegel regarded the whole of reality as being an entity of this kind.) [See "Internal relations".]

PARADIGM: A term popularized by the historian of science T. S. Kuhn, having a notoriously wide set of meanings. The basic idea is that a scientist normally will be working within a theoretical framework—a paradigm—that determines the problems that are regarded as crucial, the ways these problems are to be conceptualized, the appropriate methods of inquiry, the relevant standards of judgment, etc.

PHENOMENOLOGY: The study, in depth, of how things appear in human experience. Developed initially by Brentano and Husserl, the practice of phenomenology involves the "bracketing" or laying aside of preconceptions (including ones derived from science), in order to be able to inspect (one's own) conscious intellectual processes more purely.

PLURALISM: The view that reality is multifarious, and that many rival theories can be true of it at the one time. (In this work, it is closely associated with the view that competing paradigms (q.v.) each present their own "true" view of reality.)

POSITIVE HEURISTIC: The set of principles or rules-of-thumb that give guidance in making changes to the protective belt of a Lakatosian scientific research program. [See "Hard core"; "Protective belt".]

POSITIVISM: This term has a variety of senses which all seem to revolve around giving centrality, in the gaining of knowledge, to the methods of science. For Comte and other nineteenth-century figures, positivism also pertained to a theory of the development or progression of human knowledge through stages. [See "Logical Positivism".]

PROTECTIVE BELT: Expression used by Imre Lakatos for the portion of a scientific research program that is expendable; as evidence accumulates, changes can be made in the "protective belt" in order to deflect what otherwise would be challenges to the program's "hard core". [See "Hard core"; "Positive heuristic".]

REALISM: The view that entities exist independently of being perceived, or independently of our theories about them. (A realist may, or may not, hold that we can attain knowledge about this independent reality.)

REDUCTIONISM: The belief that a branch of science can be explained in terms of (i.e., reduced to) the propositions of another. Reductionists can disagree about whether or not a particular science is reducible; most agree that chemistry is reducible to physics, but it is controversial whether (even in principle) biology is reducible to chemistry or whether sociology is reducible to psychology.

RELATIVISM: Relativists do not hold (as is sometimes erroneously supposed) that propositions do not have the property of being true, rather, they insist that judgments of truth are always relative to a particular framework or point-of-view. Thus, relativism entails that proposition p can be true for individuals in framework of belief B1, but false for individuals in a different framework B2.

SCIENTISM: A term used in a mildly abusive way to indicate slavish adherence to the methods of science in a context where they are inappropriate (e.g. in studying human affairs). It is sometimes used in a related but somewhat different way, to indicate a false or mistaken claim to be scientific.

SEMANTIC HOLISM: The view that the meaning of a term is determined by the total network of relationships within the system in which it is located. If part of the system were to change, the meanings of all the interrelated terms would change. This view leads to the acceptance of incommensurability (q.v.).

TACIT KNOWLEDGE: According to Michael Polanyi and others, individuals know more than they are able to express in words, and it is this tacit knowledge that enables them to perform in ways they cannot explain.

THEORY-LADENNESS (OF PERCEPTION): The thesis that the process of perception is theory-laden, in that the observer's background knowledge (including theories, factual information, hypotheses, and so forth) acts as a "lens" helping to "shape" the nature of what is observed. Although Wittgenstein, Popper, and others argued for this thesis, the exposition by N. R. Hanson is best-known.

UNDERDETERMINATION: The view that what theory is true is underdetermined by the total evidence available; that is, a number of theories (technically, an infinite number) can equally (but perhaps differently) account for the same finite body of evidence.

VERIFIABILITY PRINCIPLE (OF MEANING): See "Logical Positivism".

Index